ROSE HEMPEL

THE GOLDEN AGE OF JAPAN
794–1192

translated by Katherine Watson

RIZZOLI
NEW YORK

Japanese Names
In the normal Japanese usage before 1868, family names
preceded first names (during the Japanese Middle Ages
the two names were separated by the word 'no'). Since
the beginning of the Meiji era in 1868, Japanese names
are written with the first name before the family name.

German-language edition: *Japan zur Heian-Zeit: Kunst und Kultur*
Copyright © 1983 by Office du Livre S.A. Fribourg, Switzerland

English translation:
Copyright © 1983 by Office du Livre S.A. Fribourg, Switzerland

English translation published in 1983 in the United States of America by:

*R*IZZOLI INTERNATIONAL PUBLICATIONS, INC.
712 Fifth Avenue/New York 10019

Library of Congress Cataloging in Publication Data
Hempel, Rose.
   The golden age of Japan.

   Translation of: Japan zur Heian Zeit.
   Bibliography: p.
   Includes index.
   1. Arts, Japanese-Heian period, 794–1192. 2. Arts,
Buddhist-Japan. 3. Japan-History-Heian period,
794–1192. I. Title.

NX584.A1H4513 1983   700'.952   83–42924
ISBN 0-8478-0492-5

Printed and bound in West Germany

Contents

Introduction

This book is concerned with a period of Japanese art and civilization that has been described by J. E. Kidder as 'one of the most Japanese of all Japanese history'[1]: the Heian period.

It owes its name to the new capital city of Heian-kyō (modern Kyōto), founded in 794. The period lasted for four hundred years, the longest of any in Japanese history. In the traditional periodization it is regarded as part of the Classical Era and hence as 'proto-historical'. It came to an end in the late twelfth century, when the military regent Minamoto no Yoritomo moved the seat of government—though not the imperial court—to Kamakura, in the year 1192.[2]

What made this Heian period one of the most Japanese in all the island empire's history? What new forces were brought to bear? What set in motion this blossoming of Japan's own distinctive art and culture?

The Early Heian period, reckoned from the foundation of Heian-kyō to the rupture of diplomatic relations with China in 894, already saw the introduction of new ways of thinking. This was the work of two outstanding individuals, both of them highly learned priests. In 805 and 806 Kūkai (Kōbō Daishi) and his contemporary Saichō (Dengyō Daishi) returned from China. There they had come in contact with the latest Buddhist teaching on Enlightenment and Deliverance to be received from India, and this they brought home with them. Renouncing the life of the court they founded remote monasteries in the mountains. The distinctive traits of an essentially native 'Japanese style' (wa-yō) first appeared in embryo in the forms of their architecture and the Buddhist sculpture and painting associated with it. An innate affinity with landscape and nature admitted the inclusion of Shintō concepts. Shintō is the name of Japan's traditional aniconic religion, the 'Way of the Gods', which now became logically integrated into the pantheon of the new Buddhist esoteric teaching. The quest for Enlightenment, for a Manifestation of Ultimate Reality, pervades the imagery of the entire Early Heian period.

The Middle Heian period is named after the Fujiwara, the family of regents who held effective power. Around the imperial court with its series of ritual functions there gathered a decadent society devoted to courtly elegance (miyabi) and luxury. Every nuance of clothing, of gesture and word, of perception and sensation was minutely regulated by the 'rule of taste'.[3] In the secluded world of the women's quarters, the court ladies wrote their diaries and skilfully wielded their brushes to dash off tales of fantasy or novels. About the year 1010 Lady Murasaki Shikibu published her *Genji-monogatari,* a novel of great psychological finesse depicting the life of the court. It is centred round the brilliant and adored Prince Genji and his son and grandson. And what would this amorous, flirtatious but deeply melancholy world have done without its writing and poetry? Perhaps even before the visual arts had made the themes of landscape and feeling, man and fate, their own, these had been shaped by poetry. *Wa-yō,* 'Japanese style', also came to the fore here in all that was light and delicate, everyday and diverting: in the subject matter, literary style and calligraphy of the ladies. For serious ideas, political and important matters, the Chinese style remained the norm: the style and calligraphy of men *(kara-yō).* But even the hieratic art of Buddhism was modified by the courtly ideals of *wa-yō.* Sublime elegance and tender beauty were introduced into high religious art. The aspiration to Enlightenment prevalent in the Early Heian period was followed by a more facile belief in Deliverance through prayer and invocation. Amida Buddha, Lord of the Western Paradise, promised immediate re-incarnation in his Abode of Bliss.

With ideas of the approaching period of the latter days of the Law, which is the end of time as we know it, the nobles of the court began to commission and endow composite earthly representations of paradise; these syntheses embraced palace architecture, carved images and paintings in a comprehensive iconographic programme. Hosts of artists, craftsmen and slaves worked on such projects. Few have survived the brutal power struggles of the rival knightly clans that waxed bitter in the late eleventh century: the great temple and palace complexes of Heian-kyō were destroyed by fire and slaughter, and the people plunged in misery.

The Late Heian period, after 1068, is named after the cloister government (insei) administered from temples that began in this year, when emperors who had abdicated and taken holy orders left a titular emperor and officials at court and governed from seclusion. The history is one of feuds between rival houses, of shadow regents seeking alliances with one of the rising clans, Taira or Minamoto. While the art of the court still held sway, its dream world was gradually pushed aside by the realities of power politics. Yet it was in the first half of the twelfth century, when the world of the court was already ailing, that the earliest known illustrations of court life were produced. These are in the scroll with pictures of the Genji novel, *Genji-monogatari-emaki*. It was entirely composed, painted and written by courtiers, and the painting is in the purely Japanese style, already at that time termed *Yamato-e* ('pictures of Japan'). As a result, the strongly coloured technique of composition and painting was used to produce in great number courtly tales with pictures, called *tsukuri-e* ('coloured pictures').[4] While at about the same time in literature the *Konjaku-monogatari* was written for the simple folk, with popular stories also having a Buddhist content, so other *emakimono* were produced recounting historical incidents or Buddhist miracles. Here too arose a new dramatic quality of realism. The figures are alive, active and show their feelings without constraint. A new free brush technique allowed the narrative to be depicted in broad sweeping lines on the paper of the scrolls. The new styles of Song China (960–1271) were clearly not without their influence on the painters, whose names are now unknown to us; they studied the Chinese examples and then translated the novel technique into a Japanese idiom. One of the great paintings of the world was produced in this period: the satirical animal scroll, *Chōjū-giga*. The painter, probably a priest, depicts the animals' pranks with great wit and humour and an extraordinary gift for rapid characterization and caricature, in a series of scenes in which not even Buddhist ceremonies are spared ridicule. We can see here the dawning of new spheres of thought and a new artistic freedom. The elitist culture and art of the court period were at an end.

I Japan as the Client of Chinese Culture

Yamato and its Capital at Nara

Yamato is the highest part of the country:
The mountains are green walls;
Nestling in its hills, its terraces
lie range upon range—
How lovely is the land of Yamato.

(*Kojiki,* Poem 30)

In this poem the legendary prince Yamato-takeru, son of the twelfth Japanese emperor, Keikō, celebrates the countryside of Yamato in central Japan. According to tradition, this smiling fertile land south of Lake Biwa was occupied during the fourth century A.D. by the imperial clan and other high-ranking noble clans from the island of Kyūshū. The legendary figure of this prince is a perfect example of the complexity of traits that typifies early Japan: unquestioning loyalty alongside violence, a passionate sense of communion with landscape and nature, a combination of acute sensitivity to beauty and profound melancholy, and with all these, a natural inclination to express them in poetry and melodic speech.[5]

The ruling clan had asserted itself strongly against all others in the conflicts between the rival confederations. Its head was the Tennō (King of Heaven), who ruled as the direct descendant of the Sun Goddess and had also priestly functions to perform. The Tennō were accustomed to build their palaces on sites with fine landscapes. The death of each monarch required a change of site, however, for the deities (*kami*) demanded consistent ritual purity and freedom from pollution.

In the fourth century immigrants from Korea and—coming through the northern colonies—from China were probably already settled in Yamato, and these settlers had brought in elements of continental culture that had raised the standard of life and culture of the inhabitants. Weapons and utensils of bronze, swords and mirrors as well as knives and ploughshares of iron, had reached the island empire in the first centuries of our era. But when Japan set up a basis of operations in southern Korea (Mimana), specialized craftsmen began to arrive from the Korean state of Paekche (Kudara), in lieu of tribute. The *quid pro quo* the Korean rulers sought was military aid from the battle-loving Japanese. By this exchange Japan acquired such items of civilization as stocks of silkworms, Chinese and Korean weavers, a seamstress, a brewer of *sake* and a smith.[6]

The annals also transmit the names of scholars. According to the latest chronology, they arrived at the imperial court in about 375. Achiki and Wani were the names of the noblemen who transmitted the complicated Chinese characters to the illiterate land of Yamato. In their luggage they brought the basic school texts of the Chinese: *Lunyu* (*'The Sayings of Confucius'*) and *Qianziwen* (*'The Thousand Character Classic'*). These scribes were appointed bookkeepers for the Imperial Treasuries and the National Census. The scribes' guild (*fubito*) enjoyed great respect. Later, potters, saddlers, painters and brocade weavers from Paekche followed. Such foreigners, if they were of Chinese descent (*aya*), rose to high station, if of Korean descent (*hatta*) they received appointment as craftsmen. The *hatta* clans in later times were involved not only in sericulture, iron smelting and bronze casting but even in the production of images of the Buddha. When they did not penetrate into high levels of the administration, they were assigned priestly office in important Shintō shrines.

An important event in early Japanese history is that of the introduction of Buddhism, nearly 150 years after that of Chinese writing. The first consignments of tribute to contain figures of the Buddha and texts of the sutras are dated to 538 and 552. The clans were of divided opinion on their valuation of this new foreign religion. The ambitious Soga adopted the teaching of the Buddha, but they achieved official recognition for it only half a century later, thanks to a modern-minded crown prince, Shōtoku Taishi (574–622). The crown prince employed Korean experts to lay out temples on Chinese plans and decorate them with auspicious sculptures and paintings; he also introduced political reforms. A constitution modelled on the Chinese was promulgated in 604. Four years later a study group was despatched to China to collect material for the reforms. The continental culture was adapted by Japan with almost unbelievable enthusiasm and skill.

94, 201

1
Hōryū-ji temple complex, Nara: aerial view. Wooden structure with tiled roofs. H. (pagoda) 32.45 m. Founded 607, buildings late seventh century.
In the foreground is the Chū-mon gateway; behind it stand symmetrically in the courtyard the Kondō ('main hall', 'Golden Hall') to the right and the pagoda to the left. The layout is completed on the west by the Kōdō ('Teaching Hall'). The Hōryū-ji complex is the earliest wood-frame construction in the world.

Buddhist temples arose on the most important sites in the land, most of them close to the palaces. The Shitennō-ji, dedicated by Shōtoku Taishi in 593, was followed by the Hōkō-ji in 596. There seems to have been one fire in the chief temple of the crown prince, the Hōryū-ji (607), already during his lifetime: in 670 we have proof that it burnt down. His family commissioned the casting of a figure of the Buddha Shakyamuni for the cure of the crown prince when he was ill, but he died a year before it was completed. This early bronze trinity is one of the most splendid of all Buddhist cult images to survive. It was made by Tori, the 'Buddha Image Maker' *(busshi)*, a descendant of Chinese immigrants and head of the guild of saddlers. The enthusiasm of faith and power kindled by Buddhism in Japan made every branch of art and culture blossom.

During the Asuka period (552–645) a number of different styles of Chinese Buddhist art came to Japan through Korea. The cave sculptures of Longmen appear to have influenced the bronze images of Tori-*busshi* and his school. The so-called 'Korean' Bodhisattva figures in the Hōryū-ji and Kōryū-ji are thought to be modelled on southern Chinese examples.

The moral teaching of the peaceful Buddhist creed had little effect at first however. Only after the cowardly murder of various claimants to the throne and of one emperor did the *Taika-kaishin* reforms begin to take shape, after 645 or 646. Nakatomi no Kamatari, ancestor of the Fujiwara clan, played a decisive role in their application; in the year of the Reform (645), Japan began to reckon according to the Chinese calendar with its annual symbols *(nengō)*.

The Tennō was declared absolute ruler in matters of religion and state. Religious ceremonies included nothing of Buddhism, only purely Japanese Shintō rites such as Harvest Thanksgiving and Purification ceremonies, the maintenance of shrines and oracle taking. Subordinate to the Tennō were the administrative offices and the civil service, which was strictly graded according to different 'cap ranks'. The complicated court etiquette of China was adopted; the land was declared state property and apportioned among the populace according to the numbers in each family. The emperor's court, the nobility and the temples all lived off the taxes they paid. In the Nara period there were in addition about six million slaves, without property, who were conscripted to work on the enormous building enterprises that were undertaken.

Not until 701–702 was the great work of reform completed and the Taihō Code passed. However this new system of government was hardly capable of pressing the Japanese, with their strongly rooted clan affiliations, into the new Chinese order, in which service was to count before rights of inheritance and appointed rank more than inherited status in the clan. By 682 the rights of inheritance had already taken precedence once more over talent for the allocation of posts.

In the reigns of Emperor Temmu (673–686), of his wife Jitō, crowned Tennō after him (690–697), and of their grandson Mommu (697–707) government and state were consolidated. Japanese missions to China brought back with them learned abbots and their new Buddhist sects, and these enjoyed the powerful protection of the court.

The downfall of the Korean kingdoms of Koguryo (Kōkuri) and Paekche brought new streams of refugees into Japan in 663 and 668. The thinly populated countryside with its areas of fallow land absorbed all these people without difficulty. To this influx from Korea Japan is indebted for the transmission of the Chinese artistic styles of the early Tang dynasty. In the mid-seventh century we can perceive the liberation of Japanese Buddhist sculpture from the archaic flat linearity and emotional severity of the Asuka period. The art of the Hakuhō period (672–685) shows a concern with modelled form and the beginnings of freer posture in its figures.

The earliest Buddhist temples that survive date from the end of the seventh century. They are mostly state temples promoted by vows of the imperial house. The rebuilding of the Hōryū-ji, after a fire in 670, was not 1 completed until the late seventh century. The Kondō ('Golden Hall') was decorated at that time. The Paradises of the Four Buddhas with their attendant Bodhisattvas reflect the maturity of Chinese art. The Yakushi Temple was built by an indigenous workshop at the instigation of Emperor Temmu in 680; he made a vow to the Buddha of Redemption, Yakushi, when his wife (later the Empress Jitō) was suffering from an eye malady. For the plan of the layout, the bracketing and roofing systems, models were sought in Korea.

In view of the great economic boom brought about both by the cultivation of the northern countryside and by the discoveries of silver and copper, Emperor Temmu decided to build a capital in the continental style. The plans were executed by the Empress Gemmei in 710. In the north of Yamato province the ground

List of *nengō* ('era names'),
the principal method of dating in Japan from their introduction in 645 to 1199

Taika	645– 650	Shōhei (Jōhei)	931– 938	Eichō	1096–1097
Hakuchi	650– 655	Tengyō (Tenkei)	938– 947	Jōtoku (Shotoku)	1097–1099
Saimei (Saimyō)	655– 662	Tenryaku	947– 957	Kōwa	1099–1104
Tenji (Tenchi)	662– 672	Tentoku	957– 961	Chōji	1104–1106
Sujaku	672	Ōwa	961– 964	Kajō (Kashō)	1106–1108
Hakuhō	672– 685	Kōhō	964– 968	Tennin	1108–1110
Suchō	686	Anna	968– 970	Tenei	1110–1113
Suchō/Jitō	687– 696	Tenroku	970– 973	Eikyū	1113–1118
Mommu	697– 701	Tenen	973– 976	Genei	1118–1120
Taihō	701– 704	Jōgen	976– 978	Hōan	1120–1124
Keiun	704– 708	Tengen	978– 983	Tenji	1124–1126
Wadō	708– 715	Eikan	983– 985	Daiji	1126–1131
Reiki	715– 717	Kanna	985– 987	Tenshō (Tenjō)	1131–1132
Yōrō	717– 724	Eien	987– 989	Chōshō (Chōjō)	1132–1135
Jinki	724– 729	Eiso	989– 990	Hōen	1135–1141
Tempyō	729– 749	Shōryaku	990– 995	Eiji	1141–1142
Tempyō-shōhō	749– 757	Chōtoku	995– 999	Kōji	1142–1144
Tempyō-hōji	757– 765	Chōhō	999–1003	Tenyō	1144–1145
Tempyō-jingo	765– 767	Kankō	1004–1012	Kyūan	1145–1151
Jingo-keiun	767– 770	Chōwa	1012–1017	Nimpei (Nimpyō)	1151–1154
Hōki	770– 780	Kannin	1017–1020	Kyūju	1154–1156
Tenō	781	Jian	1021–1024	Hōgen	1156–1159
Enryaku	782– 806	Manju	1024–1028	Heiji	1159–1160
Daidō	806– 810	Chōgen	1027–1037	Eiryaku	1160–1161
Kōnin	810– 824	Chōryaku	1037–1040	Ōhō	1161–1163
Tenchō	824– 834	Chōkyū	1040–1044	Chōkan	1163–1165
Jōwa	834– 848	Kantoku	1044–1046	Eiman	1165–1166
Kashō	848– 851	Eijō (Eishō)	1046–1053	Ninan	1166–1169
Ninju	851– 854	Tenki	1053–1058	Kaō	1169–1171
Saikō	854– 857	Kōhei	1058–1065	Jōan	1171–1175
Tenan (Tennan)	857– 859	Jiryaku	1065–1069	Angen	1175–1177
Jōgan	859– 876	Enkyū	1069–1074	Jishō	1177–1181
Gangyō	877– 885	Jōhō	1074–1077	Yōwa	1181–1182
Ninna	885– 889	Jōryaku (Shoryaku)	1077–1081	Juei	1182–1185
Kampyō	889– 898	Eihō	1081–1084	Genryaku	1185
Shōtai	898– 901	Ōtoku	1084–1087	Bunji	1185–1190
Engi	901– 923	Kanji	1087–1094	Kenkyū	1190–1199
Enchō	923– 931	Kahō	1094–1096		

plan of Heijō-kyō (modern Nara) was staked out in accordance with Chinese rules of geomantics. The rectangular street plan, with the Greater Imperial Palace (Daidairi) in the north, the location of temples and markets corresponded to the great example of the Tang capital at Chang'an.

We can only form a vague picture of the splendour of the palace area, the halls with columns lacquered in red and tiled roofs, spread over an area of about 1 square kilometre. Suzaku-ōji was the street leading from the south to the palace, forming an artery that divided the city into a western and an eastern section. The area was so extensive that it was divided into nine parts. The temples of the abandoned capital cities were re-erected inside the precincts, the Daian-ji in 711 and the Gankō-ji in 716, three blocks further east. The precious materials were apparently carried column by column and bracket by bracket on ox carts to their new destinations. The Yakushi-ji was rebuilt in 710 or 718 on an area of three by three insulae in the sixth street of the western

section. Its distinctive, graceful, three-storeyed pagoda, with roofs at each storey, survives today, but it is thought to have been built anew in Heijō-kyō in 730. The date of the casting of the imposing bronze trinity of the Buddha of Redemption, Yakushi, is variously interpreted. The generous modelling and free movement of the figures make the early eighth century the most likely.

Fujiwara no Fubito built a private temple compound as the family temple of the Fujiwara clan; this was the great Kōfuku-ji to the east of the city at that time. The early buildings, halls, pagodas and octagonal hall were all burnt down, however, in the power struggles of the late eleventh century.

The absolute peak of the Nara period was reached with the national-religious hubris of Emperor Shōmu (724–749) and of his daughter, Kōken-Shōtoku (749–758, 764–770). State Buddhism was a matter of 'protection of the land'. Men were press-ganged into monasteries as monks or conscripted to work on national building and craft enterprises. Only in this way could architecture and art reach such a pitch. Despite all this pious activity, the country was ravaged in 737 by an epidemic of small-pox. The epidemic was accompanied by earthquakes, and to avert these terrors Emperor Shōmu vowed to build a Chief National Temple, the Tōdai-ji. The people as a whole were called on to contribute, and every tenth person answered the call, even though the contributions were often meagre.

A monumental image (16.19 m high) of the Universal Buddha (*daibutsu*) Birushana (Vairocana) was cast in bronze as the chief cult image. The statue consumed all the bronze resources of the country. Because of repeated failures, it took four years before it was completed in 749, and the gilding took many years more. The eye-opening ceremony was performed in 752 with great pomp and the participation of countless nobles, priests and believers. The great hall where the cult image was enthroned was (and after various renovations, still is) the largest wooden building in the world. The Birushana Buddha was restored several times, most recently in 1962.

In separate subsidiary halls of the Tōdai-ji—the Lotus Hall (Hokke-dō), Initiation Hall (Kaidan-in)—and in the more southerly Shin-Yakushi-ji are preserved some very important cult images of the Nara period. Dry lacquer and clay provided the materials most suitable for modelling, colouring and gilding. Majestic Bodhisattva images and vividly dramatic figures of guards, demons and disciples survive as evidence of the art of Nara.

Towards the end of the Nara period the arrival of the blind Chinese monk Jianzhen (Ganjin, 688–763), who had been brought to Japan to teach the doctrines of the Ritsu sect, once more gave new impetus to Buddhist teaching and art. The imperial house bestowed on him the Tōshōdai-ji, a temple in the west of the city, north 3 of the Yakushi-ji. Prince Niitabe donated a hall in his palace to the great scholar. It was used as a teaching hall (Kōdō) and is now the only secular building to survive from the Nara period. Sculpture found new inspiration in the teaching of Ganjin and his Chinese following, and a school of wood carving worked in his temple.

Buddhist art was everywhere, in temple architecture, the iconography of cult images, religious painting and crafts of every kind for sacred purposes. The life-style of the imperial court and its appendages had an international character, or at least aspired to one. Many furnishings and utensils came from the continent. The missions of 733 and 736 are said to have brought back luxury objects produced not only in China but also carpets, glass, metalwork and gaming boards from Central Asia, Iran and Syria. Silk fabrics with their elaborately dyed and painted decoration, including Sasanian motifs, came from the 'West'. The magnificent musical instruments, mirrors and mirror cases inlaid with mother-of-pearl, tortoise-shell and gems in intricate patterns show an ornamental repertoire developed in China as a sumptuous adaptation of foreign motifs.

But a plain wooden bed, simple cupboards, writing instruments and paper, weapons and cult apparatus also survive. Among these are the celebrated screens with Chinese ladies under trees that are now considered to be Japanese work. This wealth of earthly treasure has remained intact since the death of Emperor Shōmu because Empress Kōmyō dedicated all her husband's property to the Great Birushana Buddha of the Tōdai-ji at a memorial service on the seventy-seventh day after his death, in 756. The temple built special storehouses

2
Tōdai-ji temple complex, Nara: aerial view. Founded 746, rebuilt several times.
In the foreground the two-storeyed gateway, Nandai-mon of 1199; in the background the temple precinct with the Daibutsu-den ('Hall of the Great Buddha') of 1709. In front of the hall is a bronze lantern of the first half of the eighth century.

for the treasure, the Shōsō-in, and their absolute dark-
ness has preserved the precious objects from wear and
destruction to this day.

The Literature of the Nara Period

Light is thrown on the life of the court by the reports in
the annals. The two early histories of Japan (the *Kojiki*
of 712 and the *Nihon-shoki* of 720) report not only on the
myths of prehistory but also give a chronological account of events in the country and at court. A compilation from them by J. and R. K. Reischauer[7] tells us of
the imperial ceremonies, the naming of crown princes,
coronations, dedications, feasts and various celebrations. The embassies from abroad are listed, as well as
those the Japanese sent. Edicts are noted concerning the
minting of coinage and the establishment of offices for
commerce and crafts (728) with the number—rarely the
names—of their members and the payment of salaries.
The foundation of temples in the provinces is recorded
side by side with the deployment of the armies sent to
fight the Barbarian *(emishi)* or to campaign in Korea.

The age-old traditional duties of the emperors were
shielded from any continental innovations. The prayer
ceremonies for the success of the rice harvest and the
rites of thanksgiving and purification for land and
people came from the ideology of the national Shintō
religion. The old shrines, especially the sanctuary of
the ancestress of the Yamato imperial house, the Sun
Goddess Amaterasu-Ōmikami, preserved their central
ritual importance. The shrine of the Sun Goddess in Ise
was rebuilt in 685 in the original style of the third century A.D. A law decreed that the buildings were to be
renewed every twenty years for reasons of ritual clean-
liness. Important national events were announced there
by imperial envoys; imperial princesses had to officiate
as priestesses. It is registered that notification was sent
to Ise of the casting of the 'Great Buddha' of Nara.

In the seventh and eighth centuries the primitive literature of Japan was set down in writing. Though Japan

3
Interior (detail) of the Main Hall (Kondō) of the Tōshōdai-ji, Nara.
H. (Birushana) 5.36 m. Third quarter of the eighth century.
The larger-than-life-sized statues in dry lacquer represent Birushana
in the middle, with the thousand-armed Kannon on his left and
Yakushi Nyorai on his right. Bon-ten and Taishaku-ten flank the
central image, and the Shi-tennō stand at the corners of the altar.

had developed no script of its own, language in poetic
form was from the first the most essential medium of
artistic expression. The melodic phrasing of the language began with love poems. The old love duets of the
young were called 'song hedges' *(utagaki);* first performed quite spontaneously, they were later transmitted as part of the cultural heritage.

This propensity towards poetic utterance is already
found in the three-volume *Kojiki.* It recounts the story
of the creation of the island empire—apparently with
some dependence on Korean myths. Chinese characters, read partly semantically and partly phonetically,
were used to write it down. The chronology of the emperors is set down up to Suiko-Tennō, the aunt of
Shōtoku Taishi. For the mythological passages the
compiler, Ō no Yasumaro, working for Empress
Gemmei, collected the orally transmitted texts of the
old man (or woman) Hide no Are, and 111 poems are to
be found woven into the text. The *Kojiki* was followed
in 720 by the first official work of history, *Nihon-shoki*
or *Nihon-gi,* wholly Chinese in conception. It gives an
account of the birth and development of the Tennō empire to the year 697 and comprises thirty volumes. The
final volumes are factual and were used as documenta-
tion by Japanese embassies to give an account of their
country. Histories of different provinces were also
written down following an imperial decree in 713.
These *Fudōki* ('Notes on Customs and Country') provide a rich source of information on customs and the
economy; unfortunately only a few of the texts survive.

The earliest Japanese anthology of poetry dates from
751. It contains 120 poems in Chinese, written in the
imperial entourage. Its title, *Kaifusō,* means 'Exquisite
in Imitation of Ancient Models'. The motifs and images
are those of the five-word verses of Chinese lyric writing, but they differ from the Chinese verses in content,
being centred on events in the life of the court. Profound philosophical and political themes were not subjects for verse in Japan.

The poems of the *Manyō-shū* ('Collection of Myriad
Leaves') are much more lively, telling of the habits and
customs, experiences and feelings of people in every
walk of life. The twenty volumes contain about 4,500
poems from the mid-fifth century to the year 759. The
work begins with an unaffected song supposedly composed by Emperor Yūryaku when he was looking for a
wife. Japanese poems *(waka)* comprise about 4,200 of
the poems in the compilation, numerically and by rank
more important than the 260 long poems and 60

19

dialogue verses. The *waka* or *uta* ('song'), also called *tanka* ('a short poem'), were in lines of 5–7–5 and 7–7 characters, and unlike Chinese lyrics were not rhymed. The art of compressing the most intimate expression into this exiguous form is already well developed in the *Manyō-shū*. It was most ingeniously written in Chinese characters, used only phonetically. The *manyō-gana*, as this style of writing is called, had already been tried out to some extent in the *Kojiki* and was fully established here. The noble-born Kakimoto no Hitomaro (seventh–eighth century) stands out among the court poets whose work appears in the *Manyō-shū*. He wrote many official poems for the imperial house. His style is rather pompous and rhetorical due to the invention of 'pillow' words *(makura-kotoba)*, to which Japanese poets now had recourse to fit in suitably and sonorously with the syllable count. Hitomaro's less high-born contemporary, Yamabe no Akahito, composed intimate nature and love poems. Ōtomo no Yakamochi (718–785) was the last compiler of the *Manyō-shū;* he contributed to the last four volumes of the anthology.[8]

The musicality of the poetry is inherently one with folk song and the cult songs and dances of Shintō. The ancient ritual dances of Japan are called *kagura* ('theatre of the gods'). Country *kagura (sato-kagura)* are those dances performed in the villages, and noble *kagura (mi-kagura)* are those of the court in honour of the imperial ancestress, danced to the accompaniment of flutes, harps and singing. In the sixth and seventh centuries with sculpture, dances and mask types, music and instruments from China, India and Central Asia came to Japan. An office for music (Gagaku-ryō) is included in the Taihō Code. The *gigaku* ('art-music') dances, performed as a part of Buddhist cult practices, used demonic skull masks. About 240 of these remain in the possession of the chief Buddhist temples.

II Japan's Culture in Transition

The New Capital City of Heian-kyō

When the son of Emperor Kōnin ascended the throne in 781 at the age of forty-four, taking the name Kammu-Tennō, he pressed forward with the removal of the capital, an enterprise supported by the powerful Fujiwara clan. The court needed to extricate itself from the pretensions and influence of the 'Great Seven' Buddhist temples of Nara. The new capital was established some 30 kilometres to the north in Nagaoka, near the navigable river of Yodo-gawa, in the land of the *hata* people, whose origins were in Korea. That the emperor's mother, Takona Niigasa, was of the royal Korean house of Paekche may have affected the choice of the site. The layout of the new metropolis, like Nara based on the plan of the Chinese capital city of Chang'an, required the conscription of 314,000 labourers, who worked on the foundations for seven months. The gates were brought from Nara. In 784 the emperor was able to move into the new imperial palace, government administration continuing unbroken the while.

Nagaoka, however, was not a success, not only because of its situation in a narrow valley but also because of ominous intrigues that weighed heavily on the imperial entourage. An influential Fujiwara was assassinated with the knowledge of the emperor's brother, Sawara, the designated crown prince. The prince was exiled to the island of Awaji but was murdered on his way there. His curse now seemed to bear down on the imperial house: the empress died, and the new crown prince fell seriously ill. This was not all: the imperial armies suffered a series of heavy defeats in the northeast against the Ezo (Ainu).

Ten years or so later, while hunting, some courtiers discovered a more auspicious site for a capital, north of Nagaoka near the village of Uda between the Katsura and Kamo rivers. There the proximity of mountains gave protection from evil demons, especially Mount Hiei to the north-west fulfilled the requirements of Chinese *fengshui* magic, which fixed the rites that had to be observed when founding a city. Emperor Kammu announced his plan for another move, first to the protecting deities of the Uda region in the Kamo shrine, and then to the Sun Goddess in the Daijingū in Ise and to the spirits of his ancestors in their respective mausolea. The great work of surveying and laying out began once again, though only a few areas within the precincts were built on immediately. In 794 the markets of Nagaoka were removed to the new town. On the twenty-second of the Tenth Month, the emperor and his train made a formal entry into the new palace. The city received the name of Heian-kyō, 'Capital of Peace and Tranquillity'. Heian-kyō, later called Kyōto, remained the official capital and imperial seat until 1869.

The area of the new city was about four times that of 4 Nagaoka, a rectangle of 4.5 by 5.5 kilometres. Like Nara it imitated the chessboard pattern of Chang'an with nine insulae vertically and eight horizontally. In the centre at the north lay the imperial palace, Daidairi, pp. 220–221 which in length covered the broad block between First Avenue (Ichijō-ōji) and Second Avenue (Nijō-ōji). In width it extended east and west across a block on either side of the main axis, Suzaku-ōji. From the Rashō-mon Gate in the south this broad avenue bore straight down on the Suzaku-mon, the main gate of the palace. In the Tennō's great palace the official buildings followed Chinese examples closely, as they had in Nara. The central court of the palace (the Chōdō-in) reached from the Suzaku-mon through the Ōten-mon; there isolated halls surrounded a broad inner court, bounded on the north by the great audience chamber, the Daigoku-den. In their proportions and their system of supports, the buildings resembled the halls of Buddhist temples. They had stone floors, green tiled roofs and wooden columns painted red. The banqueting hall (Buraku-in), west of the Chōdō-in, like the government offices—Office of Ceremonies, Office for People's Affairs and the Court of Justice—likewise the guard-rooms and stables were all to a detail exactly like the Chinese hall complexes. The imperial residence (Dairi or Kōryō) lay p. 222 north-east of the Chōdō-in. Behind its main gate, the Kenrei-mon, extended a different world. The buildings, raised on stilts, did not parade in splendid colour but were all of natural wood, with shingle roofs, polished wooden floors and swinging doors, creating an atmosphere of balance, restraint and wholly Japanese elegance. The private imperial Throne Hall (Shishin- 5 den) was an inner room with wide verandahs all round. Altogether seventeen halls composed the Dairi, arranged symmetrically but in a rhythm of different groupings to form a complex connected by covered passages. This layout is known as 'palace' or 'villa' style 47–48 *(shinden-zukuri);* in fact *shinden* means sleeping hall and refers to the living and rest rooms of aristocratic palaces. The forecourt of the Shishin-den set it at a distance with an expanse of white sand. The pool and garden, indispensable to noble palaces, lay further south for the enjoyment of court society as a whole.

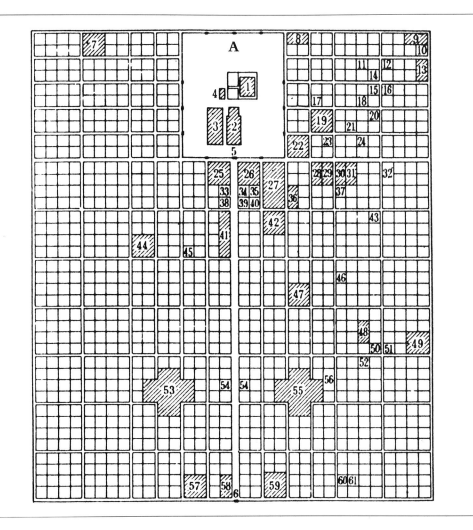

4
Map of the capital city, Heian-kyō:

A   Daidairi oder Kyūjo
      (Greater Imperial Palace)
1   Dairi (Imperial Residence)
2   Chōdō-in
3   Buraku-in
4   Shingon-in
5   Suzaku-mon
6   Rashō-mon
7   Uda-in
8   Ichijō-in
9   Some-dono
10   Seiwa-in
11   Tsuchimikada-dono
12   Takakura-dono
13   Kyōgoku-den
14   Biwa-dono
15   Koichijō-dono
16   Kazan-in
17   Hon-in
18   Sugawara-in

19   Kayano-in
20   Kon-in
21   Komatsu-in
22   Reizei-in
23   Yōzei-in
24   Ono-no-miya
25   Kokusō-in
26   Daigaku-ryō
      (University)
27   Shinzen-en
28   Horikawa-in
29   Kan-in
30   Higashi Sanjō-dono
31   Kamoi-dono
32   Konijō-dono
33   Ukyō-tsukasa
34   Sakyō-tsukasa
35   Kōbun-in
36   Mikasa-dono
37   Takamatsu-dono
38   Nishi Sanjō-dono
39   Shōgaku-in

40   Kangaku-in
41   Suzaku-in
42   Shijōgo-in
43   Rokkaku-in
44   Shōwa-in
45   Saiin
46   Kōbai-dono
47   Gojō-in
48   Korokujō-in
49   Kawara-in
50   Naka Rokujō-in
51   Tsuridono-in
52   Rokujō-in
53   Western Market
54   Kōkoku-in
55   Eastern Market
56   Teiji-in
57   Saiji (Western Temple)
58   Hanazono-dono
59   Tōji (Eastern Temple)
60   Seyaku-in (Hospital)
61   Kujō-dono

◁ 5

Shishin-den of the Imperial Palace, Kyōto. Reconstruction of 1855.
The Throne Hall (Shishin-den) is an impressive sight with the tall
curved profile of its stepped shingle roof. The hall, nine bays wide, is
entered in the centre from a wide wooden staircase with eighteen
steps. On the right when descending the stairs, stands an orange tree
(tachibana), on the left a cherry *(sakura)*. The central bay is crowned
with a medallion containing the name of the hall.

◁ 6

Seiryō-den of the Imperial Palace, Kyōto. Reconstruction of 1855.
The imperial Dwelling Hall (Seiryō-den) stands perpendicular to
the Throne Hall on the north. It opens eastwards, and two bamboos
are planted in front of the facade: a *kawatake* on the south, and a
kuretake on the north. Two narrow flights of steps lead up to the
verandah.

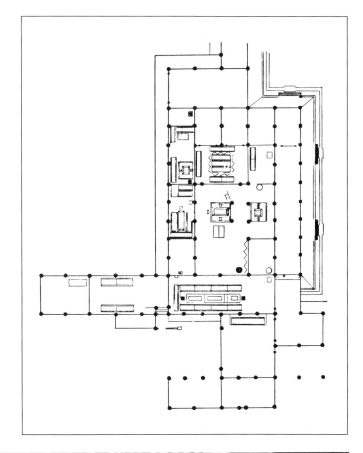

7   ▷

Ground plan of the Seiryō-den of the Imperial Palace, Kyōto.

8

Seiryō-den of the Imperial Palace, Kyōto: the emperor's private
apartments.
The rooms on the west are partitioned off by screens to form the
emperor's sitting and dining rooms. The *Asagarei* Room has a platform to sit on in the centre, and lacquer washing utensils with
decorative wall screens behind them are also visible.

9
Genji-monogatari-emaki. Chapter 49: 'Yadorigi I'. Ink and colours on paper. 21.2 × 37.2 cm. Tokugawa Reimeikai Foundation, Tōkyō. In the *Asagarei* Room of the Seiryō-den, the emperor and Prince Kaoru are playing a game of *gō* with the Princess Onna Nino Miya as the stake. The room contains lacquer furniture and a panel with silver ground, with a *Yamato-e* landscape. Two ladies-in-waiting are in the anteroom on the left behind sliding doors. Behind them can be seen a two-part lacquered wall cabinet.

6-8 A verandah led from the Shishin-den to the emperor's Dwelling Hall (the Seiryō-den) to the northwest. It opened on the east on to a small courtyard containing two fenced-in clusters of bamboo. Inside 9 the Dwelling Hall, sliding doors and screens were used to partition the various private apartments of the emperor.

Yet it was the interior courts (*tsubo*) of the Dairi that gave it its own special charm. They were called after different plants: paulownia *(kiri)*, wisteria *(fuji)*, pear *(nashi)* or plum *(ume)*. These names were then attached to their inhabitants, the imperial wives and concubines. Lower buildings lay on the outer axes and also accommodated ladies and serving maids.

In the third block south of the palace and east of the Suzaku-ōji stood the university quarter. South of the Bifuku-mon palace gate the insula between the Nijō-ōji and the Sanjō-ōji was given over to the palace garden (Shinsen-en). Its artificial lake and winding streams, composed into landscapes with little hills and groups of trees, made the ideal setting for garden, poetry and music festivals.

In contrast with Nara the axis of each market place was occupied by a national temple: in the east (*sa-kyō*) the Eastern Temple, Tōji, with the Saiji corresponding to it in the west (*u-kyō*). Both temple precincts extended to the southernmost street, Ninth Avenue. The Tōji, officially designated the Temple for the Protection of the Land (Kyōōgokoku-ji), secured its central 14 function through the great priest Kūkai (Kōbō Daishi), who was appointed its abbot in 823.

With this new capital Emperor Kammu had set up a visible emblem for the beginning of a new era. His military efforts to 'pacify the realm' against the original inhabitants are another of the achievements redounding to the fame of this energetic man. Already in Nagaoka, to eliminate the danger of further attacks, Kammu had

26

been demanding tribute in the form of military armament. The provinces of Kantō had to provide the government with leather armour, Dazaifū in Kyūshū with iron helmets, and the provinces of Tōkaidō and Tōsandō with thousands of arrows. The army, now well armed, was put under the command of the heroic and loyal General Sakanoue no Tamuramaro (758–811), and it was he who finally put down the uprisings of the indigenous population (Ezo). The emperor honoured him with the title of Sei-i Tai-shōgun ('Supreme Commander for Defeating the Barbarians'); the title was not used again until 400 years later, when it was bestowed on Minamoto no Yoritomo at the end of the Heian period. During these years of radical change an oppressive burden of conscripted labour, military service and taxation was laid on the common folk. More and more people took refuge in the city, since as servants of the court nobles or as vagrants they were exempt from taxation. Homeless vagrants are described in the early annals as *rōnin* ('wave men'), a name that in modern times was transferred to the masterless samurai.

Emperor Kammu was informed of all these wrongs by his advisors. A year before his death in 805 he officially proclaimed an amnesty, and he also posthumously promoted Prince Sawara emperor. Were these acts of clemency due to the influence of Chinese ideas of wise government, or are they to be seen as stemming from Buddhist ideals of benevolence?

Kammu-Tennō's second son, Saga, instituted a new method of government when he became emperor in 809 after the reign of the shady Heijō. To extricate himself from the legacy of the political machinations of his predecessor and his concubines, Saga set up a private imperial office through which he was able to make decisions independently, though in association with the leading nobles; these decisions had the force of law. A newly established imperial police maintained law and order. Saga-Tennō took an epoch-making step by abdicating prematurely: not only was he thus able to nominate his son as successor to his brother, Junna-Tennō, but he was also able to exercise the real power of government from behind the scenes. As ex-emperor (Dajō Tennō) he lived in his palaces, the Reizei-in in the city and the Saga-in near Kitano, and officially concerned himself with his great artistic passions. None the less he kept government closely under his control through his private office. He received a retirement pension in the form of fallow territory and families to maintain it; though it only represented about a fifth of the income of the members of the Fujiwara nobility, it was still enough to give him a not inconsiderable power basis,[9] allowing him to influence politics very strongly during the regencies of Junna-Tennō and Nimmyō-Tennō. After his death the position of regent under the following emperors fell into the hands of Fujiwara no Yoshifusa, chief of the Fujiwara clan; he was a son-in-law of Saga-Tennō and, by other family marriages, he secured de facto power and the offices of chancellor (Dajō Daijin) and regent (Sesshō).

Not until a half century later, when Uda-Tennō came to the throne in 887 at the age of twenty-one, did an emperor manage to prevail in the power struggle against the reigning chancellor, Fujiwara no Mototsune. Emperor Uda, like Saga, abdicated after holding the Tennō-ship for ten years, in favour of his son Daigo. He reigned as ex-emperor and monk-emperor (Hōō) from the Suzaki-in and from the Ninna-ji. He drew to him the intellectual, Chinese-oriented elite in the following of Sugawara no Michizane. The latter and Ki no Haseo had declined ambassadorial appointments to China in 894. Probably the collapse of the Tang empire made the mission seem unnecessary; also the men were unwilling to forfeit their influence at court by absenting themselves. Fujiwara no Tokihira, their great rival, none the less managed to get Michizane exiled to Kyūshū. The *Kitano-Tenjin-engi* of the Kamakura 161 period is a dramatic account in pictures of the tragic fate of this semi-legendary statesman.

The New Esoteric Buddhist Teaching and Shintō

For the erection of the main hall on Mount Hiei:

All you so gracious Buddhas,
So full of the highest wisdom,
Who see into our hearts,
Give your divine protection to this wood.

Dengyō Daishi (Saichō)[10]

Just as the imperial house retreated from Nara, so young intellectuals too sought to elude the superficial ritual and pomp of state Buddhism. They belonged to the six sects of the existing temples but sought an approach to Ultimate Enlightenment rather in the solitude of the mountains, in meditation and in the study of the sutras.

10

Saichō (Dengyō Daishi). Ink and colours on silk. H. 129 cm. W. 75.8 cm. Eleventh century. Ichijō-ji, Kyōto.
This idealized portrait of the great scholar and founder of Japan's Tendai sect shows him sitting in meditation on a carved priest's chair. Like other abbots he has a stole covering his head; his hands are in the gesture of meditation. This painting belongs to the famous set entitled *Shōtoku Taishi and the Ten Patriarchs of the Tendai Sect* in the Ichijō-ji.

11

Kūkai (Kōbō Daishi): posthumous portrait (detail). Kamakura period. Kyōōgokoku-ji, Kyōto.
The great priest is pictured seated on a plinth and holding in his hands the magic instruments of the Shingon sect: a thunderbolt and prayer beads. Beside the plinth, behind a pair of shoes, stands a water bottle.

10   Saichō (767–822), the son of a family of Chinese origin with rich estates on the shores of Lake Biwa, was the first notable monk to retire from the world in this way. He left the Tōdai-ji in Nara to put into practice the

novel doctrines of the Chinese Tiantai (Tendai) sect in the fastnesses of Mount Hiei. His interpretation of the *Hokke-kyō (Lotus Sutra)* impressed Emperor Kammu, who nominated him to the post of priest in the imperial palace in 797 and also enabled him to travel to China with the mission of 804 under Fujiwara no Kadono-maru. At the centre of the sect, on Mount Tiantai near Ningbo in Zhejiang province, Saichō was ordained and, after nine and a half months, returned to Japan, to the capital and his post of honour, with many copies of sutras in his luggage. He was given Mount Hiei for a monastery and built the Enryaku-ji there.

11 His rather younger contemporary Kūkai (774–835), a grandson of the poet Ōtomo no Yakamochi, came from Shikoku to the imperial university in Nagaoka, where he studied sinology. But then, in addition to the doctrines of Confucius and Taoism, he acquired a deep knowledge of Buddhist teaching, becoming a novice monk. At the age of twenty-four this brilliant young man wrote a treatise on the unity of these three teachings. At his own request he was able to join the same mission as Saichō to China and stayed there three years. Kūkai went to the Chinese capital, Chang'an. Thanks to his knowledge of Chinese he could study with the Great Master of the 'Secret Doctrine of the True Word Shenyen' (Shingon) and was designated the successor of the seventh patriarch, Hui Guo. Kūkai also learnt Sanskrit in Chang'an from an Indian Buddhist, calligraphy from the master Han Fangming, poetry and crafts. He returned to Japan with high rank and a comprehensive collection of texts and works of art. He is considered the universal genius of the Japanese Early Heian period, who laid the foundations of Japanese culture and art.

What was the novelty of Kūkai's teachings? They give a vision of the cosmos according to the *Mahā-vairocana Sūtra (Dainichi-kyō)* and the *Vajrasekhara Sūtra (Kon-gōchō-kyō)*, with the Buddha of the Highest Wisdom, Dainichi (Vairocana), at the centre. This Buddha unites the two aspects of the world, that of pure idea,
20 the 'Diamond World' *(kongō-kai)*, and that of the
22 'Womb World', world of appearances *(taizō-kai)*. The manifold manifestations of the supreme Buddha are represented in two mandala *(mandara* in Japanese): for all is Buddha. By invocation of the figures of the mandala and their conjuration through secret gestures *(mudrā)* and sounds *(mantra)* the celestial tantric powers are awakened—but only for initiates. Kūkai's interpretation made this speculative doctrine acceptable to Japanese thought by including the Shintō divinities as emanations of the Buddha as valid as the rest. The idea that Amaterasu-Ōmikami corresponded to the Buddha Dainichi and that all the nature deities had a place in the Buddhist pantheon did much to popularize the Shingon Buddhist doctrine. The magic practices and formulae had, of course, attracted the superstitious people of the Early Heian period from the start.

The Tendai sect especially produced a succession of great personalities among the priests. One such was Ennin (Jigaku Daishi, 793–864), who went on pilgrimage in China from 838 to 846 on the 'search for the law of the Buddha' and underwent great hardships. Accompanied by Korean interpreters he went on foot to the Wudaishan and on to the capital Chang'an. There he experienced first hand the brutal persecutions of the Buddhists during the years 842 to 845. Unfortunately his diaries[11] tell nothing of the vaunted wonders of the Chinese metropolis. His studies in far-off China were less concerned with the teachings of the Tendai sect than with the tantric doctrines of the Shingon sect. On his arduous return journey he brought not only Chinese works of art but also a large number of sutra scrolls, copied in part by his own labours.

After him the monk Enchin (Chishō Daishi, 30 814–891) also undertook the exhausting journey, setting out from Mount Hiei. Enchin spent the years 853 to 858 in the state of Yue (northern Zhejiang province) and studied Buddhist interpretation of the scriptures in the Qinglong Temple. After his return he grew apart from the Tendai sect and, with the energy of which his portrait also makes us aware, founded the Onjō-ji on Lake Biwa for his own tantric sect, the Jimon-ha.

The Temple Complexes of the Shingon Sect

> You ask me why I entered the mountain deep and cold,
> Awesome, surrounded by steep peaks and grotesque rocks,
> A place that is painful to climb and difficult to descend,
> Wherein reside the gods of the mountain and the spirits of the trees.
> . . .
> Futile would be my stay in the capital;
> Away, away, I must go. I must not stay there,
> Release me, for I shall be master of the great void;
> A child of Shingon must not stay there.
>
> Kūkai, poem to a noble in Kyōto[12]

Kūkai enlisted the arts in the cause of visual instruction to an extent unparalleled among the priestly fraternity. Not only did mandala painting serve his cult, but he

◁ 12
Tahō-tō ('pagoda of the treasures') of the Kongōsammai-in Temple, Kōya-san, Wakayama. Timber-frame construction with shingle roof. H. 14.9 m. 1223.

The Shingon sect developed its own form of pagoda in Japan, the Tahō-tō. It preserved the traditional Indian form of a stupa reliquary. Between two roofs a simulated round dome is inserted, surrounded by a gallery whose ingenious arrangement of consoles forms the transition to the square roof. This small Tahō-tō was donated by Masako for the salvation of her husband, Minamoto no Yoritomo. Since the three Tahō-tō of the Kongōbu-ji, the main temple on the Kōya-san, were destroyed in 994 and only one rebuilt (most recently in 1936), this elegant building along with that of the Ishiyama-dera belong to the architecturally important, early Tahō-tō.

13
Temple pagoda of the Kyōōgokoku-ji (Tōji), Kyōto. H. 55 m. 1641–1644.

The pagoda was erected on the order of Tokugawa no Iemitsu to reproduce the original building of 826. It is a gallery pagoda with five roofs, an embodiment of the pure Japanese *wa-yō* style. In the original plan the pagoda on the south-east stood as a pendant to the Initiation Hall (Kanjō-in) on the south-west.

sought to illustrate the 'Two Worlds' by the design of the layout of temple buildings and by the forms of sculpture in the teaching halls.

In 816, Emperor Saga, who particularly favoured him, bestowed on Kūkai a favorite site in the Kōya-san hills for him to build a temple. There in the untrodden solitude of nature at her most majestic Kūkai set out the plans of the temple that was to be his headquarters, the Kongōbu-ji. It was not in fact completed until the time of his successor, the priest Shinnen. Building proceeded slowly, for the region was remote and short of water. The arrangement of the buildings followed the dual mandalas: the Great Pagoda and the West Pagoda (this was re-erected in 1834) corresponded to 'Diamond

World' and 'Womb World'. The new pagoda design, perhaps his own, was close to an Indian stupa reliquary in form. These Tahō-tō ('pagodas of the treasures') 12 were of two storeys with simulated domes plastered white; they housed statues of the Buddha Dainichi and honoured relics. This type of pagoda did not oust the older multi-storeyed ones, however; they too had a place in the temple complexes and were mostly more slender in form than the original form in the Hōryū-ji.

On Kōya-san the abbatial dwellings lay among the pagodas, in accordance with the mandala scheme. The Teaching Hall (Kōdō) was set behind the inner gate, with further halls related to it. The only one to survive is the Fudō of 1197. The accumulation of private sub-

Interior of the Teaching Hall (Kōdō) of the Kyōōgokoku-ji (Tōji), Kyōto.
The hall was built in 839, endowed by Nimmyō-Tennō to fulfil a vow. Twenty-one statues stand like a mandala on a broad platform. The central group of the Five Buddhas and the central figure of the Five Bodhisattvas were restored later. The five Kings of Wisdom, the four Shi-tennō, as well as the gods of Hindu origin, Bon-ten and Taishaku-ten, however, are originals of the ninth century. They show the heavy forms characteristic of a style still deeply indebted to India and China.

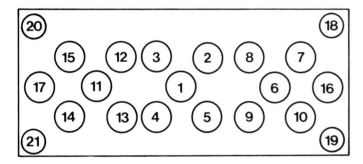

15
Plan of the Teaching Hall (Kōdō) of the Kyōōgokoku-ji (Tōji), Kyōto. The mandala ensemble of figures was dedicated in 839; six figures were completed later; the fifteen original sculptures have been drastically restored.
Central group of the Five Buddhas:
1 Dainichi Nyorai (Mahāvairocana)
2 Ashuku Nyorai (Akṣobhya)
3 Hōjō Nyorai (Ratnasambhava)
4 Fukujōju Nyorai (Amoghasiddhi)
5 Amida Nyorai (Amitāyus)
Eastern group of the Five Great Bodhisattvas (designations not unequivocal):
6 Kongōharamitsu Bosatsu
7 Kongōsatta—Kongōshu Bosatsu
8 Kongōhō Bosatsu
9 Kongōgyō Bosatsu—Kongōyakusha Bosatsu
10 Kongōhō Bosatsu—Kongōri Bosatsu
Western group of the Five Great Kings of Wisdom:
11 Fudō-myōō (Acalanātha)
12 Kongōyasha-myōō (Vajrajakṣa)
13 Gozanze-myōō (Trailokyavijaya)
14 Gundari-myōō (Kundali)
15 Daiitoku-myōō (Yamāntaka)
Centre (east):
16 Bon-ten (Brahma)
Centre (west):
17 Taishaku-ten (Indra)
Corner guardian figures of the Shi-tennō:
18 Tamon-ten (Vaishravana)
19 Jikoku-ten (Dhartarāstra)
20 Kōmoku-ten (Virūpākṣa)
21 Zōchō-ten (Virūdhaka)

temples—attracted by the proximity of Paradise, which promised a guarantee of Buddhahood—has destroyed the original scheme.

The storehouses of the mountain temple preserve quantities of works of art, Kūkai's own possessions and many of his writings, and also paintings and sculpture of the Heian and Kamakura periods, not all of them corresponding to Shingon ideas. Kūkai was able to develop further activities after 823, when Emperor Saga appointed him Great Abbot of Tōji, the eastern temple of the capital, Heian-kyō. The name of the temple was changed to Kyōōgokoku-ji ('Temple for the Protection 13 of the Land'), thereby proclaiming a nation-wide protective function for Shingon Buddhist teaching.

The temple layout had been fixed in the conventional manner at the foundation of the city. The worshipper took the path from the south gate (Nandaimon) along the south-north axis to the main hall. The south-east corner of the precinct was occupied by a five-storey pagoda with galleries, rebuilt in 1644; originally it corresponded to the Initiation Hall (Kaidan-in) in the south-west. The small altar room in the pagoda contained representations of the 'Two Worlds' spread over the pillars and walls, perhaps similar to the painting inside the pagoda of the Daigo-ji (951).

Kūkai set the Teaching Hall in the centre of the Kyōōgokoku-ji. Within it is constructed an over-life-size mandala of twenty-one wooden sculptures, stand- 14–15 ing on a plinth. The central group of four Buddhas encircling the figure of the Universal Buddha Dainichi (Vairocana) is a restoration, as is the central figure of the 'Five Great Bodhisattvas'. The 'Five Great Kings of Wisdom' (Godai-myōō) on the left survive from the early ninth century: the 'Immovable King of Wisdom' (Fudō-myōō) is flanked by four violently gesticulating Vidyārājas, personages of Indian Hinduism. On the four corners of the plinth stand the 'Four Heavenly Kings' (Shi-tennō) and, on the short sides, the Indian deities Brahma and Indra (Bon-ten and Taishaku-ten) riding on animals. The figures were not consecrated until 839, three years after Kūkai's death. In this mandala a breath of the corporeal yet magical Indian world of forms seems to have awakened in Japan to its own life.

A further temple, outside Heian-kyō, gained in importance for the Shingon sect: the Jingo-ji in the Takao mountains, where originally there had been a Shintō nature shrine. The ill-fated minister Wake no Kiyomaru built himself a private temple there in 801. Saichō

16
Pagoda of the Murō-ji, Nara. Timber-frame construction with shingle roofs. H. 16.2 m, W. 2.45 m. *c*. 800.
The small galleried pagoda, five storeys high, with widely overhanging flat shingle roofs, stands on a rock base within a thick wood of cryptomeria. The construction of its corbelling resembles the pagoda of the Yakushi-ji in Nara.

17
Kondō (Main Hall) of the Murō-ji, Nara. Timber-frame construction with shingle roof. Early ninth century.
The hall was originally five bays long and four bays wide; the addition of a Prayer Hall (Raidō) gave it a square ground plan. The elegantly curved shingle roof gives the building an intimate character. The Raidō and verandah were restored in 1672.

resided there also and gave readings of the *Lotus Sutra (Hokke-kyō)* to the court of Emperor Kammu. The temple, at that time was called Takao Sanji ('mountain temple of Takao'). Two years after the death of Saichō in 822, however, Kūkai took over the temple and reorganized it as a centre for Shingon teaching. He built a Tahō-tō pagoda and had five wooden sculptures of the Godai Kokūzō, the embodiments of the 'Womb World', set up in it. Kūkai endowed the Jingo-ji with the earliest mandala painted in gold and silver on purple damask. The influence of these works is clear in the sculptures. The twin shingle-roofed halls, the

Godai-dō and the Bishamon-dō, are (like the Kondō and the pagoda) later reconstructions. At the beginning of the ninth century the standing wooden figure of Yakushi (Bhaishajyaguru), the Buddha of Healing, came into the possession of the temple as a 'guest' from the Jingan-ji, a part of the Jingo-ji. The image is an early example of Japanese wood carving, a new and independently developing art known as Jōgan sculpture.

Towards the end of the Heian period the Jingo-ji again became a centre of interest as the refuge of Ex-emperor Goshirakawa. The ex-monarch assembled courtiers and artists about him, had a group of portraits 170, 202 of his familiars painted—allegedly by Fujiwara no Takanobu—and officiated himself at the 'Ceremony of the Lighting of the Lanterns' in the main hall in 1190.

The small mountain monastery of Murō-ji was orig- 16–17 inally, in about 700, the retreat of the hermit Shōkaku Gyōja, and it came within the administrative sphere of the Kōfuku-ji in Nara, which belonged to the Hosshō sect. The priest Kenkei is said to have laid out the

18

Sculptures in the altar room of the Main Hall (Kondō) of the Murō-ji, Nara. Wood, dressed and painted. H. (Shaka Nyorai) 238 cm. Early-late ninth century.

Beside the monumental central figure of Shaka Nyorai stand, on the right, Yakushi Nyorai and Jizō Bosatsu; on the left, Monju Bosatsu and the eleven-headed Kannon. The austere images, carved in single-block technique in the Jōgan style of the Early Heian period, probably did not originally belong together. Brightly painted 'board nimbi', surround the figures. The small figures of the 'Twelve Celestial Generals' are of the Kamakura period.

19

Shaka Nyorai. Wood with traces of gesso. H. 105 cm. Ninth century. Miroku-dō of the Murō-ji, Nara.

The seated figure, except for the hands and knees, is carved from a single block of *hinoki* wood with a few scant traces of the white coating that formed the basis of its original covering. The hair has also disappeared. The quality of the carving becomes particularly impressive as a result of this denudation. There is a hollow at the back of the image; the hands—in the gesture of 'setting in motion the Wheel of the Law'—and the knees were carved from separate pieces of wood attached subsequently. The drapery folds show the perfectly evolved 'rolling-wave' style of the Jōgan period.

temple. He was from the Kōfuku-ji and died in 793, but the buildings do not seem to have been finished before the beginning of the ninth century. The elegant five-storeyed pagoda, no more than 16.2 metres high, and 16 the Kondō, both covered with cypress shingles, illus- 17 trate the new intimate type of temple building of the Early Heian period. The valley in which the temple stood was celebrated for its rain-making processions, and legend has it that Kūkai, himself a rainmaker and wonderworker, marked it out as a mandala area. The Murō-ji did not officially join the Shingon sect until later. The small unpretentious precinct nestling in its natural surroundings heralded the spirit of the new era. Inside the Kondō, later to be extended by an ante- 18 chamber, stand five still and solemn wooden figures

20   ▷

The Diamond World Mandala (detail). Colours on silk. H. 183.5 cm, W. 163 cm. *c.* 900. Kyōōgokoku-ji, Kyōto.

In the upper central field Dainichi, the Buddha of Wisdom, bejewelled like a Bodhisattva, is seated on a lotus throne. His hands are in the *mudrā* of absolute Enlightenment; his head ornament has five Buddhas arranged like a crown; a veil-like flaming halo surrounds his head. The body nimbus is encircled with flames against the white, moon-like sphere that contains the figure.

arranged in an unorthodox hierarchy. The tall Shaka (Shakyamuni) holds the centre, and next to him on the right follow the Buddha Yakushi (Bhaishajyaguru) and Jizō (Kshitigarbha). On the left stand a Monju (Mañjushrī) and an eleven-headed Jūichimen Kannon (Avalokiteshvara). The figures are carved from the block in *ichiboku* technique, coloured and framed by richly painted aureole panels. Although the group seems to represent a local style, it is said that the Shaka and the Jūichimen Kannon date from the ninth century, and the other three figures only from the tenth. In front of this group stand small figures of the 'Twelve Heavenly Generals' (Jūni Shinshō). The histrionic naturalism of the figures has features characteristic of the Kamakura period.

The Maitreya Hall (Miroku-dō) of the Murō-ji preserves two more famous works of the Jōgan period. The Miroku, who has given his name to the hall, belongs among the very rare Chinese figurines of sandalwood *(danzo)*. This fragrant, exquisitely grained wood is especially admired by the Japanese. Japan, however, never adopted this manner of carving rich jewellery minutely out of the block. The hall also has the famous 19 seated Shaka Buddha preserved in a special shrine. It is a mature and extremely dignified example of Jōgan sculpture. With both setting and hair lost, the impressive ornamental quality of the conception and execution are emphasized all the more.

The Mandala *(Mandara)*

The secret teaching *(mikkyō)* of the new sects, especially the Shingon sect, used the pictorial arts to make the speculative vision of the Cosmos accessible not only to the understanding but to the senses of the faithful. This was why Kūkai had brought paintings and sculptures from China. The Mandala of the 'Two Worlds' *(Ryōkai Mandara)* forms the basis of meditation, magic and enlightenment. It gives a visual representation of the two aspects of the Ultimate Buddha of Highest Wisdom, Mahāvairocana. According to the texts of the *Mahāvairocana Sūtra* and the *Vajrasekhara Sūtra,* these magic diagrams originated first in India and were then given their East Asian stamp in China. In the centre of both configurations appears Vairocana. His many hundreds of symbolic forms are projected into the mandala in geometric patterns according to their degree of importance and the extent of their magic power.

The *Garbhadhatu Mandara* or Womb Mandala represents the aspect of 'unlimited compassion' in the world of appearances. Here Vairocana in his absolute aspect occupies the centre of a lotus. He is surrounded by four Buddhas and four Bodhisattvas in eight lotus petals, set towards the points of the compass. The 'Five Great Kings of Wisdom' (Godai-myōō), especially venerated

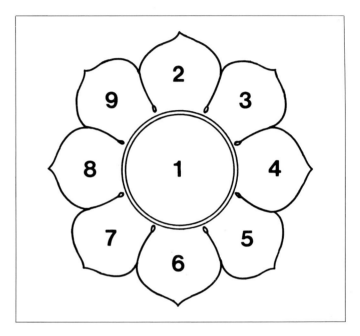

21
Diagram of the central field of the Womb World Mandala. Kyōōgokoku-ji, Kyōto.
1 Dainichi Nyorai (Mahāvairocana)
2 Hōdō Nyorai (Ratnaketu)
3 Fugen Bosatsu (Samantabhadra)
4 Kaifukeō Nyorai (Samkusumitarāja)
5 Monju Bosatsu (Mañjushrī)
6 Muryōju Bosatsu (Amitāyus)
7 Kannon Bosatsu (Avalokiteshvara)
8 Tenkuraion Nyorai (Divyadundubhimeghanirghosa)
9 Miroku Bosatsu (Maitreya)

22   ▷
The Womb World Mandala. Colours on silk. H. 183.6 cm, W. 164.2 cm. c. 900. Kyōōgokoku-ji, Kyōto.
This mandala is based on the *Mahāvairocana Sūtra.* It is composed of twelve zones with an eight-petalled lotus in the centre. The heart of the red blossom is occupied by the Buddha Dainichi in the form of a Bodhisattva. He is seated on a white lotus and surrounded by four Buddhas and four Bodhisattvas, all other incarnations of Dainichi. Above the lotus is the zone of 'universal knowledge', with the triangular symbol of absolute wisdom in the centre. Below the lotus are placed the Five Great Kings of Wisdom. In the outer zones, the manifold appearances of the Buddhas and Bodhisattvas are multiplied into a fascinating coloured mosaic.

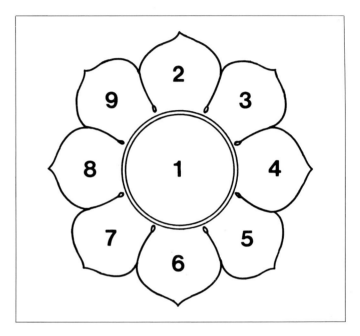

38

in esoteric Buddhism, fulfil their protective function by standing on a field below the lotus. At the corners appear the magic figures of Avalokiteshvara as the 'Thousand-armed Kannon' (Senju Kannon).

The Buddha Shaka and the Bodhisattva Monju Bosatsu occupy the spaces above. In the *Vajradhatu Mandara,* the Diamond Mandala, the 'diamond' aspect of the absolute wisdom of the Cosmos is represented by 445 beings. Vairocana occupies the top centre field of nine squares and also the centre of the eight other diagrams; next to him and surrounding him stand fabulous figures and symbols in circles. His absolute aspect in the upper space shows him sitting crowned on a lotus, with his hands joined in the *bodhyagri-mudrā,* symbolizing 'wisdom' and 'means', the two components of Enlightenment.

The *Takao Mandaras* of the Jingo-ji, brought from China, are considered to be the version handed down by Kūkai's teacher, the Patriarch Hui Guo. They are thought to date from between 824 and 833. These are probably Japanese copies; they are painted in gold and silver on purple damask in a technique recalling the end papers of sutras, which are painted on blue paper. The famous colourful mandala pair in the Tōji known as the Saiin version, is of the late ninth century.[13] This celebrated work of art illustrates not only the brilliance of Chinese painting in the late Tang period but also the virtuosity of the Japanese monk painters in copying them. The whole range of means available to Buddhist cult painting was at their command, used with confidence and delicacy: the modelling of the nude, 'reversed shading' on garments and lotus pedestals and painting with gold (the background would have originally been covered with patterns in gold openwork [*kirikane*]). The expressive faces, from the impassive frontal rendering of the exalted Buddhas to the lively or ferocious grimaces of the baser beings, are fascinatingly portrayed.

As T. Yanigasawa suggests,[14] these coloured mandalas may go back to models by the Chinese court painter Diao Qing. It is said that the priest Enchin, who stayed in Chang'an in 855, brought them to Japan first and dedicated them to Emperor Seiwa in 859.

Painted mandalas had their place, as they still do in Shingon temples, in front of the altar platform between the main pillars at the side. They were also hung up in the Shingon-in Hall of the palace during the second week of the New Year for the ceremony of the Protection of the Nation.

Jōgan Sculpture

The religious sculpture of the Early Heian period is called after the year cycles Kōnin (810–824) and Jōgan (859–876). Nowadays Jōgan sculpture (*Jōgan-chōkoku*) is a term applied to the distinctive and individual Japanese style of wood carving of the eighth to tenth centuries.[15]

The dissolution of the state and monastic sculpture workshops of the great temples of Nara after 780 at first no longer allowed the realization of large comprehensive programmes by division of labour. Because of the expense, the materials of the Nara period—bronze, dry lacquer and clay—were discarded in favour of wood carving. The trees of sub-tropical Japan provided many suitable woods. Jōgan sculptors preferred cypress, torrea nut, cherry and zelkova.

The out-of-the-way private temples tended each to have their own image-makers. Even before the esoteric sects of Tendai and Shingon brought in new esoteric figure programmes and new inspiration and models from China, new interpretations of cult images for the old sects (again and again the Buddha of Healing, Yakushi) were being carved in wood. The names of the artists are not known, but it is thought the many came from the Nara workshops. The workshop of the Tōshōdai-ji had a wooden sculpture studio run by Chinese monks who had come to Japan in the following of the priest Ganjin. There the wooden figures were mainly carved as cores for lacquered figures. The chief cult image of the seated Birushana Buddha in the Kondō is modelled in dry lacquer (*dakkan kanshitsu*), but the attendants are lacquered over a wooden core (*mokushin kanshitsu*). Numerous figures and torsi of bare wood are preserved in the temple's Kōdō. They have opulently curved limbs, and the drapery is rendered in ribbon-like, ornamentally arranged parallel folds. The influence of late Tang Buddhist stone carving can be detected in these pieces.

23
Yakushi Nyorai. Wood with traces of painting on the head. H. 170 cm. *c.* 802. Jingo-ji, Kyōto.
This cult image of the Buddha of Redemption, carved from a single trunk, is an example of the new Japanese type of expression in esoteric Buddhist sculpture. The ponderous volumes of his body and face give an impression of brooding gravity. The ornamental parallel pleats of his thin, tightly fitting robe are carved in the 'rolling-wave' style.

40

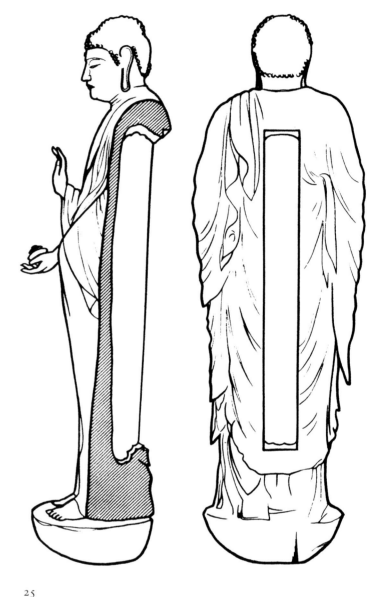

24
Yakushi Nyorai. Wood. H. 165.5 cm. Ninth century. Gangō-ji, Nara.
The standing figure of Yakushi is carved from a single block, only the head and hands are inserted. The proportions and the treatment of every detail are typical of the style of Jōgan sculpture. A comparison with the Yakushi of the Jingo-ji (Pl. 23) illustrates the influence here of the sculpture of the Nara era.

25
Drawing of the construction of the *Yakushi Nyorai* in the Gangō-ji, Nara.
The vertical hollow in the back of the statue served both to prevent splitting and to give room for holy substances.

An essential feature of Jōgan images is the single-trunk technique *(ichiboku-zukuri):* the figures are carved like columns from a block. To avoid the danger of splitting, the figures were often hollowed out vertically from the back. For projecting parts like arms, the side parts of standing figures or the knees and drapery of seated figures, extra blocks were attached.

A standing figure was naturally suited to the single-trunk technique; the round trunk was right for shape and treatment. The Japanese sculptor's elaboration of

42

novel ornamental effects showed great sensitivity for
the structure of the wood; such effects could not have
been achieved in the previous period with only the soft
modelling for bronze casting or for the lacquer and clay
figures. The drapery folds are described as in 'rolling
wave' style *(hompa-shiki);* the section shows a rhythmi-
cal alternation of high cord–like ridges and flat undula-
tions, hollowed like a teaspoon. The ornamental aspect
of the Jōgan figures is further stressed by the sharp
linear manner in which the heavy unclothed parts of the
body are juxtaposed, and the undefined and massive facial features are in some measure set against the often
elegant lines of the drapery that terminate in volutes. In
the Jingo-ji the standing Yakushi Buddha figure is the
prototype of Jōgan sculpture. The sagging heavy forms
of the head and body crowned with a bonnet-shaped
ushnīsha became the model for figures in the Gangō-ji
and Murō-ji.

The uncoated wooden figures, with only eyes, lips
and facial hair painted in colour, are called *sochi-zō*
('nature figures'). This group includes the seated
Yakushi Buddha, which is the central figure of the
Shin-Yakushi-ji in Nara.

The cosmic ideas of the esoteric sects made other
members of the Buddhist pantheon the centre of worship. Imaginary spirits and magical protective deities
now needed to be represented. Kūkai had seen such images in China, based on models with Indian features.
Hindu deities like Brahma, Indra and the Kings of Wisdom appear in the sculpture mandala of the Tōji. As an
example H. Minamoto illustrates side by side the
three-headed Bon-ten (Brahma) of the Tōji and the
three-headed Shiva Mahādeva of Elephanta of the
seventh century.[16]

The grouping of the seated Bodhisattvas in the Tōji
and of the Five Godai Kokūzō in the Jingo-ji convincingly express the gentleness emanating from these di-

(marginal references: 19, 26 — 23 — 24 — 19 — 14–15)

26
Bosatsu. Wood. H. 124.5 cm. First half of the ninth century.
Hōbodai-in, Kyōto.
This Bodhisattva is sitting in the posture of 'royal ease' with his
right leg hanging down. The pupils of the eyes in his full face and the
beauty spot *(ūrnā)* on his forehead are of incrusted amber, and his
hair is bound up like a crown. His garment falls into swirling ornamental drapery of the 'rolling-wave' type. This figure, carved in the
single-trunk technique, is among the masterpieces of the fully developed Jōgan style and is closely connected to Chinese sculpture of
the Late Tang period.

43

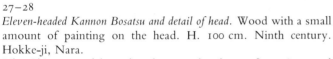

27–28
Eleven-headed Kannon Bosatsu and detail of head. Wood with a small amount of painting on the head. H. 100 cm. Ninth century. Hokke-ji, Nara.
Like Chinese sandalwood sculptures, the elegant figure is carved from one block of wood. The pose and expression, like the mannered fall of the scarf and the skirt drapery, show the culmination of the Jōgan style.

vine healers. They are very similar to the interpretations of the painted mandalas.

Their painterly quality is stressed by the partial coating of dry lacquer, which covers only the clothing, while the exposed parts of the skin are left bare. The same technique is used on the masterpiece of the 26 Hōbodai-in Temple, Kyōto, a Bodhisattva of markedly Chinese style seated in the posture of 'royal ease'.

Among these esoteric Buddhist beings is the central cult image of the Kanshin-ji near Ōsaka, a seated figure of the Nyoirin Kannon, from about 830. It is a six-armed avatar, composed in the round, which belongs

to the impressively sublime sculpture of the Jōgan period. It is ranked artistically with the Shaka Buddha 19 of the Murō-ji and the standing eleven-headed Kannon 27–28 of the Hokke-ji.

The influence of the small sandalwood figurines that had been coming from China since the Nara period is probably not insignificant either. These Tang figurines mostly represented the Bodhisattva Kannon adorned with openwork strings of jewels. On the other hand, the portable altar with a Shaka trinity in the Gandhāra

29   ▷
Face of *Tobatsu-Bishamon-ten*. Wood with dressing of lacquer and paint over cloth. H. 194 cm. From China, *c.* 800. Kyōōgokoku-ji, Kyōto.
Tobatsu-Bishamon-ten, a protective deity of Tibeto-Turkestanian origin, was adopted as guardian of the capital city and probably originally stood in the Rashō-mon city gate. The fact that the figure is built up of a number of separate wooden blocks and has eyes of incrusted obsidian shows it to be Chinese work.

style, a personal possession of Kūkai, seems to have made very little impression on Japanese figure style.

The eleven-headed Kannons of Jōgan sculpture seem to have been more affected by the iconography than by the style of the sandalwood figurines. The eleven-headed Kannon in the Hokke-ji represents a very far-reaching modification of the Chinese models towards Japanese taste. It is a paradigm of all of the stylistic traits of Jōgan sculpture.

Several monumental wooden sculptures in the possession of the Tōji even came directly from China. In addition to a set of the Five Godai Kokūzō, the mighty figure of Tobatsu-Bishamon-ten plays a national role as Guardian of the North and, moreover, of the whole country. The ferocious armoured figure with Tibetan features is said to have stood originally on the upper storey of the Rashō-mon city gate. The guardian stands, with pagoda and lance, on three demons, the middle one of which—the Earth Goddess Jiten—resembles a secular figure, a Chinese lady-in-waiting.

In the Shingon cult the 'Five Great Kings of Wisdom' (Godai-myōō) played a leading role, and among them Acalanātha (Fudō-myōō) is especially prominent as the manifestation of the Great Buddha Dainichi. With the image of this 'Immutable King of Wisdom' a new character took the centre of the stage in the tantric cult. Besides the original image in the Kondō of the Tōji, the 'secret Buddha', a sculpture of Fudō from Kūkai's dwelling hall (Miei-dō) in the Tōji, presents an even more decisive version of Jōgan style. Since the teaching of the Shingon sect brought Japanese deities into the Buddhist pantheon, Shintō gods were also represented in sculpture. Hachiman shrines, attached to Buddhist temples as Shintō protective shrines, contained groups of two or three Shintō deities in human form. Hachiman, the ancient Japanese god of war, was represented in them as a monk (Sōgyō Hachiman) as he was in the Yakushi-ji trinity of 889–897. His attendants, Empress Jingō-kōgō, or Jingū-kōgō, and Princess Nakatsu-hime are represented as court ladies in Chinese costume. No other Shintō figures show the maturity of Jōgan style as perfectly as this Yakushi-ji trinity. A cruder but earlier group belongs to the Tōji; one rather later to the Matsuo-jinja Shintō shrine. A few portrait sculptures of priests also form part of this group. For reasons of magic the rendering of the individual facial features is of paramount importance. The seated figure of the priest Enchin is a striking rendering of the forceful personality of this unusual man.

30

The Priest Enchin (Chishō Daishi): by Ryōsei. 1143. Shōgo-in Temple, Kyōto.

There are three posthumous portraits of the famous priest Enchin (814–891) of the Tendai sect who, thanks to his trip to China and his founding of the Onjō-ji, is considered one of the most important people in Japanese esoteric Buddhism. This portrait shows a strong man with a high forehead and a wide chin, sitting in meditation. Statues of Shintō gods probably influenced this picture, for Enchin was also known by a Shintō name, Sannō Daishi or 'mountain king'.

31

Empress Jingō-kōgō. Wood, dressed and painted. H. 35.5 cm. Ninth century. Yasumigaoka-Hachiman-Jingū, Yakushi-ji, Nara.

The empress belongs in a trinity of Shintō deities with Hachiman, the war god, represented as a monk, and Princess Nakatsu-hime. The goddess wears Chinese court apparel, as was fashionable in the Early Heian period, with a skirt and the brocade jacket of the upper nobility over a long-sleeved kimono. Her free-falling hair, crowned with a bun, gives the impression of being a wig. The figurine is carved in 'single-block' technique and coated with colours and dry lacquer, with a few traces of gold still recognizable.

Buddhist Painting

Like sculpture, the religious painting of the late eighth century managed to free itself from the highly developed artistic activity of the temple workshops of Nara. Painting, especially in the East Asian form of hanging or hand scrolls of silk, linen or paper, intended for only temporary display or examination, is very subject to wear and tear, and only very few paintings of the Jōgan period have been preserved. They all belong to esoteric painting *(mikkyō-ga)*.

Due to Kūkai quite a number of Chinese paintings came to Japan, either given to him by his teacher or commissioned by him from well-known painters. It was a tenet of Shingon belief that in representing a being some of its magic power might be directly awakened and transmitted to the practitioner, and thus the painting itself partook of divinity.

The original coloured set of the Mandala of the 'Two Worlds' from China survives in the Saiin (or in the Shingon-in) of the Kyōōgokoku-ji, a work we have already mentioned. The two other sets, both in linear drawing of gold and silver, stem from other models, perhaps lost iconographic sketches. The earliest pair in the Jingo-ji is dated around 824; the next, in the Kojimadera, is only eleventh century. The mandala, especially the coloured version, already shows signs of the Japanese touch. The soft brush drawing and the unexpected serenity of the lively figures of the 'lower ranks of being' are quite alien to Chinese style. The cursory brushwork of the filling of row upon row of Buddha figures suggests a division of labour in the production.

Portraits of patriarchs occupied a similarly high position in Shingon doctrine. Kūkai returned from China with five ideal portraits of the Chinese Shingon patriarchs. They are from the hand of Li Zheng, a painter whose name is quite forgotten in China. Kūkai had the portraits of the Indian patriarchs Nāgārjuna (Ryūmyō) and Nāgabōdhi (Ryūchi) finished in Japan. These two paintings are without an artist's signature, but Kūkai adorned them, perhaps for ritual reasons, with inscriptions in an archaic decorative script *(zettai-sho)* and put explanatory inscriptions on the lower borders with the date 821.

The monk painters who had been trained on the painted mandala pictures were apparently given the task of decorating temple walls directly with the sacred mandala diagrams. The figure painting on the chapel of

the Daigo-ji is very close to that of the mandala in the Saiin. The building was completed in 951 and consecrated by Emperor Murakami in 952. The figures of the mandala were laid directly on primed wooden boards; the figures of the highest rank were placed centrally on the primed 'heart pillar' of the structure. The *Taizō-kai* Mandala appears facing west and the *Kongō-kai* Mandala facing east. On the lower parts of the board walls at the sides, the Eight Patriarchs of the Shingon sect (with Kūkai as the eighth) are represented in a lowly location, closely modelled on the original images of the Kyōōgokoku-ji. Here again the inferior quality of the secondary figures compared with the chief ones is striking. Y. Yashiro[17] thinks it probable that stencils were used to help with the drawing in, and then the sketches were overpainted by hand. This would represent an early use of the method of duplication practised in secular painting, for example on the sutra fans of the Shitennō-ji.

Some hundred years before the decoration of the pagoda of the Daigo-ji, a Taishaku Mandala was painted in the main hall of the Murō-ji, hidden behind the carving of the Yakushi Buddha. Taishaku-ten (the Hindu god Indra) appears as a Bodhisattva seated between two standing attendants. On the narrow boards that serve as the ground all the spaces round the main figure are filled with innumerable dot-like little secondary figures. A step towards the complete synthesis of all the arts perfected in the Fujiwara period can be seen attempted here.

'Meditation pictures' had a similar function to the mandalas, with single figures or trinities, usually showing the demonic aspect of the Buddhist pantheon. Acalanātha (Fudō-myōō) appears time and again as a central figure. In Jōgan painting three versions were apparently already developing. The 'Yellow Fudō' (Ki-Fudō) belongs to the 'secret Buddhas' of the Onjō-ji, founded by the priest Enchin on Lake Biwa. The

32

Womb World Mandala (detail). Wall painting, colours on panel. 952. Pagoda of the Daigo-ji, Kyōto.
The core of the pagoda is lined with boards on which the mandalas of the 'Two Worlds' are represented. The western side shows the Buddha Dainichi Nyorai richly bejewelled, flanked above by two Bodhisattvas, and over him, also on a lotus throne, is the symbol of absolute wisdom: a triangle. The connection with the mandalas in the Kyōōgokoku-ji is very close, though some 'Japanization' is apparent.

33
Fudō-myōō and Two Disciples. Colours on silk. H. 205 cm, W. 150 cm. Mid-eleventh century. Shōren-in Temple, Kyōto.
Fudō is portrayed sitting on a rock base and surrounded by a wildly flaming aureole. As a Blue Fudō he holds sword and lasso like the statue in the Kyōōgokoku-ji. His young disciples, the boys Seitaka-Dōji and Kongara-Dōji, are flanking him. According to documents in the Daigo-ji the painting was supposedly done by Genchō, a priest of the Gangō-ji in Nara.

34
Gozanze-myōō. Colours and *kirikane* on silk. H. 153 cm, W. 128 cm. 1127. Kyōōgokoku-ji, Kyōto.
The terrifying three-headed and eight-armed figure of Gozanze is one of a set of cult images of the Godai-myōō, the 'Five Great Kings of Wisdom or of Light'. Dancing he hovers over the Earth goddess Jiten, and stands on a worshipping demon. The dramatically gesticulating figure is set against a background of ornamental flames. The series of paintings was displayed for worship in the Shingon-in, the palace chapel, during the ceremonies of the Protection of the Nation.

35
'The Shingon-in Chapel in the Imperial Palace': Scroll 6 of the *Nenjū-gyōji-emaki,* painting 4 (copy after the original of *c.* 1160). Ink and colours on paper. H. 45.2 cm. Private Collection.
We are shown the interior of the Shingon-in chapel with monks along the side with the entrance. Opposite are the hanging scrolls with the cult images of the Godai-myōō over altar tables, while the mandalas of the 'Two Worlds' hang on the end walls to the right and left. Before these are placed flat altars with lotus blossoms. In the right one is a reliquary shrine. The painting is done in central perspective, very seldom used in the scroll paintings instead of parallel perspective.

rigidly frontal standing figure seems to be carved from wood. The rich Indian jewellery and the shaded pigmentation of the parallel folds of his garment recall the 'rolling waves' of Jōgan sculpture. The compulsive gaze of the eyes is the strongest reminder of his magic presence.

33   The 'Blue Fudō' (Ao-Fudō) in the temple of Shōren-in, on the other hand, holds close to the representation conceived in the painted mandala. Fudō is seated in the lotus posture on a rocky plinth, holding a sword and lasso to combat evil. He is surrounded by a flaming aureole. His boy attendants stand in worship beside him: Seitaka-Dōji and Kongara-Dōji. This outstandingly composed and sophisticated painting is a version of the eleventh century. We encounter here the technical virtuosity and artistic maturity of the Late Heian period.

The third interpretation, the 'Red Fudō' (Aka-Fudō) is preserved in the Myōō-in on the Kōya-san. In spite of the archaicizing technique of 'ironwire lines' *(tessen-byō),* there are details that show this celebrated painting to be a work of the Kamakura period.

The Saidai-ji in Nara possesses devotional pictures in the Early Heian style of the ninth century in the form of twelve hanging scrolls of the Twelve Deva Kings (Jūni-ten), who function as protectors against disaster and sickness. The heavy figures, riding on animal mounts and each flanked by two worshippers, come near to bursting out of the picture space.

The Bodhisattvas of the group of the 'Five Great Bodhisattvas of Power' (Godairiki Bosatsu) appear in frightening guise. Three single elements of the group are preserved in the Junji-Hachiman-kō Temple on Kōya-san. Their aggressive frontality and bursting vitality has all the features of early esoteric painting. The flames of the nimbus are rendered with linear stylization here, unlike the free and lively flickering round the 'Blue Fudō'. These paintings are direct evidence that certain archaicizing traits persisted, probably for magical reasons, into the Fujiwara period.

Chinese Literature and Calligraphy

In writing down the Japanese-language *Manyō-shū* an-   36
thology in 759, the compilers aimed at using the Chinese ideographic script in a new phonetic manner *(manyō-gana* or *mana).* In spite of this start, at the beginning of the Heian period there was no specific script to meet the needs of the agglutinative Japanese language.

Furthermore, the Chinese language, and Chinese culture altogether, was considered indispensable for scholars, men of rank at court and priests. The two outstanding intellectuals of the Early Heian period, the priests Saichō and Kūkai, had acquired their thought and their writing skills from the book scrolls imported in the Nara period. There were, it is true, some attempts at a free cursive script, but the texts of the classics, philosophers and poets and of the Buddhist sutras, which were copied as acts of merit, were written in meticulous block characters *(rei-sho).*

The travellers in the mission to China of 804 helped forward the task of freeing the script from architectonic strictness to a painterly art of the brush. Not only the priests in the mission took part in this work but also the high-born courtier Tachibana no Hayanari, whom the Chinese are said to have addressed as a 'superlative talent'. But it was Kūkai who achieved sovereign mastery of both classical and modern Chinese calligraphy. He studied in Chang'an with the calligrapher Han Fangming and practised the exemplary style of the great Wang Xizhi (307–365). He exercised himself both in the semi-cursive *gyō-sho* and in cursive grass character 37 (*sō-sho*) and also practised artistic scripts like 'flying white'. A few lines of the epoch-making 'Treatise on Writing' *(Shupu)* by Sun Guoting[18] are preserved to this day in what is claimed to be Kūkai's own copy. His 38 own philosophical and critical writings, epitaphs and poems fill volumes. Kūkai also kept up a correspondence with Saichō, a few fragments of which remain. His basic work of Shingon teaching, 'The Ten Steps of Spiritual Development' *(Jūjūshiron)* and his work on Chinese poetry, 'Secret Treasure of the Mirror of Literature' *(Bunkyō hifuron),* have remained standard works.

Kūkai founded a school of art and science in the Tōji in 828 for the benefit of poor students; he also taught calligraphy at the court. His most distinguished pupil was Emperor Saga. With this rather dilettante emperor and Tachibana no Hayanari, who wrote name plaques for the court, for temple gates and for dedication documents, he is one of the 'Three Masters of Writing' *(sampitsu)* of the period.

The emperors of the Early Heian period considered it meritorious to publish works in Chinese. Emperor Kammu encouraged the publication of the second of the 'Six Official Annals of the Empire' *(Shoku Nihongi,* 797) by the Bureau for the Compilation of Imperial Histories under Fujiwara no Tsuginawa. The *Nihonkōki* followed in 844 under Nimmyō-Tennō. There also appeared in the early ninth century three anthologies of Chinese poetry written in Japan, all under the patronage of Saga-Tennō. The *Ryōun-shū* of 814 contained 91 poems; the *Bunka Shūrei-shū* followed in 818 with 143 poems; while the *Keikoku-shū* of 827 had as many as 900 poems, prose pieces and dissertations. Even works by Kūkai appear in it. It is difficult to judge whether the Japanese poets succeeded in expressing anything individual in the foreign language; the poetry of the Tang and pre-Tang periods was too well known not to be zealously copied. A manuscript of poems in 39 the hand of Emperor Saga survives; the poems are by Li Zhiao, an eighth-century poet quite forgotten in China.

The works of the famous poet Bo Juyi (Haku Rakuten, 772–846) were already reaching Japan during his

36
Manjō-shū (detail of Katsura fragment): Anonymous. Ink on eight kinds of coloured paper. H. 29 cm, L. 805 cm. Eleventh century. Imperial Household.
This scroll contains 309 poems from the fourth volume of the *Manyō-shū* in excellent and rapid calligraphy. Not only the juxtaposition of *kana* syllabic script with the full characters of the Chinese script, called *manyō-gana,* gives this calligraphy its rhythm, but the underlying painting in gold and silver also adds considerably to its force.

37
Inscription by Kūkai (Kōbō Daishi) on a *Portrait of a Patriarch* (detail). Ink on silk. *c.* 821. Kyōōgokoku-ji, Kyōto.
Kūkai wrote the sinicized name-characters on the portrait of the great Indian patriarch Ryūmyō (Nāgārjuna). The decorative script was dubbed 'flying white' from the broken lines of ink.

38
'*Fūshin-jō':* calligraphy (detail) by Kūkai (Kōbō Daishi). Ink on paper. H. 28.5 cm, L. 154.6 cm. *c.* 812. Kyōōgokoku-ji, Kyōto. The scroll with Kūkai's notes to Saichō (Dengyō Daishi) are called after the beginning of the text, 'Fūshin-jō'. They are dated the fifth, eleventh and thirteenth days of the Ninth Month. The Chinese characters written by Kūkai, partly in complete and partly in abbreviated script, give a clear picture of the powerful personality of the writer. (After *Shodō Zenshū,* Vol. IX, Nihon 2, Heian I. Tōkyō, 1955, Pl. 26)

39
Poem by Li Zhiao: calligraphy (detail) ascribed to Saga-Tennō (809–823). Ink on paper. H. 235 cm, W. 26 cm. Imperial Household.
Of the work of 120 poems by this Chinese poet of the Tang dynasty, twenty have survived in the copy by Emperor Saga. The style of the writer is based on the script of the Chinese master Ouyang Xiu, whose calligraphy was fashionable in Japan at the beginning of the Heian period. This poem on 'Dew' shows the bold but stylized hand of the emperor. (After *Shodō Zenshū,* Vol. IX, Nihon 2, Heian I, Tōkyō, 1955, Pl. 66)

lifetime. His fame in Japan was universal: the 'Poem of Eternal Sorrow' *(Chōgonka)* especially touched all hearts. It became the fashion to use a line from one or the other of his poems as a topos for Japanese *tanka*. His works also enjoyed a great vogue as texts for calligraphy: an example has been preserved in the uncom- 40 monly exalted sweeping hand of Daigo-Tennō.

Knowledge of Chinese literature and calligraphy was officially transmitted through the teachers of the universities. There were Doctors of Calligraphy *(shohakase)* as well as Doctors of Literature *(monjo-hakase).* These offices were mostly the prerogative of sinologi-

36

37

38

39

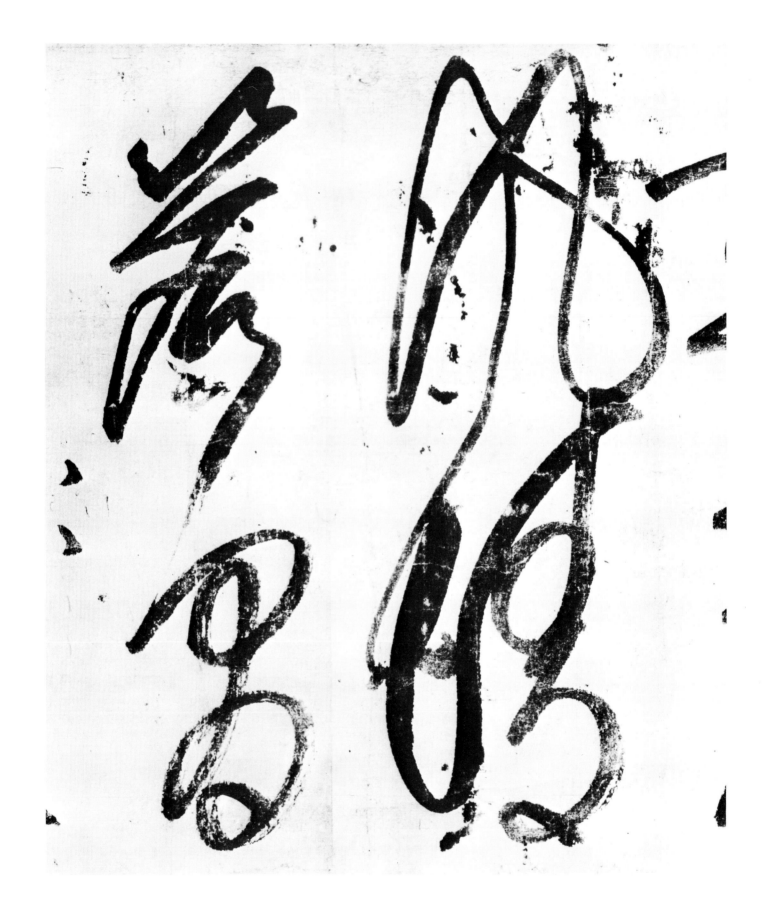

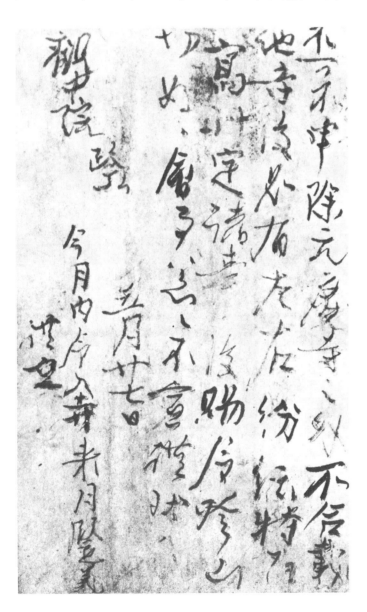

cally oriented families like the Tachibana, Ōe, Ki and Sugawara, and were hereditary.

The members of the Tendai sect who went to China as pilgrims made their mark in the ninth century as independent calligraphers. They were less interested in the religious teachings of their sect than in obtaining the practices and texts of the Shingon sect in China. The celebrated diary of the priest Ennin has probably not been preserved in the original. The calligraphy of the younger priest Enchin was more highly prized as calligraphy and treasured in the Onjō-ji founded by him. A letter from the year 890, however, shows the sprawling hand of an elderly sick person; it is shattering from a human point of view to note the difference from the early brilliant examples penned by the great man.

With the cessation of official embassies to China in 894, the Japanese court seems no longer to have been interested in direct contact with the continent, for the troubles of the declining Tang empire promised little profit either materially or intellectually. Even so the international status of Chinese scholarship at court remained as high as ever.

Japanese Literature and Calligraphy

Beside the Chinese style in literature and writing, a Japanese style was crystallizing; it did not immediately oust the continental style but developed a Japanese feminine alternative to the Chinese one, which was felt to be masculine, like the *yin* and *yang* of Chinese cosmology. At the end of the ninth century, the development of two simple *kana* syllabic scripts gave the Japanese language the cursive *hira-gana,* which joined the manly Chinese script *(onoko-de)* as its feminine counterpart *(onna-de).*

Even though Chinese script and literature was dominant during the first half of the ninth century, the Japanese short poem in 5 lines and 31 syllables *(tanka)* persisted, traditional since the *Manyō-shū,* alongside the pompous rhymed Chinese verse of 5 or 7 lines *(kanshi).* In the ninth century appeared the 'Six Poetical Geniuses' (Rokkasen), some of whose works were published posthumously by Ki no Tsurayuki in the *Kokin-shū* in 905 but in no way praised in his famous Introduction. The Rokkasen included the courtiers Ariwara no Narihira (825–888), Bunya no Yasuhide, Ōtomo no Kuronushi, the monks Bishop Henjō (816–890) and

Kisen, as well as one lady: Ono no Komachi (*c.* 850). Numerous legends are woven about her brilliant life and lonely old age. Though the *tanka* flows with flattering melody for the ear, its meaning is liable to be far from clear, for the use of hinge words *(kake-kotoba)*, pillow words *(makura-kotoba)* and associations *(engō)* were a burden on spontaneity. Despite these rules, which narrowly confined the form and content of the poetry, the world of the poet's sensibility could unfold the finest nuances in the *tanka*.

The 'Collection of Old and New Japanese Poems' *(Kokin[-waka-]shū)* of 905 stands at the head of the anthologies compiled by imperial decree. Seven more collections followed, ending with the *Shin-Kokin-waka-shū* in 1205. Uda-Tennō appears to have initiated the *Kokin-shū,* but it only came out under his son, Daigo-Tennō. Two of the compilers, Ki no Tsurayuki (872–945) and the elder Ki no Tomonori, wrote prefaces with similar contents. The celebrated Japanese text by Ki no Tsurayuki (Tomonori wrote in Chinese) went: 'The Yamato poem has the human heart as its

42–43
Kokin-shū (Honami fragment, details): attributed to Ono no Tōfu (Michikaze, 894–966). Hand scroll with ink on paper, previously printed and coloured. H. 16.6 cm. Eleventh century. Imperial Household.
On a hand scroll composed of pastel-coloured sheets of paper, pasted together and printed with mica in various coloured patterns, the calligrapher has written poems from the *Kokin-shū.* The combination of Chinese characters with linked, sweeping *kana* syllables and the somewhat irregular placing of the lines give the calligraphy a melodic rhythm. The hand scroll once belonged to the great calligrapher and artist Honami Kōetsu (1558–1637).

root and thousands of words as leaves. ... In this world, where people are employed in so many different ways, poetry consists in expressing what the heart feels by what we see and hear [and here Tsurayuki indicates the actual subject of poetry]: to fall in love with flowers, to envy the birds, to be moved by the delicate spring mist and made sad by the dew'.[19]

In contrast to the *Manyō-shū,* which contained every kind of poem and song, and set lyrics by emperors be-

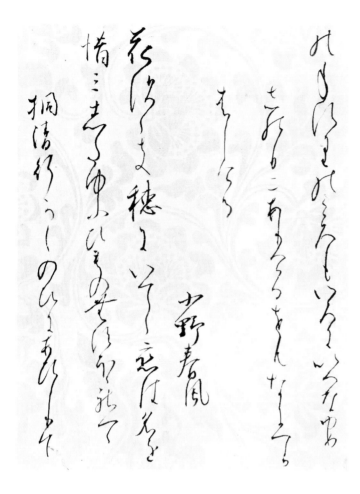

ture, which S. Kato terms the 'first turning point'.[20] After the priest Shunei of the Tendai sect returned from China in 865 as the last of the pilgrims to China, and before relations with China were finally broken off and Fujiwara no Yoshifusa was appointed regent (Sesshō) in 866, a radical change occurred in social, political and economic affairs. As a consequence, aesthetic values also began to change, and facets of Japanese thought and feeling, which have retained their validity to the present day, began to crystallize.

The writing of the brilliant statesman Sugawara no Michizane (845–903) represents another high water mark in the Chinese-style literature and poetry of the Heian period. He wrote and thought fluently in Chinese and wrote two collections of poems: *Kanke-bunsō* (900) and *Kanke-koshū* (903), both of which contained highly personal poems. His pupil Ki no Haseo (845–912) also shone as a calligrapher of Chinese characters. The latter's son, Ki no Yoshimochi, wrote the Introduction, conceived originally in Chinese, in Japanese for the anthology *Kokin-shū* referred to above. The opposition of the mighty Fujiwaras meant that the sinological families were unable to retain high positions. Michizane, a victim of intrigue, was one of the 'noble failures' of Japanese history.

The *kana* syllabary was adopted in court circles through the poet and anthologizer Ki no Tsurayuki. A manuscript of the *Kokin-shū,* compiled by him, known as the *Koya-gire,* includes certain passages attributed to his own hand. Since Tsurayuki wrote carefully precise characters, his form of *kana* is known as 'proper style' *(shin-tai).* There are parts in the same manuscript written in cursive *kana (gyō-tai)* and the virtuoso trailing forms of the grass-character *kana (sō-tai).* These, however, are of a rather later date. We can see how spontaneously the *kana* script was adapted and refined into variants that are worthy to be set alongside the hands of Chinese calligraphy. Tsurayuki left behind him a few small but highly prized pieces of calligraphy in the form of poem sheets, 'colour papers' *(shikishi).* These *shikishi* herald an art form that, in the following centuries, was repeatedly manipulated in new ways, supremely suitable for the delight in refinements of variation that particularly appeals to the Japanese. The twelve *shikishi* by 44 Tsurayuki, called *Shunsōan-shikishi* after the place where they were preserved, show his writing on select coloured 'China paper' *(kara-kami),* lavishly printed with mica powder. Each poem is on a separate sheet, written in cursive *kana* characters. Tsurayuki's pioneer-

42–43 side those of peasants and soldiers, the *Kokin-shū* is more uniform. The 127 poets chosen almost all belonged to the lower nobility. Only in one section of chapter 20, almost at the end of the collection, are twenty poems from the Imperial Office of Poetry, and only a single poem was by an emperor. A third of all the *tanka* are by unknown poets. There are two main groups of poems: chapters 1 to 6 contain 'Poems for the Four Seasons' and chapters 11 to 15 'Love Poems'. 'Congratulations and Good Wishes', 'Parting', 'Travel', 'Names of Things', 'Sorrow', 'Miscellaneous', 'Digressions' and 'Poems by the Office of Poetry' each have one chapter. The strict and demanding *tanka* form predominates with 1,102 poems, while there are only five 'long poems' *(chōka)* and four 'dialogue verses' *(sedōka).*

During the ninth century the detailed *mana* characters gradually developed into the *kana* syllabary of forty-eight characters still valid today. The abbreviations first appear, as though by chance, in a note by Fujiwara no Aritoshi. It was the beginning of 'Japanization' in litera-

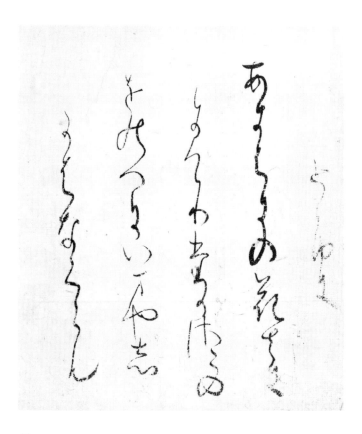

44
Poem sheet: attributed to Ki no Tsurayuki (872–945). Ink on light blue paper with mica printing. H. 12.9 cm, W. 12.3 cm. Eleventh century. Gotoh Art Museum, Tōkyō.

This poem sheet *(shikishi)* is now mounted as a hanging scroll. The noble Chinese paper, printed with a gourd scroll in mica, comes from a famous album that originally belonged to the Shunsōan Temple of the Daitoku-ji in Kyōto (hence the term *'Shunsōan-shikishi'*). Because Ki no Tsurayuki wrote the poem, the powerful *kana* calligraphy is attributed to him, but it only dates from the eleventh century.

ing work in purely Japanese calligraphy started a tradition that has persisted to modern times.

Though *kana* script was termed 'women's script' because of its simplicity and elegance, it did not prevent

Tsurayuki and other poets in the Japanese language from using this new form. Tsurayuki wrote his *Tosa-nikki* ('Tosa Diary') as though the author were a woman. It was written in 935 on his journey back to the nostalgically longed-for capital, Heian-kyō, from Tosa, the province where he had been governor. He wrote: 'Diaries, I am told, are things written by men, but I am trying my hand to see what a woman can accomplish'. The *Tosa-nikki* thus occupies an outstanding place in Japanese literature, being the first diary that is wholly personal and full of feeling and sentiment. Before Tsurayuki, the monk Ennin had written a diary of his journey in China, but Ennin (who wrote in Chinese) gave a very dry record of the stages and incidents of his travels, allowing no personal impressions to intrude.

There had been other prose writing in Japanese before the *Tosa-nikki,* but the prose tale, romance or novel *(monogatari)* did not emerge as a genre until the turn from the ninth to the tenth century. The *Taketori-monogatari* ('Story of the Bamboo Cutter') was written at more or less the same time as the *Kokin-shū* and in a mixture of *kana* and Chinese. The content and style both bear the marks of Chinese and Korean influences. While the *Taketori-monogatari* has popular traits, the famous 'Tales from Ise' *(Ise-monogatari)* is a verse novel *(uta-monogatari)* that could only have been written in the court entourage. The *Ise-monogatari* has 125 episodes recounting the amorous adventures of the Japanese Don Juan, the poet Ariwara no Narihira (825–880), who was one of the 'Six Poetical Geniuses'. Each episode begins: 'Once upon a time there lived a man. . . . .' There is no continuity of narrative but rather a series of vignettes framing one or two love poems. A third of them are poems by Narihira himself. With the *Ise-monogatari,* written after the lifetime of its hero, begins the series of charming tales that are to be regarded as the forerunners of the great epic novel of the Heian period, the *Genji-monogatari* by the court lady-in-waiting, Murasaki Shikibu.

III   The Flowering of the Heian Period

The Fujiwara Family

The power of the imperial house since the Nara period was founded on the laws of the Taihō Code of 702 and the Yōrō Code of 718, both based on Chinese models. They established the penal regulations and administrative institutions of a centralized state. In the compilation of both codes a large part was played by Fujiwara no Fubito (659–720), a son of Nakatomi no Kamatari. (Kamatari, who had won renown as victor over the Soga clan and as the originator of the Taika Reform of 645, had received the name Fujiwara as a distinction.) The codes laid down the orders and prohibitions of the young Japanese state. The land belonged to the emperor, who awarded it to his subjects. Rights of use and taxes were ordered according to households and head counts, and in theory these were reviewed every six years, for, according to the land regulations, after a death the land reverted to the state. Registers of households (koseki) were drawn up and checked by officials. Besides household lands there were rank lands (iden) for princes and the higher nobility, service lands for officials (shikibunden), merit and honour lands (kōden). The produce of post lands (ekiden) went for the national budget, and of crown land (kanden) for the imperial household. However, this system was not observed in practice. The cultivation of new territories allowed the establishment of private latifundia (shōen), not included in the fiscal returns. More and more frequently the nobles and clergy managed to dodge the land regulations through middle-men, and the state received less and less income and labour service. With its enormous estates, the landed nobility found itself wielding a new political power. Furthermore, since the peasants were increasingly exploited—exactions grew to between 40 and 60 per cent—they sank into debt to the new landowners or fled to the city to become servants in noble households.

The old clans had, it is true, been integrated into the bureaucratic system as social units, but after the Nara period they won back their independence; they organized themselves as family groups, parallel to the imperial house. Like the Tennō, the clan leaders wielded absolute patriarchal authority over all the members of their clan, which was graded into an administrative system composed of offices and ranks. The clan chiefs also held priestly authority over the Shintō shrines and temples in their territories. They presided over the clan universities and were able to procure promotions in rank at court for their fellow clansmen. At a ceremonial banquet the clan chief received the insignia of clan lordship: utensils and five tables of red lacquer, and the clan seal as the sign of absolute authority. The clan administration emulated the complex hierarchy of the imperial household: below the clan chamberlain (bettō) came an adjutant, inspectors, a tutor and a scribe to draw up documents. The head of the clan was served, moreover, by his own army of vassals (kenin) and knights (samurai) and by his personal servants (toneri). Through agents the clan head exercised his patronage over groups of artisans and craftsmen, who were paid from the clan coffers. Nowhere else but in Japan could bonds of loyalty have held this elaborate system together so effectively.

Among the eight leading clans the northern branch of the Fujiwara (Hokke) had achieved precedence over all the others by the mid-ninth century, mainly by marrying its daughters into the imperial family. 'As a rule the Fujiwara achieved their ends not by violence but by the relentless use of political pressure, which they were able to apply because of their matrimonial relations with the Throne or by means of their great wealth and consequent influence in the provinces, where their estates multiplied rapidly.'[21]

The unscrupulous dynastic power struggle for the imperial inheritance stopped neither at intrigue nor murder, and the role of the Fujiwara in it was a shady one. It is impossible to make out whether the thirst for power—personal or dynastic—alone drove them on, or whether this was compounded with loyal ties to the imperial house.

Kammu-Tennō, the founder of Heian-kyō, ruled until his death (806) without either chancellor or a regent. Among his male offspring it was a weakling, Prince Ate, who succeeded as Heizei-Tennō. Although he was forced to abdicate, he continued to reign as ex-emperor (Dajō Tennō). This institution was confirmed during the Heian period and brought the state treasury to the verge of ruin. In the next generation there were as many as three imperial courts, for Saga-Tennō, who had abdicated in 823 in favour of his brother Junna, was appointed Senior Ex-Emperor (Saki no Dajō Tennō) in 833 when Junna also abdicated. Fujiwara no Yoshifusa (804–872), who was the wire-puller, took for himself the office of regent (Sesshō) for the Emperor Seiwa, who was a minor. Previously this office has only been entrusted to members of the imperial house. When

Yoshifusa's son, Fujiwara no Mototsune, appointed himself not only Sesshō but Kampaku (civilian dictator) in 884 on behalf of the fifty-five-year-old Kōkō-Tennō whom he had himself enthroned, the reins of de facto government were firmly in the hands of the Fujiwara and remained there until 1068. The office of regent-dictator (Sekkan) also remained hereditary in the Fujiwara clan.

Uda-Tennō (867–931), who was not related by marriage or blood with the family of the regents, deliberately ruled independently. After he abdicated in favour of his son Daigo, he ruled as ex-emperor with his own entourage in the Suzaku Palace and later in the Ninna-ji, and, supported by the opponents of the Fujiwara regents, including Sugawara no Michizane, Ki no Haseo and Minamoto no Takaakira, he dominated the politics of his successors Daigo and Suzaku, although he gave it out that he only wanted to live for his artistic interests. Even after the abdication of Suzaku-Tennō, who lived with his mother, Fujiwara Onshi, in the Suzaku-in, Emperor Murakami (926–967) did not appoint a ruling regent. But under Emperor Reizei, Fujiwara no Saneyori succeeded in being nominated as Regent-Dictator, since, as the uncle of the Empress Mother Anshi, he had been able to enthrone emperors Reizei and Enyū. Even the private court administration of the ex-emperors, constructed on the same principle and with equal expense as the imperial household and the clan administrations, could not operate effectively during the period from 967 to 1068 when the Fujiwara regency was at its strongest.

The power and hubris of the Fujiwara reached a brilliant climax under Michinaga (966–1027), the fifth son of Fujiwara no Kaneie. Michinaga ruled from the Tsuchimikado Palace of his parents-in-law with the backing of his huge landed possessions and his close blood ties with three emperors. This palace he rebuilt entirely after a fire in 1016, sumptuous beyond all measure, and not only this new palace but his other town properties as well (his house on Lake Biwa and his Higashi Sanjō Palace) outstripped the Imperial Palace and the dwellings of the top nobles by far in elegance and splendour. The character and temperament of this man are easily brought to life, not only from his own

45

Murasaki-Shikibu-nikki-ekotoba: Scene 11. Ink and colours on paper. H. 20.6 cm. Mid-thirteenth century. Gotoh Art Museum, Tōkyō. On the evening of the day after the visit of the emperor, the court nobles Narinobu and Mitsunari stand on the verandah under the full moon in the palace of Fujiwara no Michinaga. Wearing brocade *naoshi,* both courtiers are looking through the *shitomi* lattice behind which Murasaki Shikibu is visible. The verandah cuts at a right angle into the garden, which lies autumnal under the silver moonlight.

diary *(Midō Tsuchimikado-nikki)* but also from the unofficial chronicles (the *Eiga-monogatari* and the *Ōkagami*) and, above all, from the observations of Murasaki Shikibu, which were recorded quite objectively in her diary. He is shown in a humanly touching light at the confinement of his daughter Empress Akiko, the wife of Ichijō-Tennō. The delivery took place, as was customary according to ritual prescription, not in the Imperial Palace but in the Tsuchimikado Palace. Michinaga emerges as a proud grandfather and the perfect head of the household. He jokes with the ladies-in-waiting and keeps the gardeners up to the mark.

He was an ardent Buddhist and imbued with the contemporary fear about the approaching latter days of the Law; therefore, he put far more of his resources into temple building than his circumstances warranted. At the burial place of the Fujiwara clan in Kobata, near Uji, he raised the Jōmyō-ji (begun in 1005) according to the prescriptions of the Tendai sect. The dedication and procession of the Burial of the Sutra at Mount Kimpusen, at which a copy of the 'Important Writings on Rebirth' *(Ōjō Yō-shū)* he had written himself was also buried for the next era, was initiated by Michinaga. When he retired from the world as a monk in 1019, he built a private temple, the Hōjō-ji, to the east of his palace. The layout and equipment seemed so exaggeratedly luxurious that his own son refused the funds for the undertaking. However, feudal dues from the provinces were sufficient to enable the building to be completed. The Amida Hall was built in 1019 in the spirit of the Jōdo faith as a Mūryōju-in, with nine monumental sculptures of the Amitābha Buddha carved by the greatest sculptors of the period—Kōshō and Jōchō. The description of the dedication of the 'Golden Hall' on the tenth day of the Seventh Month of 1022 is given in fascinating detail in the *Eiga-monogatari*.[22] Building never ceased on it, even after the death of Michinaga, but the grandiose structure was totally burnt down in 1058.

Michinaga retired in 1017 in favour of his son, Yorimichi (992–1074), who thereupon received the office of Sesshō, and in 1020 that of Kampaku. Yorimichi too married his daughters to two claimants to the throne. Under the emperors Gosuzaku and Goreizei, he ruled with absolute power. Yorimichi pursued no less consistently than his father the cult of a refined style of life, elegant entertainments and witty religious-worldly festivals. He made an enemy of the self-willed second son of Gosuzaku-Tennō, Prince Takahito. This prince's mother was not of the Fujiwara clan, and Yorimichi therefore refused him the insignium of the crown prince, the *tsubori-no-tsurugi* sword. For twenty-four years while he was prince, Takahito studied Confucian scripts, calligraphy and poetry intensively. When he was raised to the throne in 1068 as Emperor Gosanjō, there was only one thing for Yorimichi to do. He retired to his estate in Uji, became a monk in 1072 and died in 1074 at the age of eighty-two. With his end the absolute power of the Fujiwara regency was broken.

Yorimichi, like his father and forefathers, had built a private temple, the Byōdō-in. His plan followed, even 65–66 more consistently than that of the Hōjō-ji, the concept of imitating the Western Paradise here on earth. Groups of halls were spread round a lotus in a complex whole of unparalleled loveliness. The Phoenix Hall (the Hōō-dō, 1053) with its monumental carving of the Buddha 69 Amida, Bodhisattva figures floating among the rafters, 70 and wall paintings of the different degrees of the 'De- 60 scent of Amida' *(raigō)* survives today as a great and important testimony to the art of the Heian period.

The Cloister Government *(Insei)*

Emperor Gosanjō (1034–1073) ruled without assistance. He was served by three secretaries, who were nobles of inferior rank. In the place of the Fujiwara, the Minamoto clan rose to the high nobility. Gosanjō promulgated two laws in 1069, aimed at regulating the maladministration of land distribution and, in particular, returning to state ownership the *shōen* territories of the Fujiwara family of regents. In the palace an office for 'Examination of Land Titles' *(kirokujo)* worked out a redistribution by which the imperial house won back important latifundiae. Gosanjō also laid down a uniform measure for assessing rice contributions for the whole country and instituted price controls. This emperor was one of the really great personalities to reign in Japan. After three years he abdicated in favour of his son, and the period of so-called cloister government *(insei)* began.

Prince Sadahito (1053–1129) ruled as Shirakawa-Tennō for more than half a century. He also followed the example of his father and abdicated in 1086, after fourteen years as Tennō, in favour of his second son. He managed to circumvent cleverly the aspirations of his brothers to the throne. Shirakawa had built himself a place of retirement in the south of the city, at great expense and with large contributions from the provincial governors. This was the Toba-dono. He spent little time there even as ex-emperor, preferring to reside in the Ōi-dono Palace in the city and remain in the centre of things. His bureau of government employed twenty directors, four secretaries, five scribes, five assistants and eighty soldiers.[23] Shirakawa was not as effective a ruler as his father, but he had new problems to tackle. The peace of the capital was threatened by the soldier-monks *(sōhei)* of the monasteries. The Enryaku-ji on Mount Hiei, the Kōfuku-ji in Nara and the Onjō-ji on Lake Biwa had created bands of monks that tried to force the temples' demands—often a question of the ownership of property—on the Tennō and the ex-emperor. Their armies flooded into the capital and took up threatening positions at the palace gates.

It is true that Shirakawa had reinstated the Fujiwara family in favour by appointing Morozane Sekkan, but the latter was not able to achieve the same kind of hegemony that the Fujiwara had exercised a century earlier. Even though the three ex-emperors—Shirakawa, Toba and his wife Shōsi—managed to enjoy the new-found imperial might, the stability of the imperial house was still in question. Toba-Tennō (1103–1156), jealous of the supreme authority of his energetic grandfather Shirakawa, was hostile to his eldest son, Emperor Sutoku (1119–1164), who was thought to be in fact the son of Shirakawa.

Similar feuds within the family plagued the house of the Fujiwara regents, so that, it is said fanned by the intrigues of Chancellor Fujiwara no Shinzei, the Hōgen Uprising of 1156 broke out. In 1155 Fujiwara no Tadamichi saw to it, through his sister Bifukumonon-in, that the fifth son of Toba acceded to the throne as Goshirakawa. Ex-emperor Toba died, however, and in the renewed struggle a leading role was played by an alliance between the noble warrior families of Taira and Minamoto. Taira no Kiyomori (1118–1181) emerged victorious in his support of Goshirakawa and with his power much increased. Emperor Sutoku was deposed and exiled to Sanuki. Minamoto no Yoshitomo (1123–1160), who had fought for the emperor, watched the execution of his father and his father's followers. Goshirakawa only remained on the throne until 1158. Spurred on by Chancellor Shinzei, he started reforms in which a new distribution of estates came first. A rebuilding of the imperial palace was also begun, and every province was given tasks and required to send

contributions. Old traditions were revived with the new palace. Goshirakawa, who was himself an inspired poet, reintroduced the poetry contests of the First Month at the imperial court, a custom that had fallen into disuse since the reign of Emperor Goichijō in 1038. Goshirakawa ruled as ex-emperor from the town palace of Takamatsu-dono. His son, Nijō-Tennō, died at the age of twenty-three.

While at first Taira no Kiyomori rose to greater and greater power through the grace of Goshirakawa, the monarch finally conspired, though in vain, to free himself from the supremacy of his favourite. Kiyomori, however, succeeded in placing on the throne his grandson, the unfortunate child-emperor Antoku. The power conflict now rested between the Taira and Minamoto warrior clans. In the sea-battle of Dannoura in 1185 the Taira were crushingly beaten; the wife of Kiyomori, Nio-no-ama, and the child-emperor jumped into the sea. In Kyōto, however, the imperial line remained unbroken, for the victors of the conflict, the Minamoto, set the half-brother of Antoku, Gotoba-Tennō, on the throne. Goshirakawa, ex-emperor and monk (Dajō Hōō), preserved his dignity and claim to power against the shōgunate government of the Minamoto, instituted in Kamakura in 1185. Goshirakawa firmly refused to issue an edict giving Yoshitomo's son, Minamoto no Yoritomo (1147–1199), the title of shōgun, a title that could only be conferred by the Tennō.

During the last phase of the Heian period, covering the *insei* government of the ex-emperors, a system was developed that brought ever more revenues to the palaces of the ex-emperors and ex-empresses, through the allocation of territories for their maintenance. Shirakawa-Tennō, like the Fujiwara regents before him, began to build his own temple monastery for his old age. These temple monasteries of the ex-emperors, like the palaces, received *shōen* for their maintenance.

To the east of the Kamo River the 'Six Shō Temples' *(Rikushō-ji)* rose up close beside each other within the course of a century. Shirakawa founded the first of these temples in 1077, the Hosshō-ji, a fine layout comprising Amida Hall, Teaching and Lotus Halls and a large pagoda. Thirty years later, in 1102, Emperor Horikawa founded the Sonshō-ji nearby. Toba followed him in 1119 with his Saishō-ji. Then Toba's wife, Taikemmon-in, dedicated her own temple close by in 1128. The building programme came to an end with two foundations by Emperor Konoe, the Seishō-ji of 1139 and the Enshō-ji in 1149. But many more imperial undertakings were built to serve as palaces as well as temples. They made the imperial capital a city without parallel in brilliance and splendour—at least for the next two hundred years until civil war reduced innumerable temples and palaces to dust and ashes.

Shinden Palaces

sono dono wa	This house
mube mo tomikeri	Truly, truly it is splendid,
sakigusa no	Of *hinoki* wood, yes indeed,
mitsuba yotsuba	Yes, with three and four wings
tonozukeri seri	Is the building of this house.

Saibara (*The Story of Prince Genji,* Vol. I, p. 688)

The Imperial Palace was burnt to the ground in 960 for the first time after the foundation of the city. The imperial household found itself obliged to remove to a town palace, at that time the Reizei-in, which was attached to the outer palace wall to the south-east. The Tennō owned quite a number of properties with detached palaces inside and outside the city; thither, or to the palaces of their families, went the wives of the emperor for their confinements, since these constituted ritual impurity. The rebuilding of the Imperial Palace took two years. But fires became more frequent—presumably because of deliberate cases of arson, so that the palace was burnt down eleven times before the year 1048. This insecurity and improvisation was a situation that favoured the position of the Fujiwara regents and enabled them to entrench their power.

By the mid-tenth century a typical schema for the layout of the palace of an aristocrat had been worked out to provide a refined and elegant setting for the life style of the Late Heian period. In the late nineteenth century it was christened the 'sleeping-hall method of construction' *(shinden-zukuri)* by N. Sawada. Although every original palace building of the Heian period has disappeared, it has been possible to proceed with a reconstruction by consulting the texts of Heian literature and, with even more precision, the minutely detailed illustrations of the *emaki* picture scrolls.

A dwelling of a member of the upper nobility will have occupied the whole of a street insula *(chō),* a more or less square area of about 10,000 square metres. In the centre facing south lay the main hall, which was the living and sleeping quarters *(shinden)* of the head of the household. Its central space *(moya)* measured 6 bays wide by 2 bays deep (*c.* 18 × 6 m). A surrounding gallery *(en),* sheltered by overhanging roofs *(hisashi),* extended the hall in the four cardinal directions. The simple pile construction with round wooden pillars, board floors and hipped or saddle-shaped shingle roofs reflected the Dairi Palace in miniature. Double corridors led from the *shinden* to the subsidiary apartments *(tainoya),* set symmetrically on east, west and north. The *tainoya* provided accommodation for women and servants to the north and for guests and an office on the west and east. Open horseshoe-shaped corridors framed the courtyard to the south of the *shinden* hall and led to the two pavilions by the lake: the fountain pavilion *(izumi-dono)* and the fishing pavilion *(tsuri-dono).* With the plan open to the south there was a view from the *shinden* onto the courtyard and the artificial lake with its carefully placed island rising beyond a charming little bridge. The court and lake were the setting for aristocratic pleasures where nature's changing seasons were to be enjoyed in intimate proximity and in a very individual fashion. The pond was fed from a stream that ran in decorative curves beneath the palace. Poetry festivals were celebrated on its banks. Two pleasure boats floated on the lake: the dragon-head boat and the cock-head boat, and when there were performances of dancing on the island the company was enraptured with the sight of the landscape under the moon as it made music, recited poetry and drank *sake.* More intimate festivities took place in the pavilions: poetry contests, incense making and such-like.

The living quarters of the master of the house in the central space were divided into a sleeping closet and a day room. There there might be a platform with a canopy and curtains where the head of the family would work, eat and sleep. Usually however mats were spread and cushions laid out as seats. Ladies were seated behind a screen so that the soft, decoratively patterned rolls of cloth hid them from penetrating glances but allowed

46
Kitano Tenjin-engi: Scroll 1, scene 2. Ink and colours on paper. H. 52.1 cm. *c.* 1219. Kitano-jinja, Kyōto.
In the *Shinden* Palace of the Sugawara family, the scholar Sugawara no Koreyoshi is seated in the hall, the luxuriant garden spreading before him, with plum trees in red and pink blossom. A child has appeared to him, who, as is told in legend, announces himself as the scholar's future son Michizane.

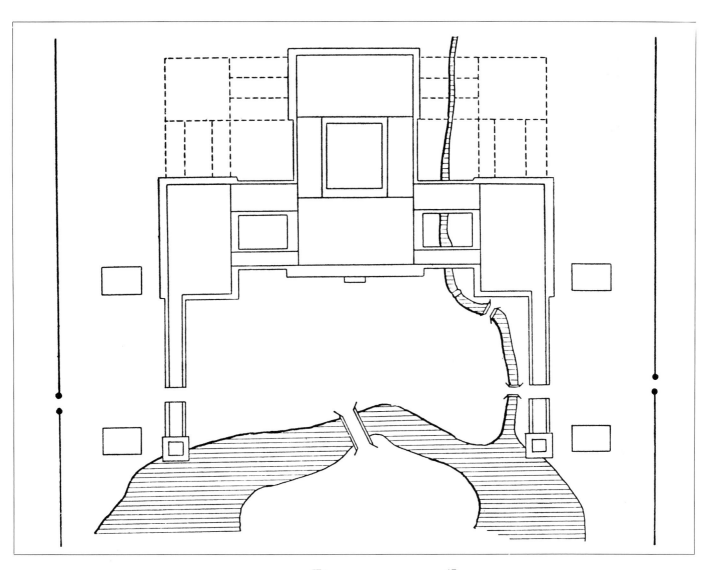

47
Ground plan of a *shinden-zukuri* layout

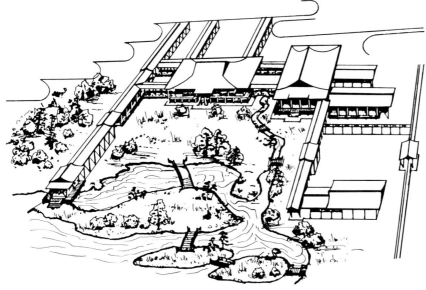

48
Reconstruction of a *shinden-zukuri* layout with landscape garden

49
Genji-monogatari-emaki: Chapter 38, 'Suzumushi II'. Ink and colours on paper. H. 21.8 cm, L. 48.2 cm. First quarter of the twelfth century. Gotoh Art Museum, Tōkyō.
A view into the Reizei-in Palace; the roofless construction allows us to see Emperor Reizei in an inner room talking to his father, Prince Genji, who is leaning against a pillar. On the verandah courtiers have settled down and hung their trains over the palings. One of them is playing on his flute in the beauty and melancholy of the autumn night.

50
Genji-monogatari-emaki: Chapter 44, 'Takegawa I'. Ink and colours on paper. H. 22 cm, L. 46.9 cm. First quarter of the twelfth century. The Tokugawa Reimeikai Foundation, Tōkyō.
On a spring night we see Kaoru on the steps of the palace of the Tamakazura. The fifteen-year-old, who is being watched inquisitively through the *sudare* by some ladies, looks at nightingales in the garden's flowering plum tree.

them to look out. Painted screens of six or eight panels allowed the central space to be further divided, yet for special occasions could be removed to clear the whole hall.

Narrow steps led down into the courtyard from the halls. During the day, thin bamboo blinds (sudare) made an airy partition for the inner chamber, while at night folding wooden lattices (shitomi) were affixed, which secured the interior while allowing air to pass. Solid swinging doors (tsumado) separated the hall from the corridors.

The compound was surrounded by white walls, and usually the main gate was on the east side. Here visitors arrived, and here too arrived the ox carriages, which were unyoked and dragged up to the gallery surrounding the hall so that the passengers could enter at ease. On official occasions the master of house alone was entitled to step through the southern gate. On these ceremonial sorties he was carried in a litter.

51

Shigisan-engi-emaki: Scroll 3, scene 4. Ink and colours on paper. H. 31.5 cm *c.* 1160–1170. Chōgonsonshi-ji, Nara.
The nun, sister of the priest Myōren, has set out in search of her brother. She is seated with a pilgrim's staff on the threshold of a village hut with a wooden roof. She and her attendant, who is standing, are questioning the young mistress of the house, while from the half windows nearby a woman with children watches and a man trys to quieten down two dogs.

The mighty regent Fujiwara no Michinaga (966–1027) resided in the most magnificent of all the palaces in this style. This was the Tsuchimikado; it extended across several *chō* at the Kōto-mon in the Kyōgoku insula. This palace too, celebrated with such high praise, was completely burnt down in 1016. The residences of other representatives of the top Fujiwara nobility lay on the street of Higashi Sanjō: the palaces of Moromichi, Tadazane (1078–1162) and Tadazane's eldest son, Tadamichi (1097–1164), and grandson, Yorinaga (1120–1156). While the high nobility built their *shinden* palaces in the manner described above, the lower nobles lived less luxuriously. The famous poet Fujiwara no Teika (1162–1241), compiler of the *Shin-kokin-waka-shū,* though he had a small property in the aristocratic Ichijō quarter, only built a single *shinden* living hall on it. He was not able to afford *tainoya* halls. A Buddha hall with a house beside it, and a servant's hall composed the dwellings of farmsteads.

The houses of the populace *(itaya, koya)* were crowded together and gave directly on the street. The front of the house was 3 bays—about 9 metres—long and was entered through an open doorway up one step into the interior. Wooden pillars supported a wooden roof, weighted with stones. The walls were clay or mats; walls of half height *(hajitomi)* allowed a view into the street through narrow upper windows. These houses with their unkempt but exuberant inhabitants are illustrated with great care in the *emaki* of the later twelfth century: the *Shigisan-engi-emaki* and the *Ban-Dainagon-ekotoba.*

Shintō Architecture

According to the records in imperial decrees, the *Engi-shiki,* during the Engi period (901–923), 573 Shintō shrines were formally under the control of the central government of Heian-kyō; the other 2,288 Shintō sanctuaries were protected by the appropriate provincial

52–53   ▷
Ujikami-jinja. Uji near Kyōto.
A row of three small shrines on stilts is joined into a Hon-den by a surrounding structure. The extended *nagare* roof makes a prayer room in front of the steps with curved bannisters that lead to the little shrines. Both as the earliest of all Shintō buildings and as an example of Shintō architecture of the Heian period, the Ujikami Shrine is no less important than the Hōō-dō of the Byōdō-in, which stands on the opposite bank of the river.

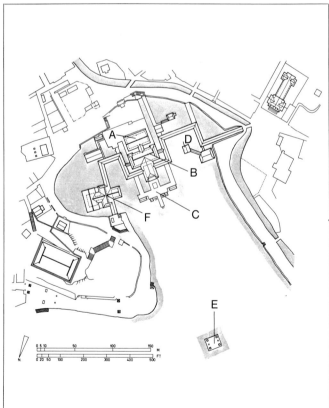

54

Itsukushima-jinja. Timber frame construction with tiled roofs. Miyajima Island, Hiroshima.

The layout of this Shintō shrine, built into the sea, is of the sixth century. It received its elegant fan-shaped form, however, some time between 1149 and 1169 from Taira no Kiyomori, who resided there as Lord of Angei. The layout is orientated towards the water with the great *torii* standing in the sea, for the shrine is dedicated to the honour of sea goddesses *(kami)*. The present building was put up about 1556, it shows the successful fusion of Shintō and Buddhist building traditions.

55

Ground plan of the Itsukushima-jinja, Miyajima Island, Hiroshima.

A Hon-den
B Hai-den
C Platform for sacred dances
D Nō stage
E *Torii*
F Marōdō-jinja (Sha-den)

56   ▷

Sha-den of the Itshukushima-jinja. Timber-frame construction with shingle roofs. 1164–1165. Miyajima Island, Hiroshima.

On the left beside the main shrine is the visitors' shrine, Marōdō-jinja, which is joined to the central building by a roofed verandah. The halls are built over the water: together with the open galleries, they are reflected in the lake with their red pillars and corbelling, so that today the visitor can still experience the effect of an elegant Heian-period building.

governments. By wisely tolerating, indeed ingeniously recruiting, the traditional Japanese concepts and mythology into the Buddhist pantheon, the time-honoured Japanese reverence for nature and ancestral gods was allowed to continue unabated.

Shintō architecture, it is true, took over certain forms from Buddhist temple design. However, the holiest sanctuaries such as the earliest form of the *jinja* in Izumo and the shrine of the Sun Goddess Amaterasu-Ōmikami in Ise were to a great extent preserved from changes for ritual reasons.

In the Heian period three new styles of Shintō building were developed. The first was that of the Kasuga-jinja, the family shrine of the Fujiwara clan in Nara. Here the characteristic placing side by side of four identical shrines, each the house of a deity, is new, but the layout approximates to Buddhist temples in that, in 1179, the *torii* was replaced by a grandiose double-storeyed gateway *(rōmon)* and the old fencing palisades were turned into corridors. In the Yasaka-jinja in Kyōto this new style was probably worked out for the first time, for there the posts and timberwork were red and the walls white, in Chinese style.

A second innovation came from the High Kamo Shrine north of Kyōto; a hall of worship was created by extending the canopy roof, supported on tall pillars, to cover the platform and the sweeping flight of steps. This *nagare-zukuri* style also was used at the Ujikami-jinja, sited on the opposite bank of the river from the Byōdō-in, and probably designed at about the same time but finished rather later. The main hall of the temple sheltered three small interior shrines, each consecrated to a different deity. Some details of the construction, for example the lattice windows and perhaps the all-over plan, are thought to show a relationship to the Byōdō-in.

52–53

The third style was evolved at the Usa shrine in Ōita province on Kyūshū, which is one of the chief shrines of the war god Hachiman. The twin halls perhaps demonstrate an influence of Korean architecture, according to A. C. Soper.[24] This arrangement was followed by the Kitano-temman-gū in Kyōto, where Sugawara no Michizane is honoured, and by the Hiei shrine in Sakamoto. At both these places an intermediary hall lay between the twin halls, anticipating the *gongen* style, which later came into fashion.

The family shrine of the Taira is the Itsukushima-jinja, raised by Kiyomori after his appointment as governor of Aki province. It lies like a dream palace in front

54–56

of Miyajima Island. Though the original building of the mid-twelfth century, like all the other Shintō shrines, has been ruined and rebuilt many times, the rich and elegant design still radiates forcefully the atmosphere of the Heian period.

The Cult of Amida

Among the religious practices of the esoteric Buddhist sects, especially that of the Tendai doctrine, belonged invocation to Amida Nyorai (Amitābha Buddha).[25] Lord of the 'Western Paradise', his 'Pure Land' *(Jōdo)*, he helped any worshipper who repeatedly called on his name with *namu Amida Butsu* to rebirth in his paradise and release from the cycle of rebirth on earth. The repetition of this invocation (called *nembutsu* for short) soon became the chief element of the faith. It was believed that if the name of Amida was recited continuously and with belief throughout a day or a week, it would ensure the grace of birth into the Western Paradise in a condition of pure spiritual bliss, though not yet of entry into the non-being of Nirvana.

57–58

This concept had always existed since the beginning of the Mahāyāna Buddhist doctrine, but during the tenth century in Japan it spread rapidly among broad sections of the populace, for it required no deep learning nor ascetic practices, good works nor sacrifices of wealth.

In China a sect of the 'White Lotus Blossom' had taught invocation of Amitābha Buddha since the year A.D. 390; they were centred on Mount Luoshan. The priest Tanhuan founded the 'Pure Land Sect' in 508 in the Chinese capital of Luoyang, from which derived the similarly named Jōdo-shū in Japan. But it was not started until 1175 by Hōnen Shōnin.

The cult of Amida was based on three Indian sutras: the *Sukhāvatīvyūha Sūtra (Amida-kyō),* the great *Amitāyus Sūtra (Muryōju-kyō)* and the *Amitāyurdhyāna Sūtra (Kammuryōju-kyō).* They all give a description of the Western Paradise ruled by this gracious Buddha; the

57
The hands of *Amida Nyorai:* by Jōchō. Wood with gold leaf over lacquered dressing. 1053. Hōō-dō of the Byōdō-in, Uji.
Amida Nyorai holds his hands in *jōin* mudra on his feet, in the centre of his body, while he sits in harmonious concentration. This pose is a symbol of his vow of redemption, which embraces all beings of the 'nine stages of existence'.

◁ 58

Amida Nyorai (detail): by Jōchō. Wood with gold leaf over lacquered dressing. H. 280 cm. 1053. Hōō-dō of the Byōdō-in, Uji. The head of this monumental seated figure of Amida Nyorai by Jōchō is an incomparable rendering of the essential radiance of the Buddha, 'Lord of the Pure Land'. His look, detached but full of gentle kindness, is directed at the worshipper with the promise of rebirth in his paradise.

59

Kūya Shōnin: by Kōshō. Wood with painted dressing. H. 117 cm. First half of the thirteenth century. Rokuharamitsu-ji, Kyōto. The priest Kūya (d. 972) wandered the length and breadth of Japan preaching the invocation to Amida, *nembutsu.* The sculptor Kōshō, the fourth son of Unkei, rendered him with great realism: his mouth is open as he walks, and six small figures of Amida float out of it.

second named recounts his forty-eight vows also, including the eighteenth, in which Amida renounces Buddhahood until all living creatures have been released from the bondage of rebirth.

Before the precise doctrine of *nembutsu* had been established in Japan, the eminent priest of the Hosshō sect Gyōgi (670–749) had preached in the Tōdai-ji that invocation of Amida was one possible way to salvation. *Nembutsu* took root in the following years particularly strongly in the teaching of the Tendai sects. Independent preachers and missionaries from the monastery on Mount Hiei spread belief in the beneficence of invocations. In the western area of the Enryaku-ji a pupil of the priest Ennin was the first to erect a double hall for Amida and Zuijii, in which meditation and *nembutsu* were both practised.

The monk Kūya Shōnin (903–972), known as the 'Saint of the Market Place', went all over the countryside evangelizing, reciting the invocation to Amida in an ecstasy, and dancing. He had a great following in both town and country. Of equal popularity was a hymn to Amida composed by the Tendai priest Senkan (d. 944). The head priest of the Enryaku-ji bore visible testimony to his belief in rebirth in the 'Pure Land': on his deathbed he had his hands attached by long threads to the hands of a statue of Amida. This death rite spread. A well-known folding altar in the Konkai-kōmyō-ji in Kyōto, of the late thirteenth century, with 'Amida Over the Mountains' *(Yamagoshi-Amida)* still shows the threads on the hands of the Buddha.

A description of the Buddhist cosmos for the common people, with its 'six stages of existence' *(rokudō)*—Hell, Purgatory, Demons *(ashura),* Animals, Men and Gods—appears in the treatise by the priest Genshin (Eshin Sōzu), published in 985. His 'Important Writings on Rebirth' *(Ōjō Yō-shū)* recall Dante's descriptions of Hell's torments. Compiled from the sutras for all to understand, the *Ōjō Yō-shū* became the religious text of the day. All could hear the consequences of evil and good deeds and the blessings brought by invoking the Buddha. The description begins with detailed horror pictures of the eight main hells and the sixteen subsidiary hells attached to them in which, for myriads of years, though not forever, the sinful being is tormented. The two worlds of hunger spirits *(gaki)* and demons *(ashura)* are described in gruesome detail by Genshin. The world of men, too, is profoundly wretched with impurity, suffering and mortality. The anatomical description of 404 diseases teaches disgust

60

Raigō of Amida: wall painting (detail). Colours on panel. 1053. Hōō-dō of the Byōdō-in, Uji.

Scenes of the Descent of Amida *(raigō)* are painted on the hinged doors of the central hall of the Hōō-dō with the 'nine stages of existence' *(kubon)*. This detail shows the ideal landscape of the Western Paradise with pavilions, rejoicing Bodhisattvas and heavenly beings, but it is also the background for a scene of the *raigō:* the Buddha with his attendants is returning to his paradise.

and loathing. Even the heavenly gods, who cannot escape decline either, exist in pain. Only the world of the Western Paradise promises fulfilment and bliss. The ar-
60 rival of Amida with his twenty-five Bodhisattvas and a host of 100,000 monks amid purple clouds, golden beams, showers of flowers, perfumes and music is depicted in detail. The Bodhisattva Kannon (Avalokiteshvara) holds the lotus seat for each new-born soul. The paradise contains golden palaces, jewel-studded halls, green groves, treasure pools with geese and ducks, surrounded by myriads of Buddhas.

Exhortations to good by fear of hell ran with the spirit of the times, for naive faith promised escape from the latter days of the Law prophesied by Buddhism.

The latter days of the Law were, according to the interpretation of the Buddhist sutras, to begin in 1052; then after the epoch of Complete Law and the epoch of Copied Law the time of trouble and unrest was to begin.

Not only strictly religious writing but profane literature as well was penetrated by thoughts of the latter days. In the *Genji-monogatari* melancholy ideas of the beginning of the end of time recur continually and colour the behaviour and thought of the characters.

The Amida cult opened up to art a new world of sacred and, at the same time, brilliantly magnificent representations of salvation. The vision of the four paradises, fixed at the four cardinal points, each with its Buddha and two Bodhisattvas, and sometimes two acolytes as well, was known already to the earliest Japanese Buddhist painting and sculpture with its compositions of three or five figures. The wall paintings of the Kondō of the Hōryū-ji (*c.* 700, burnt down 1949) show these paradises, following a Sino-Korean model. Amida's 'Western Paradise' is found in sculpture and low relief in the bronzes of the Lady Tachibana Shrine, for the belief in rebirth seems to have appealed particularly to the ladies of the court. Then there arose the

61

Raigō of Amida: three hanging scrolls. *Colours and kirikane on silk.* (centre) H. 210.8 cm, W. 210.6 cm; (right) H. 211 cm, W. 105.7 cm; (left) H. 210 cm, W. 105.7 cm. Late twelfth century. Yūshi-Hachimankō-Jū-hakka-in Temple, Kōya-san, Wakayama.

The 'Descent of Amida', on a cloud with thirty-two attendants, was originally conceived as a monumental painting; it is a splendid example of Buddhist painting of the Late Heian period. Amida appears in gold like a golden sun above a Japanese autumn landscape: he is surrounded by gesticulating and colourful Bodhisattvas and monks, rejoicing and playing music, with an Amida trinity in the far distance. The spatial arrangement of the host of attendants against the chiaroscuro of the clouds heightens the visionary character of the cult picture.

'Mandala of the Pure Land' *(Jōdo Mandara),* three versions of which are extant. In the Taema Mandala of the eighth century Amida appears in a trinity with Kannon and Seishi on a terrace, in the centre of an architectural landscape having the central-perspective arrangement of Chinese halls. In front of the terrace lies the 'treasure pool' with the reborn souls floating on lotus blossoms. At the sides are more Buddhas and Bodhisattvas, and in the foreground, heavenly beings dance on a platform. The mandala is surrounded by a border of small scenes; on the right beside the paradise landscape little vignettes show thirteen of the canonical 'Sixteen Contemplations', on the left scenes from the previous lives of the Buddha. On the lower border are illustrated the 'Nine Grades of Rebirth into the Western Paradise', with Amida descending to welcome the pious dead.

The representation of the Amida configurations as devotional images, like that of the 'Pure Land' in the *Jōdo Mandara,* follows the Chinese pattern very closely; for example, similar configurations and architectural landscapes from the seventh century are found in the cave temples of Dunhuang in Gansu province. Originally both groups of cult image were probably based on sacred images, now lost, by great painters in the Chinese capital cities. The most magnificent works of religious art were destroyed in China during the wave of persecution of Buddhists between 842 and 845.

In Japan the priest Genshin won fame as the creator of new kinds of Amida image because of his rousing writ- 61

ings; in fact, he certainly had no part in the execution of such images. The theme of the 'Descent of Amida' (raigō) was developed quite independently in Japan as the principal sacred image, freeing the representation of the Buddha from hierarchical austerity. The raigō 60 brings the Buddha and his throng down from transcendence into the human world. Thus the Buddha image became more relaxed, freer and more individual, while the background took on more of an earthly nature.

The Temple as a Composite Work of Art

Until well into the tenth century the imperial house patronized principally the temple foundations of the Shingon sect. Perhaps Kūkai had achieved highest favour by his stress on the national aspect in his teaching, finding correspondences between the Shintō deities and the various Buddha avatars. The Shingon sect had its own cult hall in the Great Palace: the Shingon- 35 in to the west of the Dairi.

The foundation of the Ninna-ji by Emperor Kōkō in 886 provided his successor Uda-Tennō with a cloister residence (in) when he abdicated. After that, the office of abbot in that temple was reserved for a prince of the imperial blood. The ritual layout of the original foundation is not known, since the present buildings date from the sixteenth and seventeenth centuries.

The Daigo-ji in the south-east of the capital had the same direct link with the imperial house. The priest Shōbō had opened up the site at the foot of Daigo hill, and Emperor Daigo protected and founded the temple. On the hill-top was the Yakushi Hall with a Yakushi 64 trinity; in 907 the emperor had made a vow to donate the sculptures. In them the heavy proportions and mannered drapery style of Jōgan carving live on, though being covered in gold the statues assume a new sheen and gentleness. The small Yakushi Hall (5 bays

62

Suribotoke ('printed Buddhas') (detail). Black ink on paper. H. *c.* 44 cm, W. *c.* 30 cm. 1047 or 1107. Formerly in the Jōruri-ji, Nara. Museum für Kunst und Gewerbe, Hamburg (1979.229).
The cult figures of the nine Amida Nyorai in the Jōruri-ji were found to contain 'sacred items' consisting of votive papers each with one hundred (ten rows of ten) small Amida figures printed on them. The papers are wood-block printed and were probably produced hundreds at a time.

63 ▷

Pagoda of the Daigo-ji, Kyōto. Timber-frame construction with tile roofs. H. 38.16 m, L. 6.63 m, W. 6.63 m. 951–952.
The construction of the pagoda in the lower precinct of the temple was planned in 931 by Emperor Daigo's widow and his successor, Suzaku-Tennō. The building was completed in 951 and consecrated in the following year. The heavy tiled roofs ponderously overhang the narrow core structure. The *suien* pinnacle is an admirable work in bronze.

wide) was put up in place of the original building between 1121 and 1124, but the Daigo-ji Pagoda, built in 951–952 to fulfil a vow made by Emperor Suzaku, stands in its original form. Above the narrow core of the building rise five wide, heavy roofs, supported on triple consoles. The high bronze ring-pole *(sōrin)* forms a third of the height of the whole building. The inner chapel depicts the Cosmos as it is manifest in Shingon doctrine in the Mandala of the 'Two Worlds'. The central bearing pillar, regarded as the world's axis, is enclosed by four panels on which are represented emanations of the Universal Buddha Dainichi. On the sides the 'Eight Patriarchs of the Shingon Sect' are pictured. The four inner pillars have images of the Shi-tennō and protectively surround the iconographic programme. Lotus and supernatural flowers adorn the timberwork. The idea of a synthesizing art is anticipated here through the medium of painting.

The temple layouts of the Middle and Late Heian periods reflect the syncretic attitude of court society to the doctrines of Buddhism. The esoteric teaching of the Shingon and Tendai sects, the 'open teaching' of the early Buddhism of the Nara period and, not the least, the concept of deliverance in the worship of Amida existed peaceably side by side. Every kind of interpretation of the world and life had its own cult hall within the temple with its own particular images, derived from the sutras, to enable everyone to achieve salvation in his own way.

The halls of meditation, first built for Tendai practices by the priest Ennin in the Enryaku-ji on Mount Hiei, grew in importance. Halls for Hokke Meditation *(Hokke-dō)* and 'Constant Walking' Meditation *(Jōgyō-dō)* were square in plan with three, five or seven bays and pyramidal shingle roofs. The scheme of the Amida halls originated from them. Already in the second half of the ninth century the Fujiwara, secure in the absolute power they wielded, were able to afford the endowment of private temples. Fujiwara no Mototsune took the lead with the foundation of his Gokuraku-ji ('Paradise Temple'). *Sesshō* Tadahira followed his example with the Hosshō-ji. One cult image has survived from this temple: the thousand-armed Kannon of 925. Nothing remains of the private temples of Fujiwara no Tamemitsu, Fujiwara no Yukinari or the mighty Fujiwara no Kaneie, all totally destroyed.

The same fate befell the grandiose buildings of the Hōjō-ji erected for Fujiwara no Michinaga. On enter-

63

64
Yakushi Nyorai: by Eri. Wood with gold leaf on lacquered dressing. H. 154.5 cm. Early Heian Period, 907–913. Yakushi-dō of the Daigo-ji, Kyōto.
The stolid seated figure of Yakushi, the Buddha of Healing, is the central larger than life-size figure of a trinity said to have been carved by the sculptor Eri, a pupil of the priest Shōbō, who founded the temple. The Jōgan style of drapery folds is relatively subdued in this work, since the lacquer and gold soften the sharp edges of the ridges.

65 ▷
Hōō-dō ('Phoenix Hall') of the Byōdō-in, Uji. Timber-frame construction with shingle roof. 1053.
The Phoenix Hall received its name as much from its ground plan as from the bronze birds on the crest of the roof. The façade opens to the east on a lotus pool, and in this resembles the buildings in the Western Paradise of Amida Nyorai. The small central hall with its airy galleries and corner pavilions is particularly light and decorative in effect. The Hōō-dō, the only surviving complex of the Heian period, gives an idea of eleventh-century court architecture.

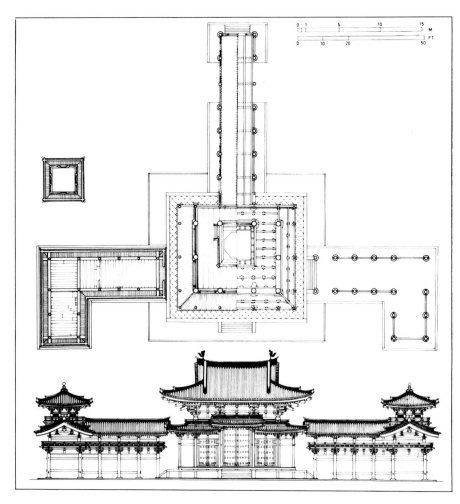

66
Ground plan and elevation of the Hōō-dō of the Byōdō-in, Uji.
The ground plan on the right is at ground level; on the left it is at the level of the board floor.

67   ▷
Phoenix in the Hōō-dō of the Byōdō-in, Uji. Bronze, cast and gilt. H. 100 cm. 1053.
The central structure of the Phoenix Hall of the Byōdō–in is crowned by two lively bronze birds. To these, as well as to the ground plan of the complex, the hall owes its name. Probably the sculptor Jōchō designed and executed the phoenix figures himself, as there is a tradition that he made a dragon-head and a cock-head as figureheads for imperial pleasure boats.

ing holy orders in 1019 he began the enterprise with an Amida Hall, named Muryōju-in after the *Muryōju Sūtra*. Nine identical seated figures of the Buddha Amida were placed side by side in this hall, an arrangement today seen only in the Jōruri-ji. The statues were of wood and gilt, and accompanied by figures (presumably standing) of Kannon and Seishi and the four painted Shi-tennō. The figures faced east. These wooden figures were all carved by the 'Buddha Master' *(busshi)* Kōshō, who had first worked for Fujiwara no Michinaga in 1005 when he made a figure of Fugen for Michinaga's Jōmyō-ji. For this work he collaborated with his pupil Jōchō. The huge commissions of the aristocracy could now only be completed at all because of newly developed and refined techniques for the division of labour *(yosegi-zukuri)*, evolved in the studios.

According to the records this Amida Hall illustrated every smallest detail of the 'Descent of Amida in Nine-Fold Form' *(kubon raigō)* to receive the soul of the dying man and conduct him to the Nine Grades of Rebirth in Paradise. Even the gates of the temple showed the Descent in nine pictures with the relevant texts from the sutras. The timberwork was gilt and set with mother-of-pearl and gems, and the figures were covered with a golden net. In the central bay of the ambulatory was an altar niche for Michinaga. Five coloured ribbons were attached to the hands of the central figure, and Michinaga held these on his deathbed, certain of immediate rebirth in the Western Paradise.

On the fourteenth day of the Seventh Month of the year 1022 Michinaga initiated the Golden Hall and the Hall of the Five Myōō (Godai-dō). The Buddhist sculptor Jōchō and his workshop had made twelve monumental statues for it. In the centre was placed the chief cult figure of the Kondō, the seated Universal Buddha Dainichi, 10 metres high, with six attendants. The Godai-dō sheltered the Five Myōō with Fudō as the central image.

The three halls of the Hōjō-ji with their galleries surrounded a large-scale artificial pond. Three bridges led to an island on which a stage for dancing and two platforms for musicians could be set up. The whole scene was like a vision of the Western Paradise as shown in the *Jōdo Mandaras,* of which devotional pictures Ennin had brought an embroidered example from China. In the halls the statues did not stand in isolation but were integrated into a ritually complete total complex through the wall paintings that depicted whichever sutra text was most appropriate. Architecture, sculpture, painting and handicrafts came together in a synthesis of the arts *(sōgō-bijutsu),* balanced in conception, precious and complete in detail, speaking not only of the wealth and power of the patron but also of his ambition for artistic and aesthetic perfection. The over-refined taste of court society, poetical and sentimental, here as in every detail of style in every-day life, laid down the most demanding criteria.

65 An idea of the character of that highly refined art is best sought today in the Phoenix Hall of the Byōdō-in at Uji, for Fujiwara no Yorimichi planned his private temple in Uji no less pretentiously than his father Michinaga. The estate had originally been laid out as a summer palace. Yorimichi converted it into a temple a year after his sixtieth birthday, in that ominous year 1052, taken in Buddhism as the beginning of the latter days of the Law. He erected the main hall facing east onto the Uji River. The chief cult image was, as in the Hōjō-ji, a Dainichi Buddha with Yakushi and Shaka, as well as two Ni-ō (Vajradhara, the two Kings) as subsidiary figures. An Amida Hall was only built second.

67 Its ground plan and the bronze birds that crowned it gave it the name of Phoenix Hall (Hōō-dō). The structure as a totality is an incarnation of the Western Paradise of Amida.

66 The plan, with a square Amida Hall, lateral wings and a wing of corridors at the back, is enclosed by water, as though on an island. Delicately curved tile roofs are superposed to create the impression that the hall and the side pavilions are two storeys high. There is nothing to compare with this small structure for graceful elegance. It is, despite unmistakeable Chinese details, a totally Japanese creation of the highest artistic order. It marks the perfection of the *wa-yō* style in every branch of art. The interior of the hall is occupied by

57–58, 68–69 Jōchō's monumental seated figure of Amida, which has been described thus by D. Seckel: 'This statue is undeniably powerful, yet despite (or because of?) the firm,

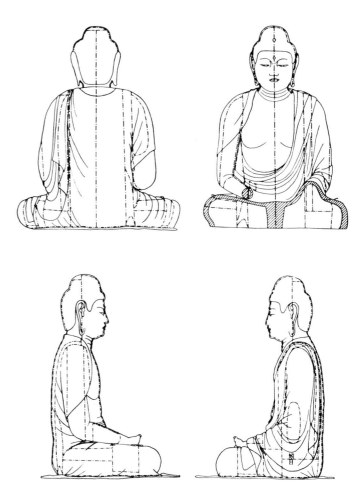

68
Construction of the *Amida Nyorai* by Jōchō (Pl. 69).

69 ▷

Amida Nyorai: by Jōchō. Wood with gold leaf over lacquered dressing. H. 280 cm. 1053. Hōō-dō of the Byōdō-in, Uji.
This Amida of *jōroku* dimensions by the *dai-busshi* Jōchō was already recognized as a masterpiece of the highest order and of absolute holiness when it was set up and dedicated in the year 1053; it has remained to this day the principle and most splendid sculpture of the entire Fujiwara period. Amida is seated in the *jōin* mudra at the centre of his Paradise on an elaborate throne, surrounded by a meticulously carved nimbus and baldachin (restored in part). Jōchō's Amida became the standard model for later sculpture.

broad and unshakeably set pose of meditation it has a floating, light quality that seems in no way to belong to the immediately tangible world of appearance and reality; the figure is powerfully present and at the same time totally withdrawn, and for all its tense spiritual and

84

70
Bosatsu with a Mouth Organ: by Jōchō. Wood with remains of a dressing. H 55 cm. 1053. Hōō-dō of the Byōdō-in, Uji.
Attached to the walls above the painted wooden doors are fifty-two small carvings of Bodhisattvas, floating attendants who make music round Jōchō's Amida. Unlike other representations of the Amida *raigō*, Kannon and Seishi Bosatsu are not distinguished by being made larger. Both appear in the northern group; this Bosatsu with a Mouth Organ belongs to the southern group. Like all the figures he is seated on a wisp of cloud in an informal pose and holds his instrument with both hands. The torso and head are in the round; the lower sections of the body are flat behind and put together from a small number of separate parts. On the back of this Bosatsu is his name, Kongo-kō.

71
Door knob of the Hōō-dō of the Byōdō-in, Uji. Iron with copper inlay. D. 9cm. 1053.
The knobs of the door leaves of the Phoenix Hall are powerfully conceived and of impressive form. The four-lobed panel is surmounted by a chrysanthemum in relief over which is a square knob pierced for the ring. The copper inlay stresses the resemblance to a flower.

72

Amida Nyorai: by Kenen in the Anraku-ji, Kyōto. Wood with gold leaf on lacquer. H. 87.3 cm. 1135-1140.
The work was originally placed in the Toba Shinmie-dō, a temple hall built by Ex-emperor Toba in his subsidiary palace in Toba. *Busshi* Kenen was a leading sculptor, grandson of Chōsei, employed in the Toba palace workshop and given the title of *hōin* on account of his works. Though the plinth and nimbus are later additions, the image radiates the celestial nobility and peace that characterize work of the *insei* period.

formal concentration it imparts a sense of relaxation. Such unity of opposites, such "non-duality" is a fundamental element of Buddhist thought, and art has succeeded totally convincingly in translating this idea into the language of form and thus making it directly perceptible'.[26]

70 Jōchō's workshop also provided the fifty-two small Bodhisattva figures that hover round Amida, attached to the walls. The leaves of the door and the wooden walls are used to support paintings of the 'Nine Degrees of Amida's Descent', a notion first carried out in the Hōjō-ji. These paintings occupy a central place in *Yamato-e,* the fully mature, purely Japanese style of landscape painting, not only as religious work but also as depictions of a natural and entirely Japanese background. The quality of the altar decoration, the nimbus and the baldachin of pierced and carved work, though in part restored, is no whit inferior to the sculptures themselves. Every bit of decoration, whether on the 71 platform or the columns and the ceiling, is of the same absolute mastery of execution, in lacquer with mother-of-pearl inlay. The ground plan of the Hōō-dō and, even more, Jōchō's sculpture of Amida exercised a strong influence on Buddhist art well into the twelfth century.

With the inception of the *insei* regime the ex-emperors and ladies of the court took over from the Fujiwara the role of patron for new large temple com-

73
Group of the *Thousand and One Senju Kannon* in the Sanjūsangen-dō of the Myōhō-in Temple, Kyōto. Wood with gold leaf over lacquer dressing. H. *c.* 170cm. 1164 and 1254-1266.
The central cult figure, a seated Senju Kannon (1254), larger than life-size by Tankei, is flanked right and left by a thousand standing life-size Senju Kannon figures, arranged in rows of ten. The huge program was completed by the Shichi-jō workshop for the second time in 1266, the original hall with its figures of 1164 having almost completely burnt down.

74
Hondō of the Jōruri-ji, Kyōto. L. 25.9m, W. 9.1m. 1107.
The Yakushi Hall built in 1047 was replaced in 1107 by a Hondō; this was moved in 1157 to the west side of the lake. This was the correct iconological position for a 'Paradise Hall' housing the images of Amida. The original shingle roof of the nine-bay hall was replaced in the Edo period by tiles, and an extension to the roof was added over the porch. The lattice windows on the façade give the little building more the look of a dwelling than of a temple hall.

plexes. The first of the six imperial 'Shō Temples' at Shirakawa was founded by Shirakawa-Tennō in 1077. His Hosshō-ji was put up at lavish expense on Nijō-ōji Street, north of the Shirakawa brook. The Amida Hall, with a row of nine seated figures of the Buddha, looked out on a lake, and its island was adorned with an octagonal pagoda nine storeys high. The sculptures were the work of *busshi* Kenkei, the 'grandson' (in terms of apprenticeship) of Jōchō. After abdicating in 1086, Ex-emperor Shirakawa began to lay out his palace in Toba, in the south-east of the city. At the same place, in 1101, there arose the Shōkoku-in Temple, with an Amida Hall having monumental sculpture by another important wood sculptor, Ensei.

In the grounds of the eastern villa of the Toba Palace, in the Anraku-ji, Toba-Tennō dedicated an Amida Hall 72 in 1147. Its principal cult image is a seated figure of Amida which, though it follows the great model of Jōchō like the rest, betrays a rather routine approach.

The Sanjūsangen-dō in the Myōhō-in Temple bears witness to the great temple foundations of the ex-emperors in Kyōto. This hall was endowed by Goshirakawa in 1164 and built south-east of his Hōjūji Palace. The hall was 33 bays long and contained an en-73 semble, based on Shingon doctrine, of 1,001 figures of the thousand-armed Kannon. The monumental seated figure was flanked by 1,000 life-size standing figures, carved by the famous *busshi* Kōjō and Kōchō of the Shichi-jō studio. The hall with the majority of its statues burnt down in 1249 in a great fire that ravaged Kyōto, and only some 120 to 150 of the original sculptures were saved. The sculptural ensemble was completed in 1266 in the rebuilt hall, by the *busshi* Tankei, Kōen and Kōsei among others.

Very few temples and halls in which the idea of the comprehensive art work was realized, that of the Jōdo Paradise or the Amida *raigō,* have escaped the depredations of the Japanese middle ages.

Of over thirty great Amida Halls with an ensemble of 74 nine Amida figures, only one survives: the Amida Hall of the Jōruri-ji. It was built in 1107 and transferred in 1157 to the west bank of an artificial lake. The remain-75 ing figures of Amida are lined up on either side of the 76 monumental central image; this central image is again reminiscent of Jōchō's Amida in the Hōō-dō. The eight subsidiary figures are monotonous in effect, though they are by no means identical. The nimbus of the main cult figure is set in the old manner with countless small, imaginary Buddhas, from among which seven larger

and four floating Bodhisattvas stand out. The subsidiary figures have panel nimbi carved in low relief. Nothing certain is known about either the artists or the workshop. The four Shi-tennō who stand at the corners 93 of the podium are of a particularly high artistic standard. The soft elegance of the shapes is an indication of the spirit of the time, a dating ratified by the well preserved colour scheme, the painting of the figures and the decoration with cut-gold leaf *(kirikane).* To the east the complex includes a small, decorative, three-storey pagoda, only 3 bays square, transferred from the Ichijō 77–78 Palace in Kyōto in 1178. The interior is decorated with wall paintings, and it encloses a Yakushi figure that is the temple's oldest image, although it is highly restored.

In the second half of the eleventh century a noble of the Fujiwara clan, Hi no Sukenari, founded a private temple in Fushimi, south of Kyōto, the Hōkai-ji. He built first a Yakushi Hall for his own personal cult image, a standing figure of Yakushi dated 1051. It was carved in cherrywood and left unpainted in the tradition of sandalwood sculpture but was adorned with the finest *kirikane.* The Amida Hall, 5 bays square with a 79 pyramidal shingle roof, was put up in 1098 and altered later. The chief cult image, however, dates from the 81 end of the eleventh century, a monumental statue of Amida on the Jōchō model. It deviates from Jōchō's work in the smooth elegance of its form and the severity of its facial expression. Integration into a total picture of the Western Paradise is achieved with wall paintings. Small bands of wall below the ceiling of the central core are painted with floating angels, the compart- 80 ments of the ceiling have ornamental scrolls and flowers. The walls of the ambulatory have row upon row of little Buddha figures. The two supporting pillars in front of the altar podium are decorated with figures of the Diamond World Mandala in strict array.

75
Nine Images of *Amida* in the Hondō of the Jōruri-ji, Kyōto. Wood with gold leaf on lacquered dressing. H. (central figure) 224.2 cm, (subsidiary figures) 139–145 cm. 1107.
The nine seated images of Amida Nyorai depict the Buddha's promise of redemption. Following the earliest group in the Hōjō-ji of Fujiwara no Michinaga, the central image shows a close relationship with the Amida by Jōchō in the Hōō-dō of the Byōdō-in (Pl. 69). Perhaps a pupil of Jōchō worked in the Jōruri-ji. The eight subsidiary figures—their hands joined in the *jōin* mudra—have individual features in spite of their formal similarity.

90

76
Amida Nyorai in the Hondō of the Jōruri-ji, Kyōto. Wood with gold leaf on lacquered dressing. H. 224.2 cm. 1047–1107.
The main cult image of the nine Amidas in the Jōruri-ji differs from the subsidiary figures in holding his hands in the *raigō* mudra. In comparison with the Amida by Jōchō in the Hōō-dō of the Byōdo-in (Pl. 69), this figure has a more thick-set body. The nimbus with seven prominent and innumerable small Buddha figures, together with four floating Bosatsu, symbolizes the worlds of the Buddha.

77–78
Pagoda of the Jōruri-ji, Kyōto. Timber-frame construction with shingle roof. H. 16.1 m. 1171.
This decorative, three-storeyed pagoda is said to have been transferred from the Ichijō Palace in Kyōto to the Jōruri-ji in 1178. The three roofs covered with *hinoki* shingles are supported on a complex system of wooden consoles. The building stands on a rock opposite the Hondō and is reflected in the pool. The lower chapel, in which a Yakushi sculpture stands, is painted.

79

80

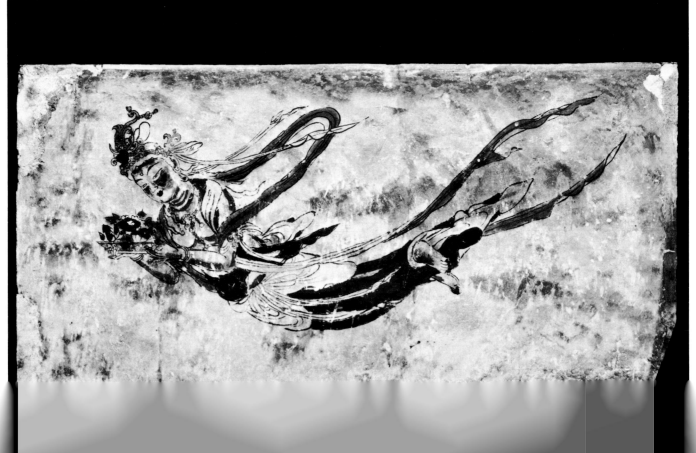

79

Amida-dō of the Hōkai-ji, Kyōto. Timber-frame construction with pyramidal shingle roof. 18.51 m. square. 1098.

A temple of the Tendai sect with an Amida Hall was built on the country property of the Hino family, part of the Fujiwara clan; it originally measured five bays by five. The verandah and its overhanging intermediary roof are said to have been added during the renovation of the hall in 1226.

80

Hiten from the Amida-dō of the Hōkai-ji, Kyōto. Wall painting on plaster. H. 46 cm, W. 92 cm. Late twelfth–early thirteenth century. The narrow bands of wall above the zone of timberwork on the inner pillars are decorated with paintings of Buddhas and flying heavenly beings called *hiten,* or *apsaras.* Similar wall paintings from the same period existed in the Nanen-dō, a hall in the Kōfuku-ji in Nara.

81

Amida Nyorai (detail) from the Amida-dō of the Hōkai-ji, Kyōto. Wood with gold leaf over lacquer dressing. H. 227 cm. 1098 (?)

This seated figure of Amida in *jōroku* dimensions follows in the succession of the Amida by Jōchō (Pl. 69) in the Hōō-dō of the Byōdō-in. The effect of the sculpture is withdrawn and heavy; the *yosegi* technique is even more refined than that used by Jōchō.

82

Hondō of the Sanzen-in Temple, Ōhara near Kyōto. Wood with bent hipped reed roof. L. 7.9 m, W. 9.1 m. Twelfth and seventeenth centuries.

The small hall, three bays by four bays wide, is said to have been founded originally by the priest Ryōnin in the eleventh century and transformed into a Paradise Hall in the twelfth century by the priest Shinnyobō. The core building with its roof and Amida trinity was preserved, and the outer shell was rebuilt in 1668.

81

82

A further Paradise Hall was apparently contributed by the priest Ryōnin (1072–1132). The Gokuraku-in was moved by the priest Shinnyobō to Ōhara and is now known as the Sanzen-in. It is small, measuring 7.9 by 9.1 metres in plan, and houses an Amida trinity, dated by inscription to 1148. Amida Buddha is attended by Kannon and Seishi, both kneeling in the pose of welcome and turned towards the faithful. The majesty of this trinity, radiant with gold, seems fit to burst through the tiny hall. The central core is likely to date from 1148, for the keel-shaped ceiling is painted with twenty-five Bodhisattvas to round off the *raigō* concept. Furthermore Shingon ideas are brought in: figures from the Mandala of the 'Two Worlds' appear in the painted programme.

The pious belief in Deliverance caused increased building activity in the provinces as well as in the capital. In the east of Japan Fujiwara no Kiyohira (d. 1128) emerged as victor in the power struggles of the military. He founded a new capital for the provinces of Mutsu and Dewa in Hiraizumi, which was meant to

83
Amida Trinity in the Sanzen-in Temple, Ōhara near Kyōto. Wood with gold leaf over lacquer dressing. H. (Amida) 233 cm. 1148.
The trinity shows the figures of Amida Nyorai with the Bodhisattvas Kannon and Seishi in the posture for welcoming the dead. The Amida, of *jōroku* dimensions, shows only a faint connexion with Jōchō's masterpiece in the Byōdō-in, however the composite concept of the *raigō* is still maintained here: the keel-shaped roof is painted with twenty-five Bodhisattvas and the back wall with the mandalas of the Two Worlds.

84
Seishi Bosatsu from the Amida trinity in the Sanzen-in Temple, Ōhara near Kyōto. Wood with gold leaf over lacquer dressing. H. 132 cm. 1148.
Seishi Bosatsu kneels to the left of Amida, on a lotus throne, with his hands folded. Like Kannon he radiates tenderness, expressive of his intention to bring Deliverance, and bends towards the believer. Though the name of the artist is not known, the date 1148 is written inside the figure.

85   ▷
Head of *Ichiji-Kinrin* from the Chūson-ji, Hiraizumi, Iwate. *Katsura* wood with painted dressing. H. 76 cm. Late twelfth century.
The realistic colouring emphasizes the beauty of this statue.

86

Interior of the Konjiki-dō of the Chūson-ji, Hiraizumi, Iwate. W. (altar) *c.* 180 cm. 1124.

The building materials used inside this tiny hall have been completely covered with lacquer and skilfully inlaid with mother-of-pearl and precious stones as well as with pierced bronze plaques, in places. Large flower rosettes have been inlaid into the beams, and the four central pillars of the middle altar, which contains a figure of the Universal Buddha Dainichi, are decorated with the finest polished lacquer. Dainichi appears in several forms corresponding to those he assumes in the mandala. Each altar holds an Amida Buddha with a Kannon and Seishi, surrounded on each side by six monks flanked by two Ni-ō. Craftsmen from Kyōto worked in the Chūson-ji, bringing the mature style of the capital with them to the far north.

87

Decorative panel on the altar plinth of the Sutra Hall of the Chūson-ji, Hiraizumi, Iwate. Wood with lacquer, mother-of-pearl inlay and chased bronze. H. (relief) 32.5 cm. Twelfth and fourteenth centuries.

The octagonal base with the figures of Monju Bosatsu and his attendants is decorated in a manner similar to the altars of the Konjiki-dō. The frames are embellished with mother-of-pearl inlay into thick sprinkled gold lacquer, with designs including *vajra* thunderbolts and blossoms, and the grounds show traces of plant motifs, while the reserves are engraved into sheet bronze. Over these reserved panels celestial bird-beings—*kalavinka*—are applied, worked in decorative relief and engraving.

equal the imperial city of Kyōto in brilliance and cosmopolitan atmosphere. The precincts of the Chūson-ji contained more than forty halls. The first hall rose in 1105; two years later an Amida Hall with nine Amida figures was erected, the central one 10 metres high, only equalled in dimensions by that of the Hōjō-ji. Of all these a 'Gold-coloured' Hall (Konjiki-dō) still stands, together with a later Sutra Hall. The Konjiki-dō was built in 1124 and dedicated in 1126, receiving imperial protection withal, with a decree from the imperial court. This hall was destined to be not only the funeral chapel of three generations of Fujiwara governors in Hiraizumi but also to assist all the fallen of the civil wars to achieve rebirth in Amida's Pure Land. It is a small hall, only 3 bays wide, and crowned with a pyramidal roof, but the interior decoration is rich beyond compare. Not only are the wooden parts lacquered and encrusted with mother-of-pearl ornament alternating with pierced-bronze patterned fittings but the inner pillars, too, bear medallions with seated Dainichi Buddhas in the most exquisite gold and silver lacquerwork. Three altars are set over the tombs of Fujiwara no Kiyohira (d. 1128), Fujiwara no Motohira (d. 1154) and Fujiwara no Hidehira (d. 1187), and the podia are as richly decorated as the pillars, with cartouches of sheets of bronze gilt, showing peacocks, peonies and butterflies. The images on the altars are

88
Shiramizu-Amida-dō (or Ganjō-ji), Fukushima. Timber-frame
construction with pyramidal shingle roof. H. 939 cm, W. 939 cm.
1166.
This Amida Hall is a classic of the type, three bays by three, developed in the Late Heian period.

89
Great Hall (Ōdō) of the Fuki-dera Temple, Kunisaki peninsula,
Kyūshū. Wood with pyramidal tiled roof. L. 770 cm, W. 930 cm.
Before 1164.
The hall is three bays by four and has a roof crowned by the sacred
pearl. The Fuki-dera alone remains of the many temples that originally were dedicated in northern Kyūshū, on the Kunisaki peninsula. Saichō, founder of the Tendai sect, is said to have preached
there before he went to China; later the Amida faith also reached
Kyūshū. The fact that the Fuki-dera is an Amida Hall testifies to
this.

90
Interior of the Great Hall of the Fuki-dera Temple, Kunisaki peninsula, Kyūshū. Before 1164.
The interior of the Ōdō has a narrow coffered ceiling that is only
raised to a keel vault over the altar. There are traces of painting on
the timber work and altar columns, faintly reminiscent of the designs in the Konjiki-dō. While the statue of Amida came later to the
temple, the raigō on the wall behind it, with a representation of the
Western Paradise, is contemporary with the foundation of the hall.

uniform: a seated figure of Amida each attended by the
Bodhisattvas Kannon and Seishi, six Jizō and two Ni-ō.
A comparison of the individual statues illustrates
clearly the change in form from the style of Jōchō, on
which these are unquestionably modelled, to ever more
delicate and smoother shapes, characteristic of Late
Heian style.

It may be supposed that many of the great provincial
nobles founded temples on their estates to emulate the
Amida halls of the capital, Heian-kyō, and those of the
Chūson-ji in Hiraizumi. In Iwaki, south of Hiraizumi,
Iwaki no Norimitsu established an Amida Hall in 1166,
ostensibly for his wife who was to become a nun. The
88 hall is known today as the Ganjō-ji, but also as the
Shiramizu-Amida-dō, because the finely proportioned
building stood on an island in a woodland lake
(*Shiramizu* = 'white water'). The hall is about twice the
size of the Konjiki-dō but restrainedly simple in spite of
the balanced wooden construction of the *wayō-degumi*
type. The curved pyramid roof is covered with
shingles. Nor is the interior to be compared with the
Konjiki-dō. There is a Buddha altar with a seated
Amida set between Kannon and Seishi and two Ni-ten;

instead of opulent lacquer and mother-of-pearl decoration only paint has been used.

As in the far north of Japan, so in the south on the island of Kyūshū, an Amida Hall of the late twelfth century has been preserved. The Great Hall (Ōdō) of the Fuki-dera measures 7.7 by 9.3 metres in plan. The original group of images in the interior has apparently been lost. Today there is a seated Amida in front of the wooden back wall, and this shows traces of the *raigō* with a recognizable Jōdo Paradise. The motifs on the timberwork only approximate to the surface decoration of the Late Heian style.

Fujiwara Sculpture

The important step that opened up the way for Japanese wooden sculpture to reach a new high point at the end of the tenth century is heralded in only a few earlier works. These are experiments in the method of systematically putting together blocks of wood *(yosegi-zukuri)* for carving, using some degree of division of labour. In Jōgan sculpture the back and head of figures carved from a single block of wood were often vertically hollowed out and closed in with a panel. Whether the inspiration to the new joined-wood technique came from China cannot be decided with any certainty. The well-known figure of Tobatsu-Bishamon-ten in the Kyōōgokoku-ji is considered to be of Chinese origin; it is composed of irregular pieces of wood joined together. The severe image of Shaka in sandalwood in the Seiryō-ji, brought back from China by the priest Chōnen, also shows an un-Japanese technique called 'split and fit' *(warihagi)*. The torso was split vertically; both sides were hollowed out and the two shells fitted together again. It had the advantage of providing a space for the holy substances and, because of the thin skin, of reducing the danger of cracking.

It is accepted that *busshi* Kōshō (active around 990–1021?) played a decisive role in the development from *warihagi* to *yosegi* technique, and that the latter was a purely Japanese invention. The structure of a Fudō-myōō of *jōroku* size, built for the Jōmyō-ji (probably by Kōshō) in 1006–1007, and commissioned by Fujiwara no Michinaga, which is now in the Dōshu-in in Kyōto, illustrates the basic form of the *yosegi* technique. The sculptor put together five blocks and panels, alternately vertically and horizontally in the manner of building blocks. After the blocks were glued together, the outer form was carved. Then the pieces were taken apart again and each hollowed into thin shells before being once more fitted together, covered with cloth, lacquered and finally coated with gold leaf or painted in colour, all according to iconographic prescription. The Senju Kannon of 1012 in the Kōryū-ji is also in *yosegi* technique. In spite of its poor state of preservation we can discern a soft elegance of expression and pose unknown in Jōgan sculpture. These traits were brought to their highest pitch of maturity in the work of Kōshō's son, Jōchō. This new approach was not without its links with the art of painting. The priest Genshin, prominent as writer of the *Ōjō Yō-shū* and herald of the Amida faith, is said also to have been a painter and, more convincingly, the inspirer of the most celebrated Amida-*raigō* paintings. Kōshō was in close contact with him and carved images for three of his temples.

Who were these Buddha masters from the late tenth century known under their names as monks and honoured with clerical rank? They were not like the sculptors of the Nara period, who worked mostly in other media and were subject to a temple office. These Buddha masters worked in guilds and had their own workshops. They received commissions from the imperial family, from the Fujiwara regents and from the top nobles, as well as from priests and temples of every sect. Thus they were engaged on the strength of their reputations as artists. They were provided with materials by their patrons and, in the manner of the time, were rewarded, for instance, with rolls of silk brocade. It is recorded that in the workshop of the Hōjō-ji the twenty 'great Buddha masters' *(dai-busshi)* each had five 'small Buddha masters' *(ko-busshi)* working under them. All together 105 qualified craftsmen worked on projects that often, when it was a case of celebrating a birth or mourning a death, had to be completed within a few weeks.

For his Hōjō-ji, Fujiwara no Michinaga ordered 199 sculptors, 15 of them from Kōshō, the rest from the workshop of the *Dai-Busshi* Jōchō. The chief cult image of the Golden Hall, a Dainichi 10 metres (32 *shaku*) high, must have been a challenge for the sculptor, both in conception and execution. The ten monumental sculptures Jōchō produced in the years 1022 to 1024 corresponded so perfectly to the religious and aesthetic aspirations of the aristocracy that he was honoured as no artist before him in Japan, with the Buddhist rank of *Hokkyō*. The higher title of *Hōgen* was conferred on him

91

Raigō of Amida. Wood with gold leaf on lacquer. H. (principle figure) 233 cm, (subsidiary figures) *c.* 90 cm. 1098. Sokujō-ji, Kyōto. This configuration is affected by the belief that Amida Buddha and his attendants escort the faithful into his Western Paradise. Amida in over-life size *(jōroku),* is seated among his entourage of life-size Bodhisattvas. Jōchō's style and plastic concepts are adopted here and interpreted in a new manner. Only ten of the original statues of attendants survive.

in 1048 for restoring images in the ancestral temple of the Fujiwara, the Kōfuku-ji in Nara.

His great talent is to be seen in undiminished splendour in the Amida of the Hōō-dō in the Byōdō-in at Uji. It is built of fifty-three separate parts, combined on the 'building-block' principle, partly of split blocks for torso and head and with many attached and inserted

pieces for arms, hands and drapery. The shell of the figure is exceptionally thin, as was ascertained during its restoration in 1955, and thus space was left for the magic substance. This consists of a disc with Sanskrit texts of the Amida invocations, resting on a painted and extremely finely carved lotus stand. *Busshi* Jōchō also designed and carved a group of the fifty-two Bodhisattva figures on the temple walls. The nimbus of the image and the baldachin, though partly restored, show the perfection reached in the techniques of relief and openwork *(ukibori).*

Jōchō's iconometric scheme for the seated Buddha set the norm for almost every subsequent image of the Heian period and later. About sixty figures of the seated Buddha are thought to have followed Jōchō's model. None of these works was a slavish copy, however. The technical details were a secret of the workshop. The

68–69

92
Jizō Bosatsu: by Jōchō. Wood, dressed and painted. H. 152 cm. Early eleventh century. Rokuharamitsu-ji, Kyōto.
This standing figure of a Jizō Bosatsu (Kshitigarbha) is thought to be an early work of the Buddha-sculptor Jōchō. Jōchō represents Jizō, the saviour of souls suffering in hell, especially children, as a young monk with a gentle withdrawn expression. The clear lines of the drapery of the monk's habit, with its long sleeves, are related to the sculptor's masterpiece, the Amida Buddha (Pl. 69) in the Hōō-dō of the Byōdō-in. Jizō's attributes – rattle and jewel – have not survived.

later sculptures of the Hōkai-ji, Jōruri-ji, Anraku-ji, 91 Sokujō-ji and Sanzen-in followed their own drafts. The tendency to ever more detailed patching together of the blocks in *yosegi-zukuri* technique and the insertion of the head gave the possibility of a new freedom of movement in the poses of the statues; however, since the iconography of the Buddha was very rigid, there still remained no real artistic liberty.

The Late Heian period found new types not only for the unshackled pose of the Buddha figure but also for the figures of the Bodhisattvas attendant on him, especially Kannon in his various manifestations who is attentive to all that passes in this world. Jōchō gave the

Bodhisattva Jizō tender feminine features in his sculp- 92 ture for the Rokuharamitsu-ji. One is reminded of the oft repeated comment on the manly heroes of the *Genji-monogatari*: '... and the involuntary thought came, "if only he had been a woman".'[27]

Even the Shi-tennō and the Ni-ō, whose protective functions required aggression and power, were given quiet or playfully histrionic gestures. The Shi-tennō of 93 the Jōruri-ji are of a high artistic level; the subtlety of the carving and of the colouring, which is adorned, in addition, with cut gold leaf, shows another facet of Fujiwara sculpture to set beside the static, withdrawn, golden figures of the nine Amida Buddhas.

The elegance of Jōchō's figure type in *wa-yō* style at this unique and unsurpassable level had a determining influence on image carving during the boom in sculpture that was started off by the enthusiasm of the ex-emperors for founding temples. The pupils of Jōchō established their own workshops, named according to their location: Shichi-jō Street, San-jō Street and Roku-jō Street schools. Other studios took the names of artists. *Busshi* Chōen (active to 1150) received the highest Buddhist title *(Hōin)* as the leading wood sculptor of the third generation after Jōchō. He worked equally for temples and the lay aristocracy. After him only Inson (1120–1198) was similarly honoured, perhaps because he collaborated in the restoration of the temples in Nara.

In Kyōto after Shirakawa-Tennō, the sculptural programme involved thousands of figures. Even the Taira generals who came to power commissioned sets of cult images: Taira no Tadamori ordered a thousand figures of Sho-Kannon on behalf of Toba-Tennō in 1132. In the Sanjūsangen-dō, which was consecrated in 1164, Goshirakawa had 1,001 images of the thousand- 73 armed Kannon set up. Both hall and three quarters of the sculptures were burnt down in 1249. In the new building dating from 1266, *busshi* Tankei and his studio

93   ▷
Tamon-ten (Bishamon-ten) in the Hondō of the Jōruri-ji, Kyōto. Wood with painted dressing and *kirikane*. H. 169.5 cm. 1107.
The Four Celestial Kings (Shi-tennō) protect the four cardinal directions, standing at the four corners of the platform with the row of nine statues of Amida. They also are carved in *yosegi* technique and very finely finished with colours and cut gold leaf. The demon base and the pierced carved nimbus add to the high refinement and soft elegance with which even these fierce guardians were endowed in the Late Heian period.

replaced the burnt statues. The smooth elegance of the restored sculpture is clearly distinguishable from the early work.

In the ancient temple city of Nara the Buddha sculptors worked mainly at the rehabilitation of the old images, but at the Hōryū-ji important new works were produced, in the traditional technique and yet of the greatest sophistication. Several are among the masterpieces of Late Heian art: *Shōtoku Taishi Aged Seven,* carved by Enkai in 1069 and coloured by the painter Hata Chitei (Munesada); a *Bishamon-ten,* and a *Kichijō-ten* in *ichiboku* technique, carved for the Saishō-e Feast in 1078. In the twelfth century a group of *Shōtoku Taishi at the Age of Forty-Five with Four Attendants* was consecrated; it differs from the earlier figures in having an element of humour in the concept. The same grotesque and humorous element is found in the 'Twelve Generals' *(Jūni Shinshō)* of the Buddha Yakushi in the Kōfuku-ji. They are unique as examples of flat relief carving *(itabori).*

95

94

96

94
Shōtoku Taishi at the Age of Forty-Five with Four Attendants (details) in the Shōryō-in of the Hōryū-ji, Nara. Wood, dressed, painted and with *kirikane.* H. (Shōtoku) 84.3 cm, (attendant) 64 cm. 1121.
The impressive portrait of Shōtoku Taishi as regent has similarities with images of Shintō deities. The prince wears official court costume with a *kammuri* cap and holds a *shaku* sceptre with both hands. The expression of concentrated wisdom in his face is enhanced by the meticulous finish in colour. His garment has a decoration in cut gold leaf over the painted pattern.

95   ▷
Kichijō-ten in the Kondō of the Hōryū-ji, Nara. Wood, dressed and painted. H. 117 cm. 1068.
Kichijō-ten (Sri Devi) is a goddess of fertility and good fortune. The image was set up with the figure of Bishamon-ten for the Saishō-e Feast. This noble figure of a Chinese lady is built up from split wooden blocks and covered with a delicate coating of colour over linen and burnt shell-lime gesso. The metal ornaments are later additions.

96
Mekira Taishō from the Kōfuku-ji, Nara. Wood, dressed and painted. H. 88 cm. Eleventh century.
The twelve guardian generals—*Jūni Shinshō*—belong to the trinity of Yakushi Nyorai of 1013 in the Kōfuku-ji. They are carved in flat relief on wooden panels and are an exception in Fujiwara sculpture: the baroque exaggeration and painterly quality of the twelve humorously conceived figures is unusual in the eleventh century. Nara, little influenced by the court in Heian-kyō, allowed independent artistic creations to be produced.

alleged that Taira no Kiyomori endowed it in 1154 for the priest Sainen. The small image is attributed to the sculptor Kenen of the San-jō school. It is one of the rarest among all Japan's treasured wood-carvings. The body is left untreated apart from a little colour on the lips, the roots of the hair and the eyes. Rich *kirikane* ornament covers the drapery and the base. The opulent jewellery—necklaces, earrings and diadem—is worked in gold and set with gems like the nimbus.

The desire to accumulate merit towards a higher status upon rebirth, which possessed every class of society in the Late Heian period, was responsible also for the less subtle creations in sculpture. There are groups of roughly carved wooden figures *(natabori)* from eastern Japan which, by their intentional naivety, present a total contrast with the art of the court.

Groups of stone figures are often found in the twelfth century, arranged in mandalas in a landscape, like the Furuzono group at Usuki in Ōita province. The stone figures, originally protected in wooden houses, sometimes show traces of a coating of lacquer and colour.

The change in sculpture from the static and over-refined style of the Late Heian period to dramatic naturalistic interpretation, especially of the lower ranks

Sandalwood sculpture also continued into the Late Heian period, apparently used mostly as images for private worship. In the Hōkai-ji, the cherrywood statue of the Buddha Yakushi is honoured as the 'image at the heart of the cult'. The expression and form possess the soft celestial gentleness of Late Heian style, while the rich elaborately patterned ornament of gold leaf *(kirikane)*, applied directly to the bare cherrywood, creates a novel effect for the work which is supremely sumptuous.

97 The thousand-armed Kannon of the Būjō-ji in the north of Heian-kyō is made in the same technique. It is

97 ▷
Senju Kannon in the Būjō-ji, Kyōto. Wood with *kirikane*. H. 31.5 cm. 1154.
This little statuette of Senju Kannon is like a jewel on its richly decorated plinth and lotus throne, which are both hung with bronze ornaments that still retain their gilding. The figure itself is also richly bejewelled; the lovely face is peaceful, and the hands gesticulate playfully. The drapery and the stand are all delicately covered in *kirikane* over the bare sandalwood. The nimbus of filigree-like metalwork is in relief and pierced; it frames the figure with a shimmering radiance. General Taira no Kiyomori had the statuette made for the hermitage of the priest Sainen in 1154. It is thought to be the work of the sculptor Kenen.

98
The Priest Rōben in the Kaidan-in of the Tōdai-ji, Nara. Wood, dressed and painted. H. 92.5 cm Eleventh century.
This posthumous ideal portrait of the first abbot of the Tōdai-ji, who died in 773, breathes the confident nobility of his personality. The carving still shows certain forms characteristic of Jōgan sculpture, but the softer more elegant interpretation of the Fujiwara period is already apparent. The figure is normally kept hidden and since 1019 has only been shown once a year in the memorial ceremony. The scepter is said to have been used by Rōben during his lifetime.

99
Dainichi Nyorai: by Unkei in the Enjō-ji, Nara. Wood with gold leaf over lacquer. H. 100.6 cm. 1176.
The noble seated figure of the ultimate Buddha Dainichi is a youthful work of the great sculptor of the Kamakura period; the concepts of the Heian period are still determinant in it. An inscription on the underside of the lotus throne states that the image was begun by Kōkei and his son Unkei on 24 November 1175, and completed and erected on 19 October 1176.

of being (demons, protecting spirits and, not the least, portraits) took place in Nara, where the cult images of 99 the Nara period continued to influence the sculptors. A new technique that rendered eyes with inset crystals was developed on the Amida trinity of the Chōgaku-ji. The bodies of this Amida and the Bodhisattvas flanking him are also given more ample forms. The pose of 'royal ease' of the seated Bodhisattvas with one leg hanging down is presumably an indication of a new in-

100   ▷
Fugen Bosatsu. Wood with traces of dressing, colour and *kirikane*. H. (Fugen) 55.2 cm, (elephant) 58.2 cm. Mid-twelfth century. Okura Shūkokan Museum, Tōkyō.
For the court nobility the *Lotus Sutra* was one of the chief texts for salvation. The Tendai sect promoted its teachings and the worship of the Bodhisattva of Highest Wisdom, Fugen, who came down from his Eastern Paradise on a elephant with six tusks. The over-refined and sentimental court society of Heian-kyō was partial to cult images with this kind of excessive charm and richness.

fluence from the mainland, for this pose was favoured in the sculpture of Song-dynasty China. The *yosegi-zukuri* method of wood carving developed in Japan enriched these new possibilities with its own particular sensibility.

Religious Painting

In the Buddhist cult it is the three-dimensional images of the Buddha that take first place in the halls of temples as manifestations of transcendental beings and powers. A chief cult figure *(honzon)* stood as the culmination and revelation of the world of the Buddha, with or without attendants, on a plinth *(shumi-dan)* that symbolized the World Mountain, Mount Sumeru. Painting fulfilled only a secondary function in the cult hall, serving the Buddhist concept of *shōgon* ('sanctification through a wealth of splendour'), as translated by D. Seckel. Its task was to decorate walls and structural members with representations or patterns. The models for wall painting in temples came to Japan by means of sketches. The Kondō of the Hōryū-ji with representations of the Four Paradises shows, at the beginning of the seventh century, a perfection that was never again achieved. In the Heian period paintings on wood, 'panel pictures' *(ita-e),* were generally preferred to decorating with water-colours on plaster. Wooden panels, door leaves, pillars and the beams of the structure were used as supports for the pictures.

Sacred paintings with magical power are also seen in the mandalas and patriarchs' portraits in the interior of the pagoda of the Daigo-ji. Even in the work of synthesis (1053) of the Amida Paradise in the Hōō-dō at Uji, the paintings of the ninefold appearance of Amida 69 play only a secondary role beside the central statue of Amida by Jōchō. Similarly the *raigō* scenes in the painted mandalas of the Western Paradise were to be found in the framing bands of the borders.

The painted image is likely to have become emancipated as an independent focus of worship as a temporary devotional picture produced for special days of celebration and commemoration. They were based on banners like those found in the caves of Dunhuang in China. The hanging scroll *(kakemono)* was painted on silk, linen or paper. Beside the beings of the esoteric sects that dominated the Early Heian period, the redeemers of the old Nara sects appear with undiminished importance, for example the Buddha Yakushi with his twelve protecting generals. Taishaku-ten and Kichijō-ten were accorded special reverence among guardian deities *(ten)* of Indian origin as bringers of good fortune and as protectors. The sixteen Rakan *(Luohan),* too, were represented as 'human' redeemers. Separate images were made of the different aspects of the Bodhisattva Avalokiteshvara: eleven-headed, thousand-armed or as Nyoirin Kannon.

Narrative didactic pictures assumed an importance almost equal to the mandalas. Events from the life of the Buddha Shaka—his entry into Nirvana or his ap- 101–102 pearance from the golden coffin—were portrayed for 107 contemplation in large-scale and artistically accomplished illustrations. A number of new themes were introduced by the *Lotus Sutra.* Its visionary descriptions inspired such scenes as the one in the Hōrōkaku Man- 103 dala, where a manifestation of Shaka and his attendants is represented in a pagoda. The Buddha's Sermon on Vulture Peak is depicted for the Hokke-kyō Mandala, where he is shown surrounded by Bodhisattvas and adored by worshippers.

The growth of the cult of Amida brought representations of his Descent to the fore, with the Buddha appearing in a trinity or with a host of his Bodhisattvas. Pictures of the 'Pure Land' as the goal of rebirth and the horrifying sufferings undergone in the six levels of existence also provided rousing and emotive themes. The introduction of all these Indian beliefs and Buddhist stories into a Japanese environment and context helped the purely Japanese *Yamato-e* to find its own pictorial language.

In the Early Heian period a belief in the beneficent properties of the model meant that painting followed closely the iconography of examples coming from China. The proportions of the figures, their poses, facial expressions, features and attributes were all adopted from Chinese models. The technique of execution—a regular 'wire-like' line drawn in red for the Buddha and Bodhisattvas, in black for the lower ranks

102 ▷

Nehanzu (detail of Pl. 101).
Behind the platform on which the Buddha lies, Bosatsu and monks stand under the shāla trees. Kannon and Fugen are portrayed with white skins, mourning with lowered gaze, while Monju, like the Buddha, has a yellow-tinted body surrounded by outlines in red. The monks on the right, with their grief-laden poses and gestures, make a strong contrast with the noble calm of the Bodhisattvas. As men they belong to a lower degree of existence.

101

Nehanzu ('Buddha's Entry into Nirvana'). Colours and *kirikane* on silk. H. 266.2 cm, W. 270.9 cm. 1068. Kongōbu-ji on Kōya-san, Wakayama. Shaka, the Buddha of the present era, went to the bank of the River Hiranyavati and entered Nirvana beneath two flowering shāla trees. He lies enfolded in a white veil with rich *kirikane* patterns, on a platform surrounded by mourners from every level of life: Bodhisattvas, monks, demons, kings and animals, who lament either calmly or in agony. At the top right appears the Buddha's mother Māyā. The Japanese painter has based this didactic work on a Chinese model, but in spite of the cartouches with inscriptions he has managed to reproduce the scene with an urgent and highly sensitive artistic force. The date 'seventh day of the Fourth Month in the year 1068' is found on the right-hand border.

103

Hōrōkaku Mandala. Colours and gold on silk. H. 144.4 cm, W. 86.7 cm. Twelfth century. Freer Gallery of Art, Washington, D.C. (29.2).

This cult painting shows the vision of the monk in the foreground. There appears to him a two-storeyed hall in which the Buddha Shaka, flanked by two twelve-armed and four-headed Bodhisattvas, is enthroned and preaching. The building is in central perspective; in front of it stand or kneel the Shitennō and the Bodhisattvas, while between them is the Wheel of the Law on a lotus throne. This unusual cult painting of esoteric Buddhism derives from a passage in the *Lotus Sutra*.

112

of figures, the convention of banded colours as well as the light, unrealistic shading of the flesh—was taken from Chinese paintings. To this was added the practice of 'reversed shading': those parts which appear dark to the eye (the inside folds of drapery, the parts of curved limbs turned away or the inner surface of the lotus thrones) were rendered not dark but light, giving the figure a visionary, floating quality. The deity seems to emanate a secret radiance. This effect was enhanced by a technique peculiar to Japanese Buddhist painting when used to this extent, a refined patterning of the figure achieved by applying the most delicate ornament of cut-gold leaf, which is reminiscent of the elegant decoration of writing paper for sutra texts and poetry. The painting was done in ink and mineral pigments of red, blue, green, yellow, shell-lime white, gold and silver, bound in glue.

The colours were lent symbolic and liturgical significance.

The different levels of existence are clearly distinguished in their colouring. The higher the rank of the divinity, the simpler and broader the colour. Many paintings of Buddhas achieve an effect of sublimity precisely in the contrast of this simplicity, which imposes beyond all multiplicities of the phenomenal world, with the rich fullness and splendour of the Bodhisattvas.... The Vidyārājas show the demonic side of colour with their sombre and sinister glow; now and again they break forth from this basic absolute colour that contains an unlimited potential, into a fortissimo that puts into relief the deep quiet of the other figures. The figures of the human sphere, especially the arhats and patriarchs, are usually rendered in quite different, more 'earthy' colours.... The choice of colour itself makes a decisive contribution in symbolizing the essential being of the different types of figure....[28]

From the late tenth century Buddhist painting, like all else, was completely subject to the influence of court taste. It is possible that the priest-painters *(e-busshi)* worked in guilds and workshops like the sculptors *(ki-busshi),* but there is no information on the subject, only on the court Painting Bureau and the pre-eminence of its painters, who had their positions in the official hierarchy and appear to have been involved also in religious painting. Fujiwara no Michinaga assigned the interior painting and the execution of hanging scrolls for his temple, the Hōjō-ji, to the priest-painter Enen, of whom it is known that he was the son of a Fujiwara courtier, Yoshikane no Ajari. The wall paintings in the Hōō-dō are ascribed (though there is no shred of evidence to support the claim) to a court painter. It is cer-

104
Portrait of Jion Daishi. Ink and colours on silk. H. 161.2cm, W. 129cm. *c.* 1061. Yakushi-ji, Nara.
The expressive portrait of the Chinese priest, an adherent of the Hosshō sect, is based on a Chinese model. It served from 951 as a cult image in Japan at a memorial ceremony, which has been held since 1061 in the Yakushi-ji. The powerful alert personality of the patriarch is fascinatingly interpreted. He sits meditating on a bench, a costly writing set beside him. On the upper border are panels with fine calligraphic inscriptions of praise.

tain, however, that many of the iconographic sketches that served as metrical models for the paintings were the work of priest-painters. The *Blue Fudō with Attendants* in the Shōren-in is probably based on a sketch of the tenth century in the Daijo-ji by the Buddha master Genchō. Similarly the idealized *Portrait of Jion Daishi* 104 from the Yakushi-ji is connected with traditional models that have survived. The group of the *Ten Patriarchs of the Tendai Set,* in the possession of the Ichijō-ji, shows the Indian teachers and the Chinese, with

106

Raigō of Amida: three hanging scrolls. Colours on silk. H. (centre) 185.5 cm, W. 146.1 cm; H. (right) 183.3 cm, W. 55 cm; H. (left) 186.4 cm, W. 173.6 cm. First half of the eleventh century. Hokke-ji, Nara.

In the centre Amida Nyorai, presented frontally, appears floating on a lotus over clouds. His hands are in the *raigō* mudra, and he looks at the worshipper through half-closed eyes. His red monk's habit with a dark lining is of the same colour as the lotus petals of his throne: it falls with spare lines round his white body. The figure, totally withdrawn and in repose, is surrounded by a double nimbus. The flanking paintings, perhaps of later date, show, on the right, a youthful standard bearer in the act of stepping out and, on the left, the Bodhisattvas Kannon and Seishi on multicoloured lotus thrones. Kannon holds his golden lotus, and Seishi holds up a canopy.

Shōtoku Taishi representing Japan; they are presented 105 partly in a hierarchical transfiguration as, for example, Nāgārjuna on the lotus throne, and partly in action as Shubhākarasimha (Zemmui) in meditative prayer and also as Shōtoku Taishi teaching his pupils.

The Amida Buddha of the Hokke-ji shows a new painterly concept, though formally it is related to the Early Heian period once again. The early central 106 painting seems to have been combined with the side wings—on the left the Bodhisattvas Kannon and Seishi, and on the right a small standard bearer—only at the end of the century, in order to make an illustration of the 'Descent of Amida'.

The great large-format narrative paintings on silk were produced in the second half of the eleventh century. *Buddha's Entry into Nirvana (Nehanzu)* (1086) is 101–102 one of the most important paintings of the entire Heian period. The Buddha in withdrawn stillness lies on a podium under flowering shāla trees. He is surrounded by mourning Bodhisattvas, disciples, gods, demons and animals, some of whom disguise their sorrow while others give it open expression. Māyā, the mother of the Buddha, floats towards them over a rocky landscape. Each figure of this populous scene is highly individualized. The ductus and colouring as well as the gauzy garments richly adorned with *kirikane* ornament are masterly. Only the labels emphasize the didactic function of the picture.

Another painting very close to the *Nirvana* is the *Resurrection of the Buddha from the Golden Coffin.* In this 107 painting the group of worshippers presses more closely together as they gather in wonder round the central figure of the Buddha. Though the method of painting is very similar to the previous work, there are particular

105

Ryūmyō (a Tendai patriarch). Colours on silk. H. 126.5 cm, W. 72.5 cm. Ichijō-ji, Hyōgo.

This ideal portrait of the Indian partriarch Nāgārjuna (second-third century) belongs to a series of portraits of partriarchs in which the Japanese Crown Prince Shōtoku Taishi was also included. Sketches brought by the priest Ennin from China are thought to have been the model for these paintings in colour. Ryūmyō is regarded as the incarnation of the Bodhisattva Jizō. He is seated on a lotus throne, wearing rich monk's apparel and holding a sceptre in his right hand and an incense burner in his left.

107
Resurrection of the Buddha from the Golden Coffin. Colours on silk. H. 159.7 cm, L. 228.7 cm. Late eleventh century. Chōhō-ji, Kyōto.

After the Buddha Shaka had entered Nirvana he raised the lid of his coffin with divine power and appeared in radiant gold to his mother Māyā, who can be seen on the right in profile with a pilgrim's staff. The Buddha is surrounded by Bosatsu and beings of every level of existence. This theme is found elsewhere only at Dunhuang in China. The influence of Song-period painting can be seen in the sweeping lines of the pouch and drapery of the Buddha.

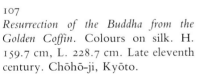

108
Shaka Nyorai. Colours on silk. H. 159.5 cm, W. 85.5 cm. Twelfth century. Jingo-ji, Kyōto.

In the *Lotus Sutra* Shaka (Shakyamuni) is the Buddha of our era, and he holds a central position in the teaching of the Tendai sect. In spite of the growing importance of the cult of Amida, Shaka continued to be held in high honour at court. In this painting the image of the teaching Buddha is represented like a sculpture on a base. The visionary apparition is heightened by the specific media of coloration and *kirikane*. The carmine-red of the garment and the white flesh are typical of the Late Heian period.

109 ▷
Kokūzō Bosatsu. Colours on silk. H. 131.8 cm, W. 84.2 cm. Mid-twelfth century. Tōkyō National Museum, Tōkyō.

The figure of the Bodhisattva of Universal Wisdom appears on a rock in the sea in front of a moon-shaped disc. This magic image of esoteric Buddhism was painted by an unknown artist in muted tones and surrounded like a sculpture with a decorative double nimbus. The delicacy of the painting with its reversed shading and *kirikane* patterning gives the figure a transparency that makes it appear like a supernatural vision.

110

Sui-ten. Colours and gold on silk. H. 144.2 cm, W. 126.6 cm. 1127. Kyōōgokoku-ji, Kyōto.

Sui-ten, the water god, belongs to a set of twelve pictures of the *Jūni-ten.* The group was painted for the Shingon Hall of the Imperial Palace and was used in the magic ceremonies on the seventh day of the First Month, together with the paintings of the Godai-myōō. The figures derive from the Taizō-kai Mandala and radiate the noble stillness of transcendant beings.

details in freer and more accentuated brush strokes. The new influence of Chinese Song-dynasty painting seems to be visible here.

From the first half of the twelfth century there has survived a larger number of devotional pictures with single figures, which must in part have come from the private chapels of high-ranking gentlemen and ladies of the court. On these *kakemono* the Buddha figure is often represented like a seated statue, on a lotus throne and a podium, and usually under a canopy. The painting of 108 the Buddha Shaka in the Jingo-ji is an example of this type. The preaching figure is rendered with the delicacy of a miniature and with great sensibility; he is shown in richly decorated monk's garb, on an intricately carved plinth, surrounded by an aureole of filigree gold scrolls.

It is comparable with the sandalwood figure of the 97 Senju Kannon in the Bujō-ji. The transcendental quality of the apparition is interpreted in the same manner for the Bodhisattva Kokūzō, an incarnation of the 109 Highest Wisdom. Kokūzō appears against a gigantic silver full moon, sitting on a rock in the sea. The sombre scale of colours stresses the magic aura of the figure, severe despite its immeasurably rich jewellery and soft drapery.

Two sets of Shingon deities from the early twelfth century are preserved in the Ichijō-ji. They stand in the tradition of works of the early ninth century that are connected with Kūkai (Kōbō Daishi). These are the *Five Great Kings of Wisdom* (Godai-myōō) and another set of *Twelve 'Ten'* (*Jūni-ten*). Both series of paintings 110 can be dated to the year 1127. While the *Jūni-ten* are painted with great delicacy and a visionary subtlety appropriate to their nature, the *Kings of Wisdom* have a much coarser impact to the superficial observer, with their terrifying aspect and flaming aureoles.

These figures are far from any direct address to the faithful. With the ideas from the *Lotus* and *Amida* sutras, proclaiming deliverance from the cycle of rebirth, worship came to be centred on new avatars. The Bodhisattva Fugen (Samantabhadra), for instance, plays a leading role in the Tendai cult, for his vow in the *Lotus Sutra* meant salvation, i.e. rebirth in Paradise even for women. Fugen is found here and there on his white elephant, a beast armed with six tusks; when seated on the lotus he takes the form of a youth in prayer who gazes gently down on the worshipper. He is often depicted in the latter pose, with a redeeming function, on the title pages of sutra texts.

In the Amida cult the early representations of Paradise and of the 'Pure Land' mandalas were followed by new versions that only reached a definitive form, for 111 example in the *Chinkai Mandara* of the National Museum, Nara, in the eleventh and twelfth centuries. Directly after the Fujiwara rule the Paradise compositions (with their palaces, jewel trees, crowds of Bodhisattvas dancing and playing instruments) and the lotus blossoms growing out of the jewel pond, each bearing a new-born soul, took on a new meaning as the model for the synthesis expressed in temple layouts.

In the second half of the twelfth century the joy in fantasizing new themes grew in strength. The absolute peak is reached among the pictures of the Descent of Buddha Amida by the *Amida Appears with the Host of His Bodhisattvas (Amida shōju raigō),* now preserved on

118

III

Fugen Bosatsu (detail). Colours on silk. H. 159 cm, W. 74.6 cm. First half of the twelfth century. Tōkyō National Museum, Tōkyō. The Bodhisattva appears beneath a floral canopy between falling blossoms; his lotus throne is carried by an elephant. On the elephant's head stand three small figures, emanations of the Bodhisattva. The figure is painted with outstanding delicacy of detail in colour and line; the interior lines, rays and nimbi are covered with cut gold leaf. The feminine manifestation of Fugen pleased the ladies of the court, who paid special honour to this Bodhisattva, for he preached deliverance for women.

the Kōya-san. This is a powerful work of art, consisting of three painted panels, 4.2 metres wide. The almost square centrepiece shows a shining gold Amida, floating on purple-white clouds, and before him the Bodhisattvas Kannon and Seishi on wisps of cloud. Round the central figure are gathered twenty-three more Bodhisattvas joyously making music, three solemn, quiet monks and, in the far distance at the end of the left-hand band of cloud, a remote red-robed Buddha with his two attendants. Here the artist has used every artistic device to heighten the celestial radiance of Amida: the back of the figure has gold leaf glued to the support. The *kirikane* ornament of his garments is wrought with the utmost delicacy, and the colourful attendant figures show movement, expres-

sion and humour. Far in the background an autumn landscape is suggested in masterly fashion with the lightest of tones. The theme of the Descent of Amida is treated in this painting by an unknown artist as a moment of supreme magnificence. In the Kamakura period there arose new variations on the theme.

The Writing of the Sutras

In the fifth and sixth centuries the imperial court and the Buddhist clergy had received all their writing materials—papers, inks and brushes—as tribute from China and Korea. In 610, as recorded in the annals, during the activity of the devout Crown Prince Shōtoku Taishi, a Korean priest called Donchō gave instruction to the Japanese in the production of inkstones, paper and ink. These materials were not only in demand for the temples. The government and the imperial court also needed their own writing materials for correspondence with foreign embassies, for bookkeeping, for registering tribute revenue and for recording population and tax statistics.

The Treasury's bookkeeping was in the hands of the writers' guild *(fumi-be)*, descendants of the nobles of Chinese origin who had emigrated from Korea in the late fourth century before the introduction of Buddhism.

In Japan simple papers were soon being made on the Chinese model from hemp fibre *(mashi)* and straw *(kokushi)*. They were usually coloured yellowish with a dye obtained from oak bark *(kihada)* and made smooth with beeswax. For writing the elaborately structured strokes of the Chinese characters brushes of hare's fur were used to produce a soft responsive line. Stiffer brushes of badger fur were used for writing the characters of titles, and for ruling lines deer bristles were found to be the most suitable. From the sixth century onwards nine Japanese provinces supplied paper as well as silk to be the imperial court as tribute.

In the Nara period the great temples—for example the Tōdai-ji, the Yakushi-ji, the Daian-ji—all had their own scriptoria *(shakyō)* for copying sutras, and not just the court and the top nobility. There trained copyists worked as well as title calligraphers, line rulers, correctors, specialists in gold characters, painters and binders. Alongside them worked craftsmen concerned not with the texts but with the mounts, decoration and cases.

The writing and commissioning of texts of the holy scriptures were considered as acts equally meritorious for the future life as the recitation of sutras and also useful as a prophylactic against bad luck and illness and, by transmission, for the protection of the country. For this reason these holy acts were performed en masse and in circumstances of ritually uncontaminated purity.

In 651 Emperor Kōtoku commissioned at great expense the copying of the whole canon of Mahāyāna Buddhism *(issai-kyō)*. Two thousand one hundred monks and nuns worked at the opus of more than 2,000 scrolls. Another complete set was ordered by the excessively pious Emperor Shōmu at the height of Buddhist enthusiasm in the Nara period. The earliest of these sutra texts bear the date Tempyō 6 (Year 734) and are signed with postscripts by officers of the Imperial Scriptorium. Four scrolls of this work survive, written in India ink on plain paper.

In copying the sutras the copyists kept very close to the Chinese models because of the need to preserve and perpetuate the redeeming and healing power inherent in the original. The arrangement of the text in vertical columns of seventeen characters each goes back to Chinese models supposedly of the fourth century A.D. From China also came the idea of gluing different coloured papers side by side into scrolls and then writing over them without regard for the joins. Above all was counted the production of dark blue indigo papers *(konshi)* or papers died purple *(shishi)*, which were inscribed with gold and silver characters *(kingin-ji)*. These colour schemes must have appealed particularly to the aesthetically sensitive Japanese, especially since, in Buddhist thought, beauty in itself was capable of enhancing holiness. Thus the Imperial Scriptorium produced several hundred copies of the *Golden Sutra (Konkōmyō-saishōō-kyō)* for the country's provincial temples. They were written in the year 740 in gold characters and on gold lines on purple paper. Emperor Shōmu ordered this work of copying because the sutra promised the pious ruler the personal merit resulting from its protection of the land and the consolidation of Buddhist doctrine.

After the removal of the imperial court from Nara to Heian-kyō, this fanatical copying at first died down, since the protection of the court was withdrawn from the powerful old temples around Nara for political reasons.

The teachings of the esoteric Tendai and Shingon sects, brought from China by the priests Saichō and Kūkai, placed other canonical texts in the forefront and brought with them other religious practices. Furthermore, these two men were powerful personalities, and their extensive education and individuality gave the art of writing an original style of calligraphy for the first time.

The teaching of the Tendai sect was centred on the *Lotus Sutra* 'of the wonderful Law' *(Myōhō-renge-kyō)*. It describes in prose and verse the sermons of the Buddha Shaka. His pronouncements and parables are given in a gripping visionary language that all can understand. It was translated into Chinese in the third century and revised more than once, and it reached Japan early, so that by 606 Shōtoku Taishi was already writing a commentary on it. The *Lotus Sutra* declares that every living being can obtain Buddhahood through faith in Buddha and in the *Lotus Sutra*. It describes the merciful acts of the Bodhisattvas, who offer redemption to the believer and enable him to attain ultimate Nirvana, after transmigration through the ten grades of Deliverance into the Pure Land. Redemption is open to all beings; even lower forms of life and women are promised rebirth. The earliest blue and gold sutras with pictures on the frontispieces come from the Enryaku-ji on Mount Hiei. The same formula is known in the famous *Diamond Sutra* (printed in China in 868) from Dunhuang, now in the British Museum, London. The temple treasure of the Enryaku-ji in Kyōto contained copies of blue and gold sutras from China and Korea, which could have been copied in the tenth and eleventh centuries. The painters of the frontispieces came from among the scribes and did not belong to the guild of religious painters. They mostly painted one motif in calligraphic brush style: the Buddha with two Bodhisattvas preaching on Vulture Peak, surrounded by pupils, devas, attentive monks and secular (Chinese) kings. The pictures are not always literal illustrations of the contents of the sutras.

The core text of the Shingon sect, on the other hand, was the *Sutra of Perfect Wisdom (Dai-Hannya Haramitta-kyō)* and the *Mahāvairocana Sūtra (Dainichi-kyō)* 'not directed to men'. Both texts address themselves to reason for understanding of the Absolute and not, like the *Lotus Sutra,* to faith. 112

The free artistic development of sutra manuscripts can be observed within the broad stream of universal 'Japanization' of all the fine arts that began in the mid-Heian period because all diplomatic and clerical links with the continent were cut. The emancipation from Chinese models only went apace very slowly at first.

Sutra writing tended thereafter to bend to the influence of the taste and aesthetic elegance of the court and its aristocracy, which set the social tone. Texts of outstanding quality of execution were produced, but they were dainty rather than devotional, seeming to concern themselves only by the way with the central religious message.

The people of the tenth century were wholly taken up with the doctrine of Deliverance given by the *Lotus*

112
Sutra of Perfect Wisdom (Dai-Hannya-Haramitta-kyō). Small text scroll with gold and silver paint on dark blue paper. H. 4.4 cm, L. 200 cm. Probably twelfth century. Formerly Jingu-ji, Sumiyoshi, Ōsaka. Museum für Ostasiatische Kunst, Stiftung Preussischer Kulturbesitz, Berlin (214).
The more than fifty miniature scrolls have frontispieces with scenes of the Preaching Buddha and covers with *hosoge* flower stems. This unusual set of miniature sutras is mentioned in the illustrated printed guide-book *Settsu Meisho zue* of 1796 and falsely ascribed to Empress Kōken (eighth century).

113
Sutra Box. Gilt bronze. H. 41.5 cm. *c.* 1116. Excavated in Fukuoka. Private collection, Tōkyō.
This elegant box comes from a sutra grave, which was intended to preserve texts of the holy *Lotus Sutra* for the approaching new Buddhist era. The octagonal case has on its sides the titles of the chapters of the *Lotus Sutra*. The flower-shaped lid is topped with a jewel mounted in bronze flames. The base is in the form of a lotus, and ornaments with glass beads decorate each leaf tip.

Sutra and the ever more pressing belief in rebirth in the 'Pure Land' of the Buddha Amida. This was natural, since it was believed that the period of the latter days of the Law was approaching as the era of the Buddha Shaka drew to its close, and men therefore sought to save themselves by crossing into the future era of the new Buddha Maitreya.

The feverish quest for salvation by the aristocracy resulted not only in temple building and the execution of holy images but also in the creation of earthly paradises

based on the correct iconography. Even sutra graves 113 (*kyō-zuka*) were laid out. The mightiest ruler of his time, the regent Fujiwara no Michinaga, copied out the *Lotus Sutra* in his own hand in the year 998. A few fragments of this text survive, written in gold characters on indigo blue paper. They show a statesman's rather awkward, schoolboy hand, the writing of a man who had an office of scribes at his disposal and was only likely to take up a brush himself very rarely. With great ceremony and conducted by Tendai priests, the scrolls were enveloped in bamboo cases and then encased in bronze cylinders and buried with other holy objects on Mount Kimpusen in Yoshino near Nara. This act facilitated his rebirth in the next Buddhist era.

From historical works, from the diaries of the court nobles, as well as from the lively wealth of literature of the court ladies, we learn of the writing of sutras at court, of sutra ceremonies and readings at births, deaths, memorial services and during sickness; these facts are told in *nikki, monogatari* and *zuihitsu* (random jottings, 'following the pen') alike.

While calligraphy had consciously emancipated itself from the strict forms of Buddhist style and reached a peak in 'Japanese-style' poetry in the work of the poet Fujiwara no Yukinari (972–1027), a contemporary of Michinaga, the hand used for Buddhist texts, doubtless for pious reasons, did not attain such freedom. Perhaps it was for this reason that the fashionable elements appear in the accessory details and not in the form of the text. 'Ornamental sutras' (*sōshoku-kyō*) were made, commissioned by the powerful and wealthy noble families of the inner court circle and by a few provincial nobles. We are acquainted with the beauty of the gigantic sutra library that was a gift of the northern branch of the Fujiwara clan in Hiraizumi for their Chūson-ji. Fujiwara no Kiyohira, prince of Mutsu and Dewa provinces, had made discoveries of gold on his estates and had the wherewithal to attract hundreds of craftsmen from Kyōto to the north and to build temple complexes to rival Heian-kyō. The Golden Hall and the Sutra Hall survive as testimony of this enterprise.

114   ▷
Sutra: *Kanfugen-bosatsu-kyō.* Gold and silver paint on blue paper. H. 25.4 cm, L. 76.9 cm. First half of the twelfth century. Freer Gallery of Art, Washington, D.C. (68.60).
The frontispiece of the *Kanfugen-bosatsu-kyō* shows the apparition to a worshipper of the Bodhisattva Fugen on his six-tusked elephant; Fugen comes floating over a Chinese-style landscape.

Immediately Kiyohira ordered a set of the *issai-kyō* in five thousand scrolls to be written for his 'Paradise Temple' of 1125. Each one of the indigo-blue scrolls has a title picture with a scene from the contents, for which there is a corresponding cover on the outside adorned with holy flowers.

The text itself is written in characters coloured alternately gold and silver. Only fifteen scrolls of the early set are still in the Chūson-ji, while the majority are in the Kongōbu-ji on Kōya-san. Of the three sutra sets dedicated to the temple, in about 1176, by the grandson of Kiyohira, Prince Hidehira, 2,739 scrolls remain in the Chūson-ji. A number have also arrived in western museums and private collections.

114

While the sutras with gold and silver text on indigo paper continued very much along the lines of the Chinese model, the Japanese craftsmen and patrons were thinking out new variants of decorative style. Sometimes the different characters were piled together into pagodas *(ichiji-hōtō-kyō)* or each character was placed separately on a lotus throne, underlining its parity in holiness with the Buddha figure. This decorative device is called 'one-character lotus-throne sutra' *(ichiji-rendai-kyō)*.

The paper too was decorated in the most refined manner. Gold and silver foil was stuck on to it in the form of mosaic, irregular flecks, sand grains or hair-thin wire. As on Buddhist paintings and sculpture, gold leaf was cut into intricate patterns. Stencils with plant and animal motifs were used over softly tinted paper; sometimes they were sprayed with metal powder. Decorative techniques appear here that are, as far as can be judged, entirely the product of the Japanese imagination. Only in lacquerwork are they also found, but not until a much later period. The quality of paper had improved since the middle of the Heian period; firm *torinoko* paper was obtained from the fibres of *kōzō* and *gampi,* and stiffened and smoothed with fillers.

New kinds of cover and title pages were attached to the display papers. The canonical sutra picture with hieratic scenes of Buddhist scripture gave way to purely Japanese illustrations. In the *ichiji-rendai* copy of the *Lotus Sutra* the text is preceded by a scene in *Yamato-e* style: we see into a mountain temple where monks are reciting the *Lotus Sutra*. The composition with a roofless house, parallel perspective and strongly coloured, chubby-cheeked figures is designed like the *monogatari-emaki* in *tsukuri-e* style, with a linear preliminary drawing on gold-decorated paper.

115

The set of the *Lotus Sutra* of 1141 from the Kunō-ji belongs in the court milieu. The frontispiece shows a melancholy courtier with an open umbrella sitting in a landscape under a shower of silver, a rain of grace. Of about the same date is the *Heike-Nōkyō,* the famous sutra of the Taira family, where we see the art of the ornamental sutra brought to its highest level. Taira no Kiyomori (1118–1181) with his family donated this set of thirty-three scrolls to the Itsukushima-jinja in 1164. It comprises a *Lotus Sutra* of twenty-eight scrolls, the *Muryōju-kyō* and *Kanfugen-bosatsu-kyō* that frame it and, in addition, the *Amida-kyō* and the *Hannya-shingyō.* These texts were partly commissioned and partly written by Kiyomori and his family in person; there is a dedicatory text *(gammon)* also belonging to them. The entire work is preserved in a metal case in three parts, adorned with the most exquisite engraving, which is probably work commissioned in Kyōto.

116–118

The hands of many different scribes can be distinguished in the *Heike-Nōkyō.* The decorative papers are not uniformly executed either. Most of them have a ground, coloured tea or purple, with the most diverse designs on the text side. The designs often show additional ornamental pictorial elements on the upper and lower borders. The reverse sides also are lined with decorated papers.

Many motifs are used that stem from the Buddhist repertoire; often too there are single rebus-like characters embedded in the designs. The end papers—cover paper and title picture—are attached with other supporting leaves that are alternately painted very sparsely or very elaborately. Here too there are scenes illustrating the beneficent deeds of the Buddha in Japan. Seven title-pages of the set show court gentlemen and ladies worshipping the *Lotus Sutra* and touched by the

116

115 ▷

Ichiji-rendai copy of the *Lotus Sutra*. Ink and colours on paper decorated in gold and silver leaf. H. 21.1 cm. Twelfth century. Yamato Bunka-kan Museum, Nara.

This copy of the *Lotus Sutra* is named after the characters, each one *(ichiji)* of which rests on a lotus throne *(rendai)*. The introductory illustration shows the roofless interior of a mountain temple in which four monks are reciting the *Lotus Sutra*, while a group of travellers participates standing outside the verandah. The painting has all the features of *Yamato-e* and is very close to the style of the *Heike-Nōkyō* and Kunō-ji sutras.

妙法蓮藥紅疊賢苾陵救藥品

第二十八

尒時普賢菩薩以
自在神通力威
德名聞與大菩薩
無量無邊

感德名聞與大菩
薩無量無邊諸
國

不可稱數從東方來所經諸國

◁ 116

Sutra: *Heike-Nōkyō*. Colours and ink on patterned paper. H. 26.6 cm. 1164. Itsukushima-jinja, Hiroshima.
The frontispiece of the first scroll of the *Lotus Sutra,* 'Jōbon', is a picture in *Yamato-e* style with a view into a roofless house with courtiers and a priest at a reading of the *Hokke-kyō*. An ascetic is praying in the garden in his grass hut. Two groups of grass characters are placed rebus-like in the garden and refer to salutary practices. Rays of grace fall from heaven onto the people.

salutory golden rays of the Buddha as they say their 117 prayer beads. Other cover papers and title pictures show Chinese scenes. Landscapes and figures are built 118 on the Chinese blue-green style and are reckoned to belong to the China style *(Kara-e)* in Heian painting. Lastly there are simple end-paper pictures where the decorative element is foremost: lotus blossoms, musical instruments, Sanskrit letters and abstract repeat patterns.

The precious papers were given suitably carefully wrought mounts. The rods with the tie ribbons are of 119 pierced silver with the finest engraving, the toggles are of semi-precious stones, metal and lacquer, shaped into Buddhist motifs of the most varied kind.

The imminence of the latter days of the Law made everyone seek for new forms to extend by symbolic means the salvation of the *Lotus Sutra* or of other salutary sutras and magic formulae over all things belonging to this world. This attitude led to characters being written in the orthodox, strict forms and arrangements, over contemporary genre scenes having no apparent connexion with the holy texts. The pictures here were simply background pictures *(shita-e)*. Sutras in book form *(sōshi-kyō)* belong in this group. The papers used as ground for the text were particularly exquisite. In the famous album of the Gotoh Art Museum, Tōkyō, 120 China paper with pressed ornament in mica alternates with papers painted over with delightful court scenes, entirely Japanese in style and content.

Even everyday objects served as a support for the *Lotus Sutra*. Fan sutras *(semmen-kyō)* are painted with 121–122

117
Sutra: *Heike-Nōkyō*. Colours and ink on patterned paper. H. 26 cm. 1164. Itsukushima-jinja, Hiroshima.
The frontispiece of chapter 27 is painted in classical *Yamato-e* style with two court ladies who raptly tell their prayer beads. Lotus petals and heavenly rays fall over a waterscape with stylized and symbol-laden motifs.

118   ▷
Sutra: *Heike-Nōkyō*. Ink and colours on patterned paper. H. 26.5 cm. 1164. Itsukushima-jinja, Hiroshima.
The title page of chapter 21 shows a scene with many elements of *Kara-e*. A hermit rapturously recites the *Lotus Sutra* in his hut on a cliff. Rocks, trees and even the lotus pool show the Chinese tradition.

119
Sutra scrolls of the *Heike-Nōkyō*.
Paper scrolls on wooden rods
with metal mounts and knobs of
metal and crystal. H. 28–30cm.
1164–1167.   Itsukushima-jinja,
Hiroshima.

The set of thirty-three sutra
scrolls prepared at the command
of   Taira   no   Kiyomori
(1118–1181) and his family for the
Shintō shrine in Itsukushima
shows the high competence of
Japanese court craftsmanship in
the Late Heian period. The multi-
plicity and variety of the
goldsmith's work can be seen in
every detail of the mounts.

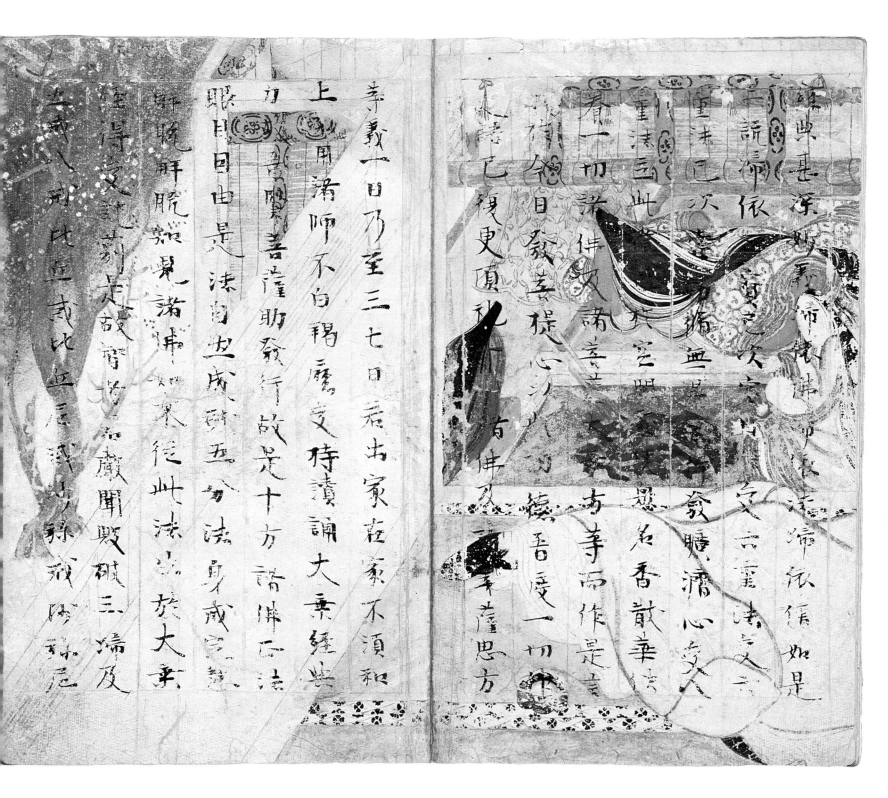

120
Hokke-kyō-zasshi with *Kanfugen-bosatsu-kyō* written over a genre scene. Colours and ink on printed paper. H. 18.8 cm, W. 23 cm. Mid-twelfth century. Gotoh Art Museum, Tōkyō.
This little album on China paper *(karakami)* is a perfect example of the tendency towards a composite work of art, with its mixture of secular illustrative motifs and a religious text. The background picture shows a domestic scene in *Yamato-e* style illustrating a poem by Ki no Tsurayuki. The calligraphic text written over it is taken from the *Kanfugen-bosatsu-kyō.*

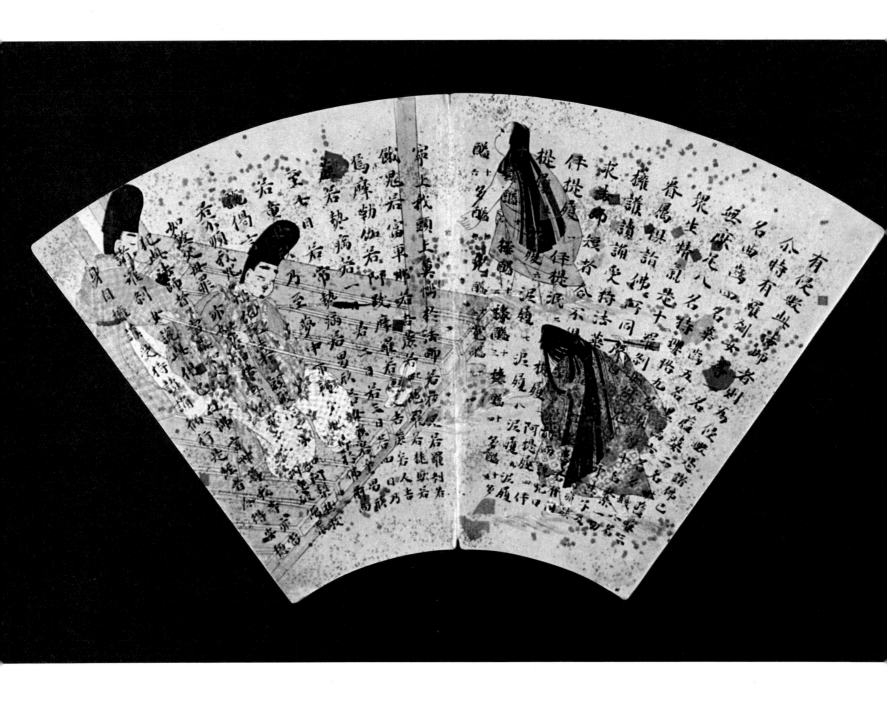

121
Sutra Fan. Colours and ink on decorated paper. H. 25.6 cm, L. 49.4 cm. Second half of the twelfth century. Tōkyō National Museum, Tōkyō.
Religious enthusiasm led even to fan paintings being written over with the holy *Lotus Sutra;* the pictures were of scenes from the daily life of the common people, partly done in colour-block printing.

Five such albums are in the possession of the Shitennō-ji in Ōsaka; one is in the Tōkyō National Museum. Paper, picture and calligraphy create a refined composite work typical of the Late Heian period. The background of the fan's decoration shows court servants cleaning the house verandah. Over this domestic scene are arranged radiating bands of text from the *Lotus Sutra*.

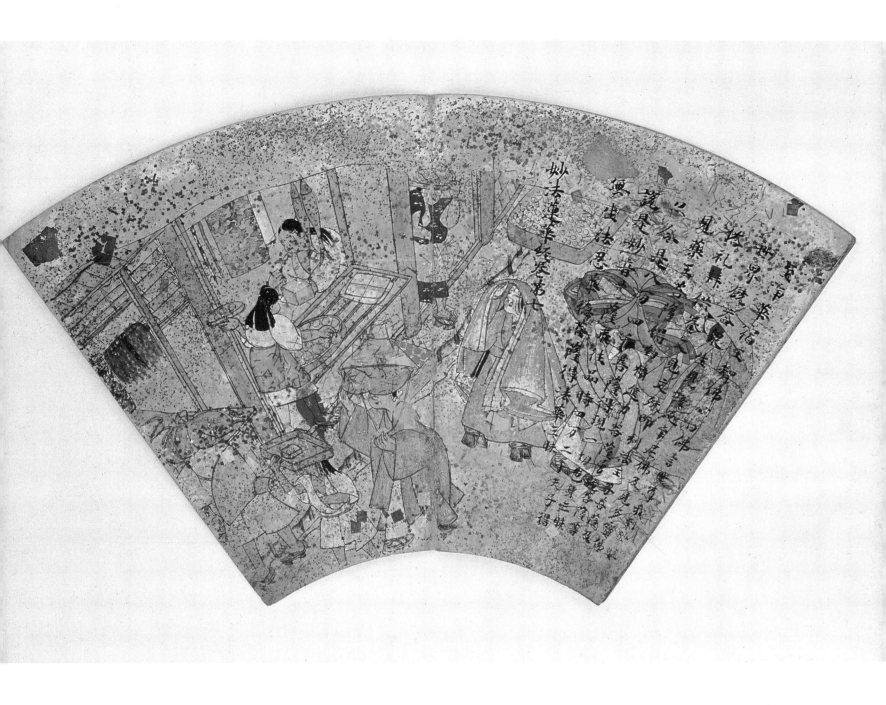

妙法蓮華經卷第七 [various columns of Japanese/Chinese sutra text]

122
Sutra Fan. Colours and ink on decorated paper. H. 25.2 cm. Second
half of the twelfth century. Shitennō-ji, Ōsaka.
Chapter 7 of the *Lotus Sutra* is written over a fan painting of a lively
scene at the market in Heian-kyō. The starkly naive drawing, partly
executed in colour-block printing, gives the scene a gripping
vitality.

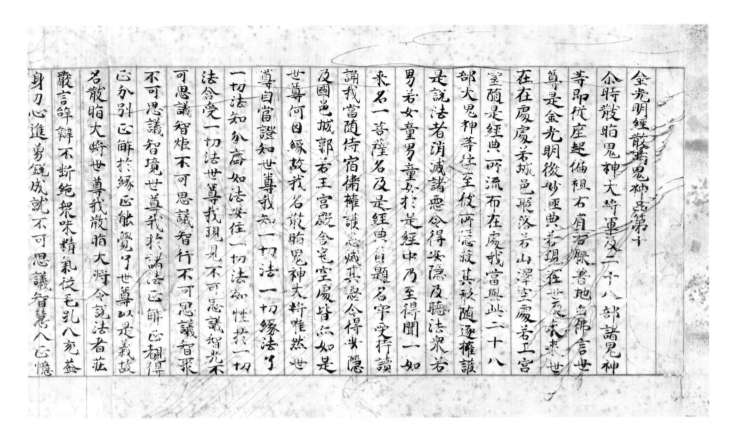

123
'Eyeless Sutra': Section 10 of the *Golden Sutra*. Ink on paper. H. 26 cm. Before 1192. Kyōto National Museum Kyōto.
The Ex-emperor Goshirakawa commissioned a nun to paint *monogatari-e*. As the work was unfinished at the time of his death —only the 'eyeless' outlines completed—it was overwritten with the holy text of the *Konkōmyō-saishōō-kyō (Golden Sutra)* as a votive offering for the deceased.

specially lively genre scenes. Folding fans—a Japanese invention—are said to have been exported in large numbers to China in the Heian period. This is probably why they are found with partly painted background pictures and single figures re-appearing repeatedly in different groupings. The fan sutras came originally from the Shitennō-ji in Ōsaka. There were 115 fans on which the whole of the *Lotus Sutra* and its accompanying texts were written by hand in radial arrangement. Here again the paper is decorated with gold and silver leaf, and the *tsukuri-e* technique of painting was used. The representation of numerous scenes from the life of ordinary folk makes the *semmen-kyō* an invaluable document for social history.

The group of *shita-e* sutras is closely related to the so-called white-painting sutras *(hakūbyō-e)* and the 'eyeless sutras' *(menashi-kyō)*. In these only the linear placing of space and figures can be made out in the background pictures. A copy of the *Golden Sutra* of 123 before 1192 is probably the earliest work in this group; for the funeral of Emporer Goshirakawa, the texts of the sutra were supposed to have been written on the unfinished scrolls.

In the following period this art form, both religious and courtly, faded away. The enormous expenditure on magnificient manuscripts whose purpose was directed towards the next world could hardly be expected to enter into the interests of the following generations of military dictators.

The Blossoming of Literature

Yamato-uta michi asaki ni nite
fukaku yasuki ni nite katashi
wakimaeru hito mata
itubaku narazu.

'The art of *Yamato-uta* seems shallow
but it is deep, it seems easy, but
it is difficult. There are few who
understand it.'

Fujiwara no Sadaie (Teika)[29]

In 951 the imperial court created an Office of Poetry, for the art of composing *waka* ('Japanese poems') had spread like an obsession that gripped every member of the court and of elegant society. *Waka* were composed for the expression of personal feelings and knowledge, especially in a question-and-answer formula that was the inescapable language of love, both official and private. Composing was also done in regulated ceremony in the poetry competitions *(uta-awase)*.

Poetry contests on a set theme came, with their rules, from China, and they were taken up and expanded with enthusiasm in Japan. As in other *awase* games, in which iris roots, pictures, shells or incense were the subjects of competition, one or several judges stood between the two parties. The left was always the first, the right the second to play. The poems were read out by reciters, alternately of one side then the other, judged according to the rules of poetics and given awards. It was a special honour to be included in one of the official anthologies of poetry. The earliest *uta-awase* was held in the house of the poet Ariwara no Yukinari between 884 and 887, the next in the Kampyō period (889–898); both were superseded by the contest in the Teiji-in Palace of Ex-emperor Uda in 913. A few poems from this event are preserved in the *Kokin-shū*. Between it and the famous contest of 960 in the imperial palace more than a hundred further *uta-awase* were held. The earliest practical texts on poetics after Fujiwara no Kintō (966–1041) were written by poets at the end of the Heian period. Fujiwara no Shunzei (1114–1204) declared the 'secret profundity' of a poem to be his ideal. His son Fujiwara no Sadaie (Teika) (1162–1241) distinguished rather the style of 'deep feeling' and advanced the concept of 'enchanting grace' as the highest requirement.

In the palaces the sliding doors *(shōji)* and folding screens *(byōbu)* were another inspiration to poetry. Sometimes a sheet of calligraphy with a poem was stuck on a screen; sometimes it was the painting on a screen that called for praise. Folding screens are known to have been adorned with sheets of poems in aesthetic arrangement. The screens for Chinese poems were about 1.50 metres high, those for Japanese, 1.20 metres. From these poems *(byōbu-uta* and *shōji-uta)* we get an idea of the secular painting of those days, for the original paintings are generally lost.

Prose in the second half of the tenth century was varied both in form and content. It would seem that the Chinese novel of the seventh century *Wanderings in the Caves of the Immortals (You Xiangku)* was not without its influence on the writing of tales. A trend of storytelling also followed the *Ise-monogatari;* these are called 'song-stories' *(uta-monogatari)*. Among them are the *Tales from Yamato (Yamato-monogatari),* which is composed of 173 separate episodes, some of them treating of the highest persons, like Ex-emperor Uda and his beloved, Ise, who was a famous poetess. Each short story, in which more than a hundred characters play a part, culminates in love poems.

The *Tales of Heichū* belong in this category also. Heichū is a tragic figure in his love adventures, already referred to in the *Genji-monogatari* as a joke. Another story in verse is about Ono no Takamura who lived in the ninth century. It is not his career that is described, however (how he refused an appointment as envoy to China and was exiled), but simply his amorous attachments to his half-sister, and after her death, to his deeply devoted wife.

Several tales of the tenth century even lead into the religious sphere. The *Tonomine Shōshō-monogatari* has Fujiwara no Takamitsu as its hero, a brother of Fujiwara no Kaneie. His parting from the world, and from his family, his adoption of the life of a monk on the Tonomine on Mount Hiei is reported as though from a diary, while the *Diary of Ionishi* gives an account of a pilgrimage to the Kumano shrines.

The *You Xiangku* and the song-story were a determining influence on two romances interspersed with historical, moralistic and romantic elements, which can be looked upon as the forerunners of the greatest novel of Heian Japan, the *Genji-monogatari*. These are the *Uchikubo-monogatari* and the *Utsubo-monogatari,* whose authors and precise dates are unknown. Though germs of realistic portrayal are sure to be noted by literary critics, the unity of the narrative is not consistent.

In contrast to these works a court lady who became known as 'Mother of Michitsuna' created a completely new style. She was a concubine of the great Fujiwara no Kaneie and wrote a diary that she called *Diary of an Indian Summer* and also *Diary of a Mayfly (Kagerō-nikki)*. In the words of E. Seidensticker: '... it is the first attempt in Japanese literature, or in any case the first surviving attempt to capture on paper, without evasion or idealization, the element of a real social situation. The author sets down her purpose and declares her independance of her predecessors in the opening sentences of the diary. Referring to herself in the third person she says: "... as the days went by in monotonous succession, she had occasion to look at the old romances, and found them masses of rankest fabrication. Perhaps, she said to herself, even the story of her own dreary life, set down in a journal, might be of interest; and it might also answer a question: had that life been one befitting a wellborn lady?".'[30]

The writer is a well known beauty of her time, and she is consumed with jealousy over her own husband, Prince Fujiwara no Kaneie. He had married her as a junior wife and then shamefully neglected her, she who desired 'a husband for all thirty days of the month'. The diary entries begin in 954 and end abruptly on New Year's Eve of 974. The more bitter and biting the descriptions of the events of her monotonous days and her reflections, the more mature her prose style becomes.

The Kagerō-nikki heralds the beginning, in Japan, at the end of the tenth century, of a blossoming of women's writing, of 'court ladies' literature' such as the world has never seen elsewhere. These ladies, mostly from the ranks of the lower provincial nobility, lived as companions of the empresses in the palace. Their chief task, as can perhaps be read between the lines of the Pillow Book (Makura no Sōshi) by Sei Shōnagon, was to entertain their empresses and provide them with amusements, stimulation and reading matter. 'They had no power to chance the world; they observed and interpreted it.'[31] It would not be possible though, to understand the great women's literature of around the year 1000 without considering the other component of Japanese literature, that written in Chinese by the male members of Japanese society.

For Chinese poetry the works of the Tang poet Bo Juyi remained an unquenchable source of inspiration; the embassy of 838 had first brought them to Japan, and a printed edition came directly in 1012. But the poets demonstrated the ambivalence of their talents in a new way also: Chinese poems had Japanese attached to them. The classic of this trend was compiled by Fujiwara no Kintō (966–1041) around 1013, the Wakan-rōei-shū, an anthology of Chinese and Japanese poems for recitation. The work was modelled on China's famous anthology Wen Xuan, of the sixth century. Of the 588 Chinese poems of the Wakan-rōei-shū, 354 are by Japanese poets, but 234 are taken from the classical poets of China, though much abbreviated. Among them are also 218 purely Japanese waka. Such an intellectual and formal alternation presented a strong challenge both to reciters and to calligraphers who had to show great flexibility of spirit and hand.

The earlier official historical works found their sequel and extension in the unofficial chronicles, which approximated slightly towards the Japanese style of narrative. The Eiga-monogatari describes the period from 887 to 1092, the Ōkagami the period from 850 to 1025. Both works give more or less finely coloured pictures of the Fujiwara rulers.

Court etiquette required that the official diaries of the leading statesmen be written in Chinese. Only a poet could be allowed the freedom to write in Japanese taken by Ki no Tsurayuki in the Tosa-nikki. The Fujiwara nobles—Michinaga in his Midō-Kampaku-ki, Fujiwara no Sanesuke in Shoyū-ki and Fujiwara no Yukinari in his Gon-ki—have left us dignified pictures of their time, none the less full of interest for cultural history.

Though Sei Shōnagon uses not a word of Chinese in her Pillow Book, her perceptive and amusing chatter has a number of Chinese traits. Her father, Kiyohara no Motosuke (908–990), was a poet distinguished enough to be among the compilers of the Gosen-shū anthology and to belong to the circle of poets called 'the five of the Pear Grove'. Her great-grandfather Fukayabu appears in the Kokin-shū.

Sei (Kiyohara) Shōnagon (State Councillor, second class), so called after her father's title, was at court in the service of Empress Sadako, wife of Emperor Ichijō and daughter of Fujiwara no Michitaka. Nothing is known of the life of Sei Shōnagon except that she entered the service of the empress in 990 and remained at court until the latter's death in 1000. She called her miscellaneous thoughts a Pillow Book. In 994 she had received from the empress a pile of notebooks that Minister Korechika had presented to Empress Sadako. 'Let me have the paper to make a pillow, I said. Now I had plenty of paper and began to fill the books with the most varied stories from the past and anything else however trivial. I concentrated on things and people I found interesting; my notes are filled too with poems, and with observations about trees and plants, birds and insects.'[32]

The contents of this book, no less lively today than when it was written, are divided by Mark Morris into three types.[33] We have the diary-like reminiscences of events of court life under Empress Sadako, essays with observations and reflections on people, things, nature and the world, and thirdly there are the 'lists', unique in Japanese literature, which comprise half of the 300 chapters.

What are these 'lists'? Sei enumerates things that relate to critiques of natural phenomena, geography,

124
Genji-monogatari-emaki: Chapter 36, 'Kashiwagi I' (detail). Ink and colours on paper. H. 21.8 cm, L. 48.3 cm. First quarter of the twelfth century. Tokugawa Reimeikai Foundation, Tōkyō.
Ex-emperor Suzaku sits full of sorrow at the sickbed of his daughter Onna Sanno Miya, who is deciding to become a nun.

125
Genji-monogatari-emaki: Chapter 40, 'Minori' (detail). Colours and ink on paper. H. 21.8 cm, L. 48.3 cm. First quarter of the twelfth century. Gotoh Art Museum, Tōkyō.
Murasaki no Kami, the beloved concubine of Prince Genji, is lying on her deathbed. Inside her room, containing a curtain on a rail alongside her, she is leaning on an arm-rest to receive her husband. Despite her illness she is wearing the official *jūni-hitoe* court costume with multiple kimonos, one over the other, and hides her face in distress with a kerchief.

buildings, animals and plants, religion, art and conversation, clothes and diseases. This kind of listing and criticism was taken from Chinese literature, the earliest works of the genre are the *Erya* and the *Shiming,* aids to reading the classics. In Japan Minamoto no Shitagō had produced a similar encyclopedia of the Japanese language, called *Wamyō-ruijushō,* in 934. Sei certainly knew it and also the many 'miscellaneous texts' of popular Tang literature, which compiled, in fives, humorous assemblages of positive and negative things or pictures. Sei was able to shine in these 'pillow notes' by the strength of her prose; only fifteen poems by her are known, and she found no delight in the fashionable *waka* poetry. She depicts the visible world from the self-confident and presumptuous point of view of the aristocrat who despises the common folk because she does not know them.

Contemporary with Sei Shōnagon, Empress Akiko, daughter of the great Fujiwara no Michinaga, had another gifted writer in her service. This was Murasaki Shikibu, who for years was writing the powerful novel *The Tale of Prince Genji (Genji-monogatari).* 'Few works of narrative prose fiction can rival the *Genji-monogatari:* it is literature of the highest quality and complexity, and has enjoyed uninterrupted popularity in Japan since its appearance in the early eleventh century.'[34]

The writer came from a subsidiary branch of the ruling Hokke clan of the Fujiwara. As daughter of the secretary of the Office of Ceremonies of Fujiwara no Tametoki she was given the name Shikibu. She probably travelled to Echizen when her father was made governor of that province. She married late, after her

126
Genji-monogatari-emaki: Chapter 49, 'Yadorigi III' (detail). Colours and ink on paper. H. 21.5 cm, L. 48.9 cm. First quarter of the twelfth century. Tokugawa Reimeikai Foundation, Tōkyō.
Prince Niou sits in the Rokujō-in Palace beside his wife Lady Nakanogimi and tries to reconcile her after an estrangement by playing the *biwa* lute. The colour composition of the figures and of the autumn garden stresses the deep melancholy of the scene.

return in 998, a much older relative by whom she had a daughter in 999. It was not until after the death of her husband that she came to the court in the service of Empress Akiko. She gives a lively, exhaustive but very sober account of this time in her diary, *Murasaki Shikibu-nikki*. After the death of Ichijō-Tennō in 1011, she seems to have stayed on at the court of the empress. It is thought that she died in 1015.

Her life's work, the novel of Prince Genji, consists of fifty-four chapters covering a span of about seventy-five years, giving the life of the 'shining Prince Genji', his son Yūgiri, his putative son Kaoru and his grandson Niou no Miya.

It has been discovered that the present sequence of chapters has been altered, that some are missing and that one ('Takegawa') was added later. The final Uji chapters were probably written down later also; when, or whether they were still by Murasaki Shikibu herself,

is not clear. The earliest complete texts come from the end of the Heian period, though fragments of it accompany the splendid painted scrolls of the early twelfth-century *Genji-monogatari-emaki*.

The subject of the novel is the love life of Prince Genji, who in the manner of his time and milieu made conquests of one woman after another, thanks to his beauty, gentleness and cultivation; but his deep and forbidden love was, first, for his stepmother, Empress Fujitsubo, and then for her niece Murasaki, who was still a minor. The latter was only his concubine but remained bound to him with deepest love until her death. The writer describes the atmosphere of court life in masterly fashion, the festivities and the human situations, but most of all the delicate relations, never twice the same, between Genji and his different loves. The *Genji-monogatari* is regarded, as a result, as the earliest psychological novel in the world's literature.

In an undercurrent the Buddhist view of life pervades the narrative with its belief in cause and effect, in pre-destination through deeds in a previous existence and with the deep melancholy engendered by the knowl-edge that the latter days of the Law were approaching. It is a fascinating account of the small circle of that period that represented the epitome of an over-refined culture, 'the culture of taste', as G. B. Sansom has named it. The hero himself seems to us to remain a shadowy character, like his first imaginary portrait in the *Genji-monogatari-emaki*.

The passionate description of true feelings in *Izumi Shikibu-nikki* was the achievement of a third woman writer of the time at the turn of the millennium. Izumi married the provincial governor of Izumi, Tachibana no Michisada and came to court in the service of Em-press Jōtomon-in. She gives an account of her affairs with Princes Tametaka and Atsumichi, the brothers of Sanjō-Tennō (1011–1016)—which provoked scan-dal—with burning and passionate explicitness. It was her poems that brought her the greatest fame. One thousand four hundred of her *waka* are preserved in the anthologies.

The *Sarashina-nikki* on the other hand is not to be compared with the diary of Izumi Shikibu; the later, largely grotesque writings of the court ladies of the fol-lowing period fall far short of the splendid masterpieces of Sei Shōnagon, Murasaki Shikibu and Izumi Shikibu.

A completely different sphere of life and thought gave rise to a traditional collection of stories called *Kon-jaku-monogatari* ('Stories of Then and Now'). The collection comprises thirty-one volumes, to all appearances written by a single author. It is a book of the people, something entirely different from the court literature previously described, perhaps directed at edifying the clergy by being read aloud. It includes stories of the miracles of the Buddha and of the consequences of good and bad deeds from the Buddhist point of view. Many of the stories recount events that are located in China. The *Konjaku-monogatari* also has secular stories from Japanese popular tradition. The lively humorous tales, full of wit and wisdom, are so entertaining to read and so naturalistic that modern authors and film-makers have drawn on them for material, for example for *Rashōmon*. This volume of tales shows clearly how the court elite no longer dictated the entire literary scene. A new current of the times is manifest in the *Konjaku-monogatari,* one that restructured political and social life so far that it spelt the decline of the Heian period.

The Calligraphy of the Late Heian Period

'We live in a degenerate age,' said Genji. 'Almost nothing but the "ladies' hand" seems really good. In that we do excel. The old styles have a sameness about them. They seem to have followed the copybooks and allowed little room for original talent. We have been blessed in our own day with large numbers of fine calligraphers.... Do whatever you feel like doing, reed work, or illustrations for poems or whatever.'

(*The Tale of Genji,*
translated by E. G. Seidensticker, p. 517)

In the mid-tenth century the 'Three Brush Artists' of the Early Heian period were succeeded by another three outstanding calligraphers, known as the 'Three Footmarks' or 'Pacemakers' *(sanseki)*. It was they who created the mature *wa-yō* style of writing, Japan's individual calligraphy.

127 These calligraphers belonged to three successive generations. The earliest master, Ono no Tōfu (Michikaze) lived from 894 to 966 and was appointed master calligrapher *(nōsho)* at court by Daigo-Tennō. He was given the office of a Master of the Treasury and rose to the rank of director of the fourth rank, second class. His tasks as *nōsho* were: to write name plates for the halls and gates of the palace, for imperial temples and shrines, also calligraphic teaching texts from the sutras

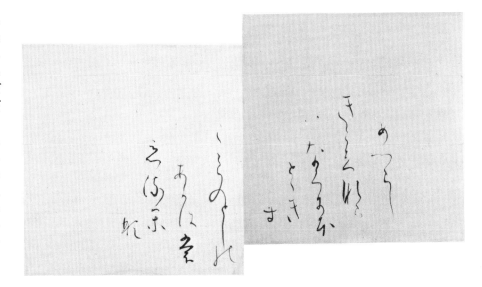

127

Poem sheets *(tsugi-shikishi)* mounted as a hanging scroll: calligraphy attributed to Ono no Tōfu (Michikaze) (894–966). Ink on two papers, each tinted in a different shade of brown. H. (each sheet) 12 cm, W. 12.8 cm. Gotoh Art Museum, Tōkyō.

These sheets belonged originally to a poem album for which Michikaze selected separate poems from the *Kokin-waka-shū*. He wrote them onto two sheets: the upper section of the poems on the right-hand sheet, the lower section on the left-hand one. The *kana* characters are placed according to aesthetic considerations, scattered here loosely, there densely. The poem illustrated, by Ki no Tomonori, celebrates the 'Call of the Cuckoo' (*Kokin* 357).

to be fastened up in the temples to explain the paintings on walls and doors. This kind of inscription is seen on the Amida-*raigō* paintings in the Hōō-dō of the Byōdō-in, but cannot be attributed with certainty to any specific calligrapher.[35] Then imperial decrees and memoranda had to be written out in fair copy from the drafts of the doctors of literature. It was also incumbent on the *nōsho* to write out elegantly the poems that had been selected for the screens for the Daishō-e Feast or for coronation festivities. The sixth task was the composition of dedicatory inscriptions for sutras, the calligraphic texts of which had been written by professional copyists.

In Ono no Tōfu's hand there is a collection of Chinese poems, intended for a screen, preserved in the imperial collection, also a decree for the priest Enchin in fair copy and texts of the poems of Bo Juyi whose 128 work still remained central to *kambun* writings. Here Tōfu's powerful distinctive hand is demonstrated in the breadth of variations of the *kai* and *sō* printed and grass

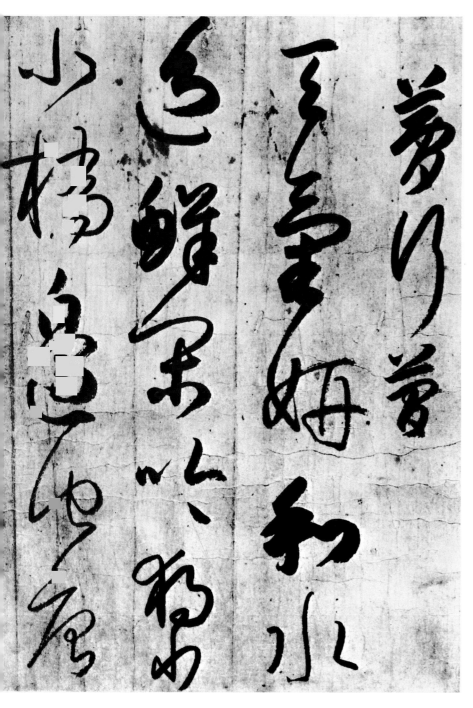

128
Scroll (detail) with poems by Bo Juyi: calligraphy attributed to Ono no Tōfu (Michikaze, 894–966). Ink on paper. H. 30 cm. Formerly Kōnoike Collection.
Michikaze wrote the poems, which are by Bo Juyi, the Chinese poet of the Tang period most famous in Japan, in three kinds of script: print, cursive and grass character. His extremely powerful brush line seems to be reminiscent of the calligraphy of Emperor Saga. Michikaze probably wrote the poems as a model for calligraphic studies. (After *Shodō Zenshū*, Vol. 12: *Japan III, Heian II*, Fig. 26).

characters. His work, in the form of writing called 'women's hand', with simple *kana* syllabic characters, is represented in unsigned and undocumented double poem papers. The poem papers are of medium size, tinted in three different colours, and each bears half a poem. The characters are 'scattered' to form rhythmic groupings of loosely connected sequences of characters with supreme concern for the aesthetic effect.

Nor are the *kana* writings of the succeeding eminent calligraphers convincingly authenticated. The brilliant calligrapher Fujiwara no Sari (944–998) was *nōsho* to the emperors Enyū, Kazan and Ichijō. Due to the fact that the fame of his calligraphy reached as far as China he rose in Japan to the upper third rank of the top nobility. Fascinating among his work are a few letters dated 981 and 982 that he wrote virtually with a whip of the brush and signed with his title of office.

The great genius among the *sanseki* was the youngest, Fujiwara no Yukinari (972–1027). His talents were widely dispersed. As a friend of Fujiwara no Michinaga, promoted official *nōsho* by emperors Sanjō and Goichijō, he was made 'vice-counsellor' with the upper rank at court. As a calligrapher he felt himself to be the pupil of Ono no Tōfu; furthermore, he perfected his hand in copying poems of Bo Juyi. Although his Chinese characters reveal the dignity and clarity of his form of writing the characters—in contrast, for instance, with the unruly ductus of Fujiwara no Sari—Yukinari is above all regarded as the man who brought to perfection the purely Japanese style of calligraphy. Even the fact that he put his name seal before the text of a letter written in Chinese—a letter of thanks for his promotion in 1020—is a unique and entirely novel, purely Japanese method of signing that came in with the *sanseki*.

Among the many fragments of manuscripts in 'women's hand' with soft flowing characters, every variant of style is represented that could possibly be devised in this period that marks the high point of Japanese culture. A few copies of the *Wakan-rōei-shū*, 129 compiled by Fujiwara no Kintō in 1013, are ascribed to Yukinari. There are indeed a few fragments of what is thought to be original text by the compiler, but it is surpassed by Yukinari's elegant calligraphy; his contrasting distribution of stressed brush strokes, heavy Chinese against light Japanese poems, is quite outstanding. His style of writing remained the exemplary model for generations, for he was the founder of the Seson-ji school of calligraphy, active at court.

138

Many exquisite works of calligraphy were produced during the Late Heian period under the influence of Yukinari's style. Perhaps even more than the poem itself, writing was an indication of a person's cultivation and character for the aesthetically hypersensitive aristocrats of the Heian period. Again and again we find judgements of men and women in the works of Murasaki Shikibu and Sei Shōnagon that are based exclusively on their writing hand. The choice of a suitable letter paper, folded and sealed with the right twig or spray to convey the correct implication and message, was also subject to fastidious rules of taste.

129
Poem sheets from the *Wakan-rōei-shū:* calligraphy attributed to Fujiwara no Yukinari (972–1027). Ink on paper printed with colours and mica; glued binding. H. 20 cm, W. 12 cm. Mid-eleventh century. Imperial Household.
Fujiwara no Kintō had complied the *Wakan-rōei-shu,* the 'Collection of Japanese and Chinese Poems for Recitation' in 1013. The work became the universal favourite in dual-language literature and was often read aloud and written out, for it had both the complicated Chinese *kanji* and the plain Japanese *kana* characters to be copied for calligraphy. This edition, ascribed to the poet Fujiwara no Yukinari, has noble coloured paper printed with mica, known as *karakami* ('China paper'), as the ground for the poems and thus gives a doubly rich effect.

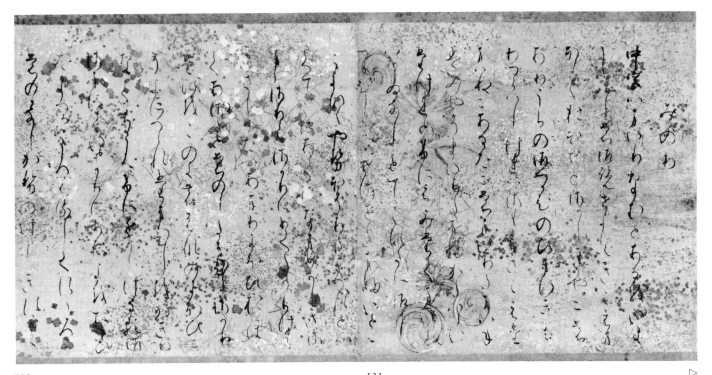

130

Genji-monogatari-emaki: Chapter 40, 'Minoru'. Ink on decorated paper. H. 21.8 cm. First quarter of the twelfth century. Gotoh Art Museum, Tōkyō.

Of the chapter 'Minoru' there survive sixty-nine characters of the text on five sheets, with the one picture (Pl. 125). The manuscript is ascribed to the first calligrapher of the five whose texts of the *Genji-monogatari-emaki* survive. The softly tinted paper is especially splendid with its gold and silver ornament and, in addition, painted emblem-like patterns.

131   ▷

Page of calligraphy from the *Ishiyama-gire*. Ink on decorated paper. H. 20.3 cm, L. 16 cm. *c.* 1112. Freer Gallery of Art, Washington, D.C. (69.4).

This fragment formerly belonged to the anthology of poems *Sanjūroku-nin-shū* in thirty-eight volumes, which was in the possession of the Nishihongan-ji in Kyōto. Two volumes, one with poems by the poetess Ise, the other with poems by Ki no Tsurayuki, were split up and ended up in various collections. This fragment is an example of the most refined handling of paper: prepared with torn work and collage, colour printing and painting, and ennobled by the stylized calligraphy. This deluxe edition is thought to have been dedicated to Ex-emperor Shirakawa (1053–1129) for his sixtieth birthday.

The most priceless writing papers came from China. When trade resumed with the Northern Song dynasty, rolls of paper could be imported. Chōnen himself, priest at the Tōdai-ji, brought back fifty rolls of Chinese paper with him from a journey to China in 897. This *karakami* was bamboo paper treated with shell-lime and tinted, and decorated in woodblock-, mica- or heat-printing with heraldic or textile scrolls. In Japan these papers were immediately copied and the patterns altered to suit Japanese taste: scatter designs of plants and animals of poetic import. Paper from the Japanese paper mills was also highly prized. Ladies loved the very white *Michinoku* paper or paper made with cloud patterns in soft colours.

In the mills near the capital the paper was either dyed or coloured by hand with a bristle brush. Another process was to mix in previously tinted fibres at the filtering stage, resulting in clouded paper. If little clouds of colour were inserted the paper was called 'flying cloud paper' *(tobigumo-gami);* thin fibrous paper with a gauze-like wave pattern was called *ramon*. The patterning called 'ink soak' *(sumi-nagashi),* when colours were allowed to run and spread, though in a controlled manner, in the damp paper, also seems to have been a purely Japanese invention that was particularly suited to Japanese paper *(washi)*. Even more refined effects were achieved by gluing cut or torn gold or silver foil, or small pieces of foil, by scattering metal powder or by using strands of metal as thin as hairs. Sometimes a pictorial design was added as well, in ink and gold or silver paint. Often the characters of a poem or 'grass-character pictures' *(ashi-de)* were included in the designs.

140

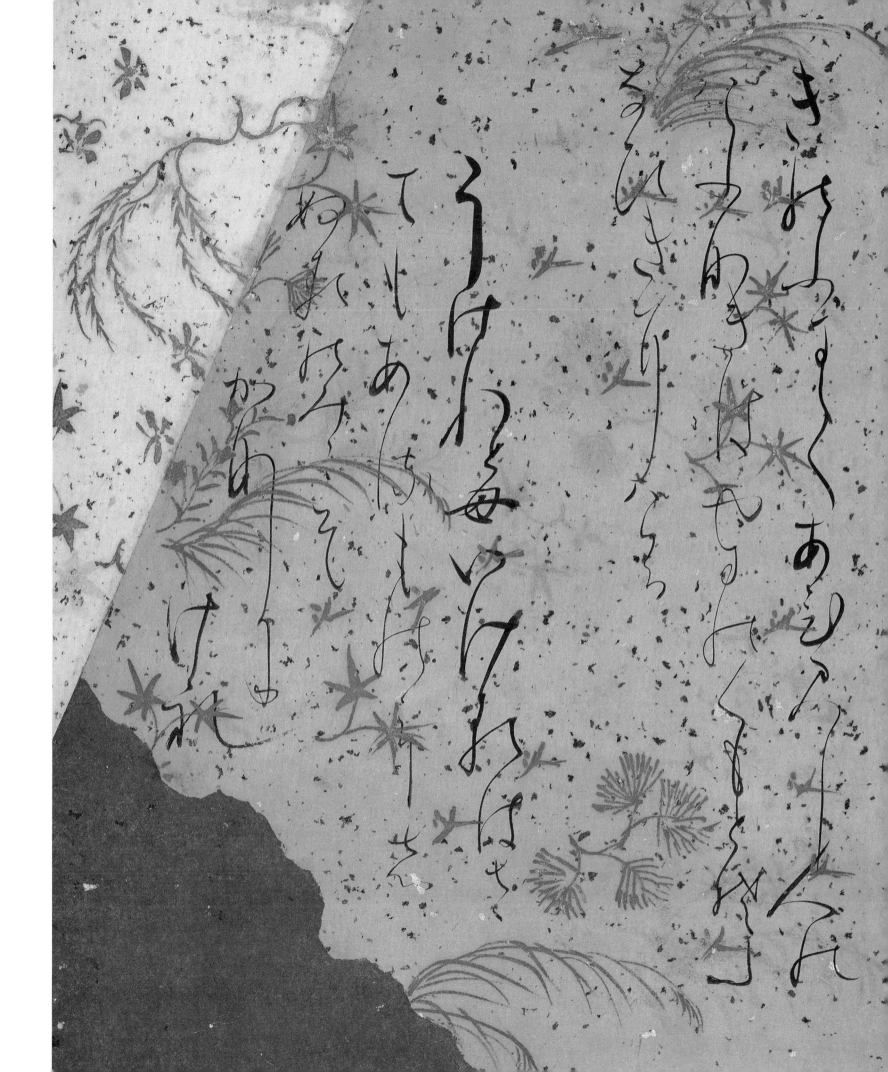

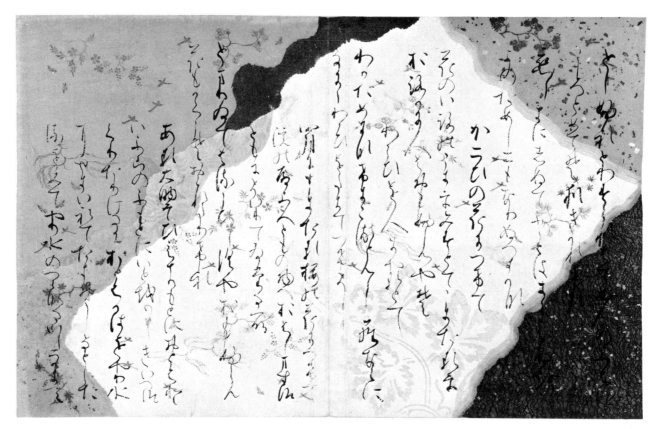

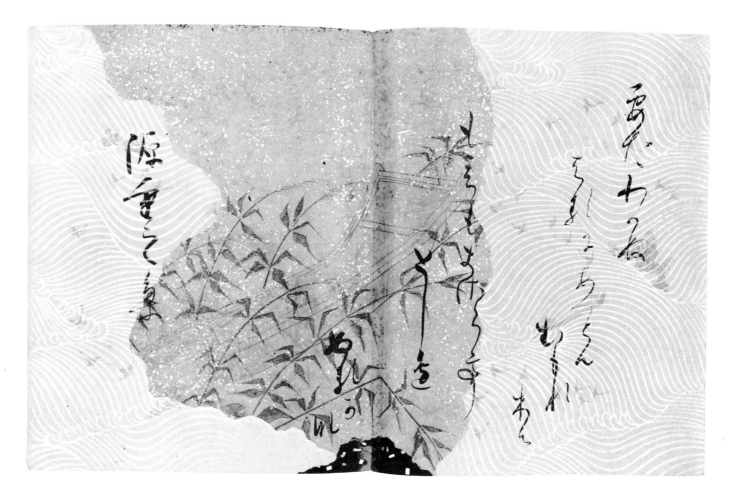

132
Page of calligraphy from the *Ishiyama-gire*. Ink on decorated paper. H. 20.2 cm, W. 31.8 cm. *c.* 1112. Hikotaro Umezawa Collection, Tōkyō.
This sheet is from the album with poems by the poetess Ise; it is compounded of many coloured papers joined together by collage. The cursive *kana* script harmonizes formally with the decorative printed and painted embellishments in powdered metal.

134
Sanjūroku-nin-shū: poem by Minamoto no Shigeyuki. Paper collage with mica printing and drawing, writing in ink. H. 20.1 cm. L. 31.8 cm. *c.* 1112. Nishihongan–ji, Kyōto.
Three sheets of decorated paper gummed together to make a page. Chinese paper, with waves printed in mica, frames a river bank of metal-sprinkled paper. A boat is painted with ornamental lines, lying among reed stems. The calligrapher has written a single poem by Shigeyuki in free characters harmoniously scattered over the picture.

133
Sanjūroku-nin-shū: poems by Yamabe no Akahito. Paper collage with painting in silver and writing in ink. H. 20.5 cm, L. 32 cm. *c.* 1112. Nishihongan–ji, Kyōto.
Six poems by Akahito are written over this sheet; first very close together, at the top right corner, then more and more loosely. The sheet is decorated with an ornamental coastal landscape. A tongue of land stretches into the deep green water—it is strewn with little silver leaves—while the banks show above and below. The edges of the banks, the fir trees and the wild geese are painted with metallic colours, showing to perfection the decorative world of motifs in Heian art.

In the unique deluxe edition of the *Sanjūroku-nin-shū* ('Collections of the Thirty-Six Poets'), the anthology compiled by Fujiwara no Kintō (966–1041), every one of the papers just described is found. The work is alleged to have been produced for the sixtieth birthday of Ex-emperor Shirakawa in 1112. Six hundred and eighty-seven different kinds of paper were used for it. The decorative effect of many of the separate sheets was made even more exquisite by the use of the collage technique: different papers, up to five layers at a time,

143

133–134 were torn or cut and reassembled with their edges displaced so that multicoloured narrow bands, like those of the superimposed garments of the ladies of the court, were visible. There now survive 136 of these collage pages from the original, which contained more than 140 examples. Albeit the deluxe copies of sutras also include many of the decorative techniques mentioned, the *Sanjūroku-nin-shū* surpasses any other writing papers in originality and beauty. The work was kept originally in the Nishihongan-ji and consisted of thirty-eight separate volumes, since the poems by Ki no Tsurayuki and Nakatomi no Yoshinobu each occupied two volumes. Thirty-two of the volumes remained together in

135

Sarashina-nikki (details): Calligraphy by Fujiwara no Sadaie (Teika) (1162–1241). Ink on paper. Volume with original cover. H. 16.3 cm, W. 14.5 cm. Imperial Household.

The diary *Sarashina-nikki* was written by the daughter of Sugawara no Takesue, a provincial nobleman, and chronicles the period between 1021 and 1058. The contents recount the restless life of a woman whose head had been turned by novel reading; she had no success at court and was widowed in early life. The earliest copy of this diary is by the great poet Fujiwara no Sadaie (Teika). The famous poet and critic writes an unconventional hand, in *kana* script with emphases made by introducing *kanji* characters.

the temple, lost ones have been added in modern times. Some of the missing volumes and single sheets were finally sold in 1929. Several single sheets are also to be found in American collections.

Twenty calligraphers are said to have shared the task of penning the 6,438 poems. The calligraphy—a few volumes with the poems of Ki no Tsurayuki (volume 2), Minamoto no Shitagō (volume 26), Princess Nakatsukasa (volume 36)—can be attributed with a high degree of probability to a successor of Yukinari, Fujiwara no Sadanobu (1088–1156). The poems of Mitsune are supposed to have been contributed by the wife of Ex-emperor Michiko (Dōshi) herself.

Beside the Seson-ji school that continued to copy works of Japanese literature in the style of Fujiwara no Yukinari for court and nobility, Fujiwara no Tademichi (1097–1164) founded the Hosshō-ji school of calligraphy. This temple had been founded by Emperor Shirakawa in 1077 as the first of the 'Six Shō Temples'. From it was launched a counter-movement in calligraphy that greatly preferred once more the powerful Chinese tradition. This trend was joined by the great poets and critics of the Late Heian period: Fujiwara no Shunzei and Teika. The new burgeoning knightly 135 ideal, championed by the landed nobility against the

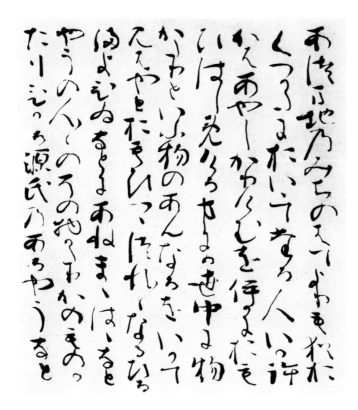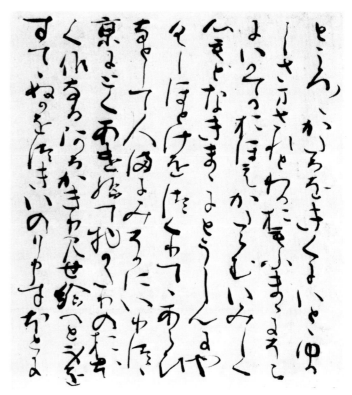

aristocratic life of the court, found an appropriate form of calligraphy in the Gokyōgoku school of Fujiwara no Yoshitsune (1169–1206). The radical change of thought is seen expressed in changes in calligraphy, even though in imperial court circles the elegant *kana* scripts formed in the Heian period have remained to this day the ideal models for *wa-yō* calligraphy.

Secular Painting: *Kara-e* and *Yamato-e*

Nothing survives of secular painting from the Early and Middle Heian periods. We can, however, obtain some idea of it from literature, especially from the introductions to the poems of the *Kokin-shū*. In the environment of the court and high nobility, painted sliding doors *(shōji)* and folding screens *(byōbu)* formed part of the elegant decoration of the living quarters. They provided a perfect ground for pictures and gave colour and light to the rooms of the interior, darkened by shutters on the outside and inside by the ceremonial curtain-stands, placed beside the ladies and dignitaries, which added to the gloom. The motifs of the pictures lent the desired atmosphere, formal or intimate as the case required. Formal occasions were best suited by pictures in the Chinese style *(Kara-e)*; Japanese style *(Yamato-e)* was for intimacy. The imperial house already had standing screens in the Nara period, made with different kinds of materials and decoration. The Shōsō-in Treasure Hall received 105 screens from Emperor Shōmu's effects in 756; sixty-eight of them are mentioned still in 856, and today there are only eleven in existence.

After the completion of palace building in Heian-kyō in 808, the Office for Painting and Interior Decorating was reduced in size; only two full-time painters remained in employment with ten assistants. Interest in painting for decorating the palace halls was on the increase, however. In 818 Emperor Saga had life-size ideal portraits of Chinese sages painted on the sliding doors of the Shishin-den Hall in imitation of those in the Chinese imperial palace in Chang'an. The emperor's living quarters too, the Seiryō-den attached to the right-hand corner, were decorated with painted screens in the Chinese style showing, for example, a 'View of Gunming Lake' and 'Rough Ocean Waves' from the Chinese *Classic of Mountains and Lakes (Shanghaiqing)*. There is mention also of horses and portraits of

great Chinese poets. All the paintings were strict copies of Chinese models, 'China pictures' *(Kara-e)*. The name Kudara no Kawanari (783–853) has come down as one of the prominent artists who must have been closely involved with the imperial projects. In 840 he received the court rank of *ason*.

After the mid-eighth century, however, a change came about in painting in the train of the change in literary fashion: painters ventured to use Japanese subjects. Many forewords to the poems of the *Kokin-shū* state that the poem was written about a screen painting. Five hundred and ninety-three have been counted in the *Kokin-shū* alone.[36]

There is talk of screens with pictures of the Tatsuta River near Kyōto, one of the classic beauty spots in autumn. For example the monk Sōsei wrote a poem (*c.* 890) on a screen in the East Hall of Empress Nijō no Kisaki, wife of Uda-Tennō. The screen showed a view of the Tatsuta River with red autumn leaves floating on it:

momiji no ha
nagarete tomaru
minato niwa
beni fukaki namida ya
tatsuran

'Where the autumn leaves
pile up as they flow in the stream,
there at the river mouth
there will be dark red (perhaps like tears?)
waves.'

(*Kokin-shū*, Poem 293)

Another screen painted with the Tatsuta River stood in the palace of Emperor Uda, the Teiji-in; the poem describes how rider and horse shy away for fear of trampling the autumn foliage.

These natural themes, at once deeply nostalgic and full of colour and pictorial potential, were to be found in the mansions of the nobles as well as in the imperial palace. It is surely not fortuitous that the earliest pictures of purely Japanese sentiment to be celebrated in poetry are those telling of spring and autumn, with the beauty of its flowers or its falling leaves. The tender melancholy of *mono no aware,* of 'being deeply touched by things' (O. Benl), a central feeling of Heian-period life, appears in a twofold artistic expression, both in painting and in poetry. By the end of the ninth century, it has been convincingly shown by T. Akiyama, the purely Japanese painting called *Yamato-e* had already taken shape in many themes. There were already land-

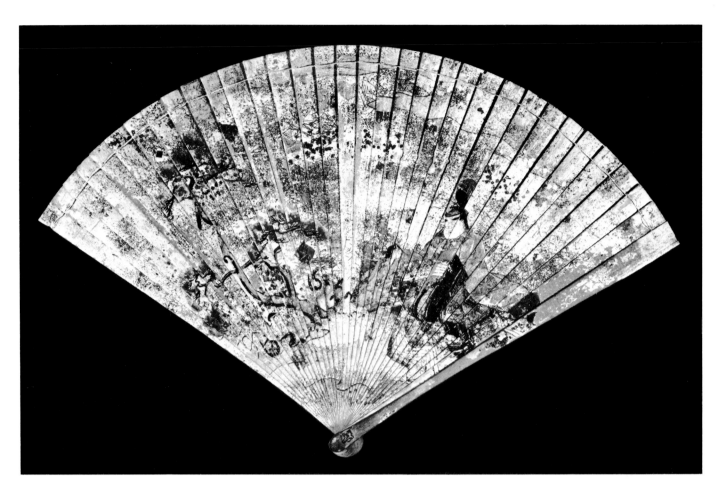

136

Hiōgi Folding Fan. *Hinoki* wood with colours and ink. H. 28.7cm, L. 48.5cm. Second half of the twelfth century. Itsukushima-jinja, Hiroshima.

The ground is sprinkled with gold and silver leaf; over it is a powerful painting in *tsukuri-e* style: a nobleman with his wife and daughter out of doors near a fir tree. In the trunk and branches of the tree are characters in 'reed script'. On the back the purely decorative effect is even more striking: plum blossoms, scatter motifs and characters are loosely arranged.

137

Nenjū-gyōji-emaki: Scroll 5, picture 4 (copy after the original of *c.* 1160). Ink and colours on paper. H. 45.2cm. Private collection. After the Naien banquet a dance by court ladies takes place in the East Garden in front of the Ryōki-den Hall. Six of the ladies dance in unison on a platform. A female orchestra sits in the adjoining rooms. Courtiers and torch bearers press round the stage, which is marked off by curtains and drawn in central perspective.

138

Senzui-byōbu (six-part folding screen). Ink and colours on silk. H. 146cm, L. 258cm. Eleventh century. Formerly in the Kyōōgokoku-ji; now in the National Museum, Kyōto.

The centre of the wide expanse of landscape is occupied by the grass hut of a hermit who sits on his porch to receive an honourable visitor: a scholar with a horse. The figures represent Chinese people, perhaps the celebrated poet Bo Juyi. The landscape, though towering, has its gently poetic moments that come closer to Japanese concepts. This screen, thought to have been used for initiation ceremonies in the Kyōōgokoku-ji, is an important example of *Kara-e*.

scape and figure representations in 'season pictures', pictures of the sequence of the months and pictures of famous views. The choice and formulation of these series was so deeply instinctive with the Japanese spirit that, in the nineteenth century, popular woodcut designers like Andō Hiroshige were still taking inspiration for landscape woodcuts from the same subjects.

In the tenth century the range of purely Japanese subjects began to widen enough to include illustrations to novels *(monogatari-e)*. We know from the journals and stories that hand scrolls *(emaki)* and narrative pictures *(sōshi-e)* came into fashion, alongside the great screen paintings, in small formats for intimate contemplation. In these subjects the painters of the Kose school took the lead. They belonged to the Painting Studio newly founded at court in 886, whose administrator generally made the appointments. We have their names—Kose no Kanaoka, Kose no Ōmi, Kimmochi and Kintada—but none of the originals survives.

The *emaki* with illustrations of court life provide the best means of studying the various folding screens, rigid sliding doors and even silk curtains with landscapes. In the *Genji-monogatari-emaki* and *Nenjū-gyōji-emaki* it can be seen how close *Yamato-e* and *Kara-e* often were. The *Genji-monogatari-emaki* has a preponderance of landscapes with trees in flower or in autumn, and

139
Senzui-byōbu (six-part folding screen). Colours on silk. H. 110.8 cm, L. 245 cm. Early thirteenth century. Jingo-ji, Kyōto. Despite its secular subject this landscape screen had its place behind the abbot's throne in the Kanchō initiation ceremony in the rites of the Shingon sect. This is the second *senzui* screen that has come down to us; it shows a complete Japanization of the landscape. Not only the scenery (part mountainous, part extensive and kindly) but also the bands of mist and lowering cloud show the mastery of painting in *Yamato-e*.

figures composed into them as accessories. Often too there are representations of colourful poem papers *(shikishi-gata),* with or without recognizable calligraphic inscriptions, stuck over the picture like mosaic in a most refined manner, adding a new dimension to the work of art with the suggestions of the art of poetry.

137 The *Nenjū-gyōji-emaki* shows a scene of a dance being performed in front of the empress's Ryōki-den Hall. The dancers wear Chinese costume, and in the side rooms to the left, the nearer room has folding screens with *Yamato-e* landscapes. In it are ladies in Japanese costume, while in a back room ladies in Chinese and Japanese dresses are playing instruments. It can be clearly made out that the wide curtains that partition the back room are painted with scenes containing figures of Chinese, probably famous poets. In this section the figures occupy a weightier space in the picture.

These curtains resemble the most well-known work of *Kara-e,* the six-part landscape screen *(senzui-byōbu)* 138 formerly in the Kyōōgokoku-ji. Here a poet, thought to be Bo Juyi, is surprised by visitors in front of his solitary hut. The screen was used in initiation ceremonies of the Shingon sect.

A second *senzui-byōbu* is preserved in the Jingo-ji. In 139 contrast to the previous one, we see here deep into a purely Japanese landscape that is animated with noble palaces and scenes from the life of the Heian aristocracy. Banks of cloud are used to articulate the picture surface. The *senzui-byōbu* of the Kyōōgokoku-ji is now dated in the twelfth century, and that of the Jingo-ji not until after 1200. The screens are important in the history of Heian art as examples of early landscape painting in both styles. As in the examples in the *Genji-monogatari-emaki,* we find once more *shikishi* poem sheets glued on the screens.

148

Decorative Arts

Ever since the earliest rich payments of tribute that arrived at the imperial court in the sixth century and during the Nara period, the Japanese had been convinced of the superiority of Chinese decorative art. Even in the Heian period the nobility preferred still to acquire things of Chinese origin. The official missions and monks travelling privately alike looked on the mainland not only for religious texts and cult objects but also for such treasures as brocades, paper, ceramics and metalwork, paying in gold so as to be able to bring them back to Japan. There was also an unofficial commerce in Chinese articles carried on by the more sea-faring Koreans and Chinese. It is reported that the imports were even sold in the markets of Heian-kyō.

By the beginning of the tenth century Japan was forming its own style in the decorative arts. There arose, not at all in isolation but in the general current of Japanization of life style and taste, an autonomous craft activity in materials that were those preferred in Japan even in later periods: metal and lacquer.

In the realm of ceramics, however, Japan came nowhere near the perfection of the Chinese monochrome stonewares and porcelains. The Chinese originals were much appreciated at court. Sei Shōnagon in her *Pillow Book* describes how a celadon vase with branches of flowering cherry in the Seiryō-den Palace was able to cause the terrifying *Kara-e* pictures with 'waves of the ocean and long-legged monsters' to be forgotten through the elegance of the pot and the blossoms.

Japanese pottery in the Heian period was of a standard far inferior to the Chinese and the Korean. Plain

140
Four-footed Jar. Stoneware with yellow glaze. H. 16.3 cm. Ninth century. Jishō-in Temple, Kyōto.
This *sue*-ware jar is of a form that is quite rare. The four feet are carried up vertically to the mouth and pass over three horizontal ridges. The brilliant yellow glaze is thought to be a deliberate application of silicate and not a chance result of wood-ash glazing occurring in the kiln. By analogy with dated finds in graves, this type of jar is thought to have been fired during the Kōnin period.

141
Vajra Bell. Bronze, H. *c.* 18 cm. Cast in the ninth century (?). Tōkyō National Museum, Tōkyō.
Among the magic instruments of the Shingon sect are a set of thunderbolts and a bell with five jagged *vajras* joined together. Around the wall of the bell are the characters for the Sanskrit names of the Five Buddhas instead of images of them.

earthenware *(haji)* served the needs of ordinary folk and the kitchens of the great for plates, dishes, water pots and storage jars, or the vessels were of hard-fired stoneware *(sue-mono),* now also with a wood-ash glaze, in shapes that originated in Korea. In the Heian period the *sue-mono* developed individual features, both of form, in the slender profile of the vessels, and of decoration, in scratched ornamental drawing. In 1955 a Heian-period kiln was excavated at Sagayama near Nagoya; it produced pots suitable for cult purposes, either as flower vases or as ritual vessels.

Only a few pottery vessels from the Heian period that were not buried have survived; most of what survives comes from sutra burials. There were kilns at Bizen, Settsu, Sanuki, Mino and Owari producing simple *sue* ware. Brick kilns must have been working in the neighbourhood of Heian-kyō and Nara, for the palaces and temples required plain, decorated and some glazed tiles, even though the mountain monasteries and city palaces showed a growing preference for shingles of cypress bark in the Japanese style.

In the realm of sacred art, bronze still played an important role, though Buddhist sculpture of the Heian period was done almost exclusively in wood. But the emperor or regent commissioned silver, not bronze statuettes from the sculpture studios for special occasions.

For the Early Heian period, temple lanterns and large temple bells show that the art of bronze casting had not been forgotten. Many of the bells are dated: one in the Saikō-ji to 839, one in the Daiun-ji to 858, the great bell of the Jingo-ji to 875 and one in the Eizan-ji 917. These bells are of such historical value that they are registered as *kokuhō* ('National Treasures').

In the Shingon cult the priest needed a set of magic bronze objects: thunderbolts, bells, a wheel of the Law, a sceptre, as well as symbolic figures for the altar and placques to hang up. The priest Kūkai had brought back the first set from China, and to ensure that the magic persisted, the original forms of the objects had to be perpetuated carefully in Japan when further sets were made.

143 ▷

Mirror. Cast white bronze (nickel, zinc and copper). D. 12.4 cm. Eleventh-twelfth century. Tōkyō National Museum, Tōkyō.
This mirror comes from a grave; it shows typical Heian decoration with softly modelled cranes and pine branches. This style is known as *wa-yō* ('Japanese style') as opposed to the more compact Chinese type of design.

142

Keman Pendant. Bronze, partly silver-plated. H. 28.5 cm, W. 32.8 cm. First half of the twelfth century. Shinshō-ji, Shiga.
In the Late Heian period altars and holy objects were decorated with *keman* pendants of leather or bronze instead of with flower garlands. Two *kalavinka* or *karabingyō* (Buddhist creatures in the form of birds) stand against a decorative flower scroll; they hold offerings and are executed in openwork, relief and engraving. A cord in relief emphasizes the earlier form of a posy, and the loops are attached to a very finely punched mount.

144
Kedachi Sword. Wooden sheath with lacquer and mother-of-pearl.
L. 96.3 cm. Twelfth century. Kasuga-jinja, Nara.
This particularly richly mounted sword has a pommel with fine
gold relief in the form of openwork scrolls over gilded ray skin. The
sheath is covered with sprinkled gold lacquer. The mother-of-pearl
inlay depicts sparrows in bamboos, chased by a cat. In addition
green and white glass, black lacquer and ivory are used in the decoration. This sword is a perfect example of the exquisite refinement of
craftsmanship that prevailed at the end of the Heian period.

Bronze was also the appropriate material for reliquaries. The idea that the latter days of the Law were
approaching resulted in the burial of sacred texts, especially of the *Lotus Sutra,* in bronze cylinders, so that
the donor's soul would be saved to new life in the new
era of the Buddha Miroku (Maitreya). Fujiwara no
Michinaga was responsible for the earliest sutra burial
in 1007 on Mount Kimpusen in Yoshino near Nara.
Reliquaries from sutra burials also came from Fukuoka
on Kyūshū. A cylindrical pagoda containing two small

Buddha figures can be dated to 1116. Another reliquary
from Fukuoka lay on a lotus throne and was crowned
with a glass jewel.

The Tang-dynasty style of decoration associated
with Buddhism was kept alive on bronze gongs and
pierced jewellery and on the metal facing of altars, but a 142
nuance of typically Japanese aesthetic taste is to be dis-
cerned in a subtle increase in sensibility, seen most
clearly in the decorative programme of the Konjiki-dō 86
in northern Japan, executed in 1124. Small pieces like
goldsmith's work became more frequent as decorative
fittings for sutra scrolls and for their metal containers.
The great *Heike-Nōkyō* set of the Taira family of 1164
has the most ambitious bronze fittings, knobs and 119
mounts in every kind of metal technique, all set with
gems. The household effects of the aristocrats also had
metal fittings; writing cases, toilet boxes and even the
sparse furniture of wood and lacquer had gilt trim-
mings. The same guild of goldsmiths made the decorative parts of armour and, above all, the noble and pre-

cious ornament required for the hilt and sheath of a sword.

But of all the bronze work of the Heian period it is the mirrors that show the most decisive step towards a Japanese style. In place of the heavy all-over patterns of Tang mirrors, the backs of Heian mirrors have delicate, dainty, natural motifs placed like *ashi-de* script: flowers and birds of the Japanese landscape. These elegant objects remind us of the patterns on writing papers or of the lively yet stylized rendering of meadow motifs on lacquer. A poetic delight in flowers and creatures in their habitat and seasonal context comes to the fore in the Late Heian period in a very Japanese manner. We should note, however, that these mirrors were often withdrawn from their profane use and engraved on the blank face with religious pictures: they then were placed among the treasures dedicated in the sutra burials.

The art of sword-making ranked in Japan as a craft of a high, almost religious order. The smith *(kaji)* submitted to the proper observance of Shintō rites before embarking on his work, with ablutions, abstinence and invocations on the godhead.

The smithy itself was fenced off with straw rope to make it a holy precinct; the smith donned the white robes of a Shintō priest and, with one helper, he often spent weeks at a time isolated from the world, working alone according to the strictest prescriptions.

By the beginning of the tenth century sword blades had reached unprecedented perfection. Sword smithies in the Early Heian period were located in the remote provinces of Buzen, Bizen, Hōki and Yamashiro near Heian-kyō. In the far north of Honshū and in the south at Satsuma on Kyūshū there were workshops subject to the powerful clans of the knightly nobility, who accumulated an arsenal of the best swords on their estates in case of war.

144 The swordsmith's art reached its first great climax under Emperor Ichijō (980–1011), just the period of the *Genji-monogatari*. But it is evident from the court literature that the effete heroes, bent on their amorous ad-

146
Back Board of a Quiver. Red sandalwood with inlay of lacquer and mother-of-pearl. H. 32 cm. *c.* 1131. Kasuga-jinja, Nara.
This small ceremonial quiver is decorated with lacquer in a technique used only here. The back, of sandalwood with an applied yellow metal plate, is decorated with incised scatter motifs of rocks, grasses and birds, which are then filled with black lacquer. The sides, on the other hand, have inlays of mother-of-pearl and mounts of bronze.

ventures and exquisite poetic reunions, had nothing but scorn for military principles and ideals.

At this time smiths were already signing the tangs of their blades. Many smiths are known by name, the five most famous worked in Bizen province. In Heian-kyō also Sanjō Munechika (938–1014) began to found a school; even the swords themselves had personal names. Moreover, swordmaking was the only manual activity considered worthy of an emperor: Gotoba-Tennō practised it. The fame of Japanese blades was so

◁ 145
Blue Armour. Iron plates and coloured leather thongs. H. (bottom section) 39.9 cm. Twelfth century. Itsukushima-jinja, Hiroshima. This armour with blue leather thongs is said to have been given to the shrine of the Taira clan, with its helmet, by Taira no Shigemori (1138–1179.)

great in the eleventh century that Chinese merchants bought up Japanese swords for China. The great Chinese poet Ouyang Xiu (1007–1072) wrote a poem on Japanese swords.[37]

Armour was prepared by the masters of the platers' guild *(katchū-shi),* mentioned in the book of ceremonies, *Engi-shiki,* of 927. Japanese armour consists of narrow iron plates bound together with coloured cords to make pads of various sizes to protect arms, thighs and belly. These pads allowed the greatest possible freedom of movement. Only the breastplate was solid and covered with coloured leather. There was also a cap-shaped knobbed helmet with attached flaps of pads, like the armour for sides and back. In the civil wars of the eleventh century the knight's armour proved to be splendid in colour, costly and effective. The great clan leaders and war lords dedicated their arms and armour, deemed holy, to the Shintō shrines of their ancestors. Today the shrine of the Taira clan, the Itsukushima-jinja, preserves its heritage, the Kasuga-jinja that of the Fujiwara, and the Ōyamazumi-jinja in Ehime has the armour of the ill-fated hero Minamoto no Yoshitsune (1159–1189).

Lacquer played a very important part in architecture, sculpture and the applied arts, prized both for its lustre and colour and for its strength. Early in the Heian period, in 808, the Offices for Painting and for Lacquerwork were amalgamated into the Palace Bureau. According to Beatrix von Ragué the art of lacquerwork in the first century of the Heian period was modelled on the techniques that had become known in the Nara period through the Chinese lacquers in the Shōsō-in (756).[38] The framing parts of the Taima Shrine, built for the celebrated tapestry with Amida's Western Paradise (second half of the eighth century), show scatter motifs of classical Tang style painted in gold and silver as additions on a lacquer ground. They are dated about 800 and form a bridge to the applied art of the Early Heian period.

At the beginning of the tenth century the lacquer craftsmen evolved a new independent Japanese technique of decoration, that of sprinkle-painting *(maki-e).* The first evidence of it is on an arm-rest with flowers and butterflies. Gold and silver powder is sprinkled into the still damp lacquer over motifs previously drawn. In a further stage of refinement the surface is covered over with black lacquer and then polished until the scatter motif reappears. The surface is then protected with a new coat of transparent lacquer. This technique appears

147
Box for Buddhist Texts. Dry lacquer with gold and silver *togidashi*. H. 8.3 cm, L. 37 cm, W. 24.4 cm. 919. Ninna-ji, Kyōto.
The slight rounding of the lid gives this flat box a graceful shape that is enhanced by the dense scroll work in 'polished lacquer' in which *kalavinka* spirits hover among plant scrolls. In the central field is an inscription stating that the box was made for texts of the Shingon sect that Kūkai had brought from China.

145

146

154

148

Sutra Box. Wood with black lacquer and gold and silver *togidashi*.
H. 16.7 cm, L. 32.7 cm, W. 23.3 cm. Late eleventh century. Fujita
Art Museum, Ōsaka.

On the sides of this box are depicted scenes from different chapters
of the *Lotus Sutra* which the box was intended to contain. One long
side shows Buddha in a previous life as a king, waiting on an ascetic,
bringing him wood for his fire and collecting fruit for him. Chinese
models can be recognized, but there are details—especially the or-
namentation of the upper side—that show that Japanese motifs have
been adopted.

149

Table. Wood with lacquer and inlaid of mother-of-pearl. H.
77.5 cm, L. 66.5 cm, W. 33.5 cm. Early twelfth century. Chūson-ji,
Iwate.

This altar table from the sutra library of the temple is made with the
same perfection of craftsmanship as the interior decoration of the
Konjiki-dō. Scroll medallions of *hosoge* flowers in mother-of-pearl
make a specially splendid effect against the ground of black lacquer
mixed with gold dust.

150
Mirror Stand. Wood with black lacquer. H. 67 cm. Eleventh century. Kasuga-jinja, Nara.
This decorative stand is on four curved feet; the two arms to hold the metal mirror repeat the same form at a sharper angle. Carved scrolls give the stand a decorative silhouette, reminiscent of Chinese forms. The black lacquer ground is decorated with gold scatter and with patterns in gold and silver foil.

147 on the manuscript case in the Ninna-ji, dated to 919. The inscription shows that the case was destined to hold the texts brought back from China by the priest Kūkai. The core of the rectangular case is of hempen cloth, with a typical Tang-period surface pattern of floral scrolls with clouds and flying mythological creatures—executed with great care in thinly scattered gold

and silver (*togidashi*). The black-lacquer ground has a sparse sprinkling of gold filings. This ground is characteristic of almost all Heian lacquers.

The case for priests' sashes in the Tōji, hardly later than the scroll case, is less indebted to hieratic Buddhist ornament. Waves, water animals and birds cover the surface of the case, and only the heads of two dragons indicate the centre of the lid. The small jewel box, also belonging to the Ninna-ji, which is said to come from the belongings of Emperor Uda who died in 937, is especially charming. The density of the sprinkled gold achieves an effect of metal, with a design of lively fantastic flowers and birds. Of the three cases dated in the eleventh century, the sutra box of Fujita Art Museum in 148 Ōsaka is exceptional, for its walls have scenes from the previous lives of the Buddha. We see here the beginning of the use of sprinkled lacquer for illustrative pictures.

The writings of court ladies around the year 1000 have plenty of information about lacquer utensils and furnishings, but it is in the *Genji-monogatari-emaki* and the *Ban-Dainagon-ekotoba* that the most important furniture, fittings and objects of noble households are most faithfully illustrated. Stands and tables, cases for 149–150 toiletries, mirrors, combs and writing materials are portrayed by the painters as lacquer objects decorated with patterns in gold and silver.

The Middle and Late Heian periods brought the first high point of purely Japanese lacquer working. Gold lacquer and mother-of-pearl brought celestial radiance into the halls of the temples, enhancing the redeeming qualities of the golden statues. The Hōō-dō of the Byōdō-in at Uji has lost its original mother-of pearl and lacquer decoration on the altar, but the interior decoration of the Konjiki-dō in the Chūson-ji at Iwate, from 86 about seventy years later, survives. The main pillars have twelve medallions with the figure of the Universal Buddha Dainichi from the mandala. They are executed in densely sprinkled gold lacquer, which leaves the outlines free. The spandrels have scrolls in the same tech-

151 ▷
Saddle. Wood with mother-of-pearl inlay. H. 27 and 30 cm, L. 44 cm. Twelfth century. Tōkyō National Museum, Tōkyō.
The front and back attachments of the saddle are decorated in mother-of-pearl inlay with long panicles of flowering *hagi* clover that grow in the middle from a cobweb. The cross boards have *hagi* plants on the edges and in the centre, inlaid in fine mother-of-pearl into a black-lacquer ground. *Hagi* clover arouses poetic and military associations and fits into the repertoire of images of the Heian court.

152
Cosmetic Box. Black lacquer ground with gold lacquer and mother-of-pearl inlay. H. 13.5 cm, L. 22.4 cm, W. 30.6 cm. Twelfth century. Tōkyō National Museum, Tōkyō.
This is at present the earliest cosmetic box to survive. It has a decoration of sprinkled lacquer and shows the poetic, ornamental motif of cart wheels seasoning in water. The lines of the water and of the wheels are rendered in *togidashi* lacquer; the wheels are partly inlaid with mother-of-pearl. The inside with flowering plants and birds of the Four Seasons makes a refined and highly stylish contrast with the outside.

153

Small *Karabitsu* Trunk. Black lacquer with *togidashi* and mother-of-pearl inlay. H. 30 cm, L. 30.5 cm, W. 39.9 cm. Twelfth century. Kongōbu-ji on Kōya-san, Wakayama.

This trunk was made to hold cult objects. On the lid and sides are portrayed swampy meadows with flowering iris, water plants and flying plovers, reminiscent of the designs on writing paper. The lines and surfaces are most delicately executed in a variety of tones of *togidashi*. Separate details are inlaid with mother-of-pearl, enhancing the sheen of the surface. The inner tray also has a marsh motif on the sides, but the base is pierced with medallions and filled with gold bronze scrolls.

nique. As a contrast the intermediary bands and all the beam work have ornamental cartouches in mother-of-pearl inlay, sometimes alternating with pierced bronze plaques. The bases of other sculptures and the temple's altar tables are probably from the same workshop with rich inlay of mother-of-pearl.

In addition to weapons and armour, four cavalry saddles survive from the Late Heian period. They too are decorated with the same mother-of-pearl inlay subsequently strengthened by coats of lacquer. Here is scope for profane and poetical motifs: branches of oak and screech owls, clover *(hagi),* sprays of peony and ornamental waves. This complete freedom of design appears on the only surviving cosmetic box of the Late Heian period. It is decorated with *togidashi* lacquer and inlay of mother-of-pearl and precious metal foil in one

154
Karabitsu Trunk. Black lacquer with *togidashi* and mother-of-pearl inlay. H. 59cm, L. 92.3 cm, W. 67.7cm. Late eleventh century. Tōkyō National Museum, Tōkyō.
The walls and lid of this Chinese-type trunk are decorated with circular phoenix emblems, inlaid in mother-of-pearl into the black lacquer ground. Consistent with the style of the period, the black lacquer is lightly sprinkled with gold dust *(heijin)*, the inside of the emblems more densely and the small emblems on the legs so thickly as almost to cover the surface. Thus a variety of glitter effects is added to that of the mother-of-pearl.

of the favourite motifs of the time: cart wheels soaking in water to season. The same subject is found on poem papers in the *Sanjūroku-nin-shū* collection. Even freer natural motifs are allowed on the small trunk with an iris swamp and plovers owned by the Kongōbu-ji on the Kōya-san. In a light *ashi-de* hand, the whole lyrical Japanese vision of a landscape is vividly rendered in *togidashi* lacquer with a few flashes of mother-of-pearl—here and there a bird or a blade of arrow grass—to animate the scene.

Among liturgical furniture the link with Buddhist style remains stronger. A new decorative element in the form of heraldic devices arose in the lacquer work of the twelfth century. The Chinese-type chest on six feet has powerful phoenix emblems in staggered repeats of mother-of-pearl inlay, distributed over the surface of the lid; emblems are repeated in miniature on the feet. In addition there is sprinkled gold in three different grades, but even so the forceful decorative style of the design is but little mitigated thereby.

Music and Dancing

...The most renowned virtuosos from the high and middle court ranks were chosen for the flutists' circle.... The forty men in the flutists' circle played most marvelously. The sound of their flutes, mingled with the sighing of the pines, was like a wind coming down from deep mountains. 'Waves of the Blue Ocean' among falling leaves of countless hues, had about it an almost frightening beauty.

(*The Tale of Genji,* translated by E. G. Seidensticker, p. 133)

In the wake of the diplomatic missions Japan became acquainted with forms of music and dance from the continent, and these were adopted with enthusiasm because of their exotic character and fascinating artistic content. *Gigaku* music and dance took a back seat after the end of the Nara period. 'Elegant music' (*gagaku*) became the fashion. It was taken under imperial patronage and performed on ceremonial occasions as festive entertainment. Dances with musical accompaniment were called 'dance music' (*bugaku*). Distinctions were made according to the country of origin of the instrumentation, choreography, costumes and masks among the apparently earlier Central Asian and Korean, the later Indian and South-East Asian, and the Tang-period Chinese dances. Ancient Japanese Shintōistic and popular dances were also developed into *bugaku*.

Appropriate instruments were used for each style of music. Indian and Chinese music was played on bamboo flutes, bamboo oboes, mouth organs, a bronze

gong, a side drum and a big kettledrum. With them the two kinds of string instrument—a bass lute (*biwa*) and thirteen-stringed reed zither (*sō no koto*)—were employed. The instruments for Korean music were different in combination. These comprised the Korean flute, bamboo oboe, bronze gong and a side drum. Instruments of the Japanese tradition are the small reed zither (*wagon*) and batons used in the *kagura* dances of the Shintō cult.

Music performed by an orchestra was based on short, folk-song like melodies of 16 to 32 bars in which every instrument played a part. In *bugaku,* the dance is only accompanied by flutes and percussion.

Music and dancing became a personal concern of the emperors. Emperor Saga, the son of Kammu-Tennō, reorganized and expanded the old Office for Music in 809. It now included four teachers each for dance, music and flute-playing; twelve teachers for Korean music, and two each for the exotic music from Dora, Wu and India.[39] The number of music teachers exceeded greatly that of those for other disciplines such as literature. Later the office was reduced again and received its final form under Emperor Nimmyō in the reform of 848. Ambassador Fujiwara no Sadatoshi returned from China, where he had studied music, bringing back twenty to thirty new scrolls with musical notation. *Gagaku* court music was based on two five-tone scales, *ryō* and *ritsu*. There were three kinds of notation: a tabulature for string instruments, indications of the exact pitch for wind instruments and a kind of linear neume for vocal music, all three taken from the notation of Buddhist hymn recitation.

With the reform, music and dances were modernized. A square stage was used for performances. Two music tents, one each to east and west, housed the musicians of the different ensembles. North of the stage stood the two large kettledrums. In the terminology of the time, left-hand and right-hand music alternated. The left-hand music included Tang music, Indian music and also the new national Japanese dance music. It was performed by the Left Imperial Body-Guard of the fifth grade in red court costume. The right-hand music was traditional Korean music and the obsolete *gigaku;* they were played by members of the Right Imperial Body-Guard of the sixth grade, who in accordance with their ranks, wore green, blue or yellow garments.

The choreography of the dances was also differentiated. There were war dances and literary dances, the

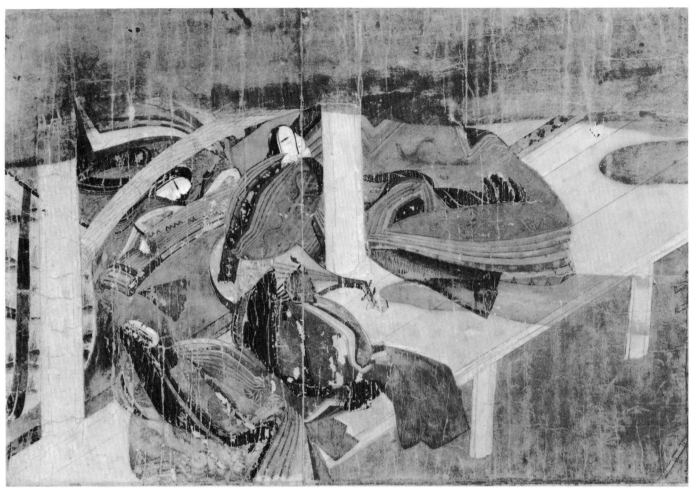

155

Genji-monogatari-emaki: Chapter 45, 'Hashihime'. Ink and colours on paper. H. 22 cm, L. 48.9 cm. First quarter of the twelfth century. Tokugawa Reimeikai Foundation, Tōkyō.

By the light of the full moon Prince Kaoru looks through a fence overgrown with red ivy at the ladies of Uji who are playing music. Behind the verandah we see Ōigimi with her *koto* zither and Nakanogimi with her *biwa* lute. Silver clouds hang over the scene.

156

Koto Zither. Black lacquer with *togidashi* on wood. L. 152 cm, W. (top) 26.5 cm. Eleventh century. Kongōbu-ji on Kōya-san, Wakayama.

On the long sounding board of the thirteen-string *koto,* between the lost mounts of the edges, are irregular curving lines like 'running ink', representing rocks around and over which plants, flowering trees, birds and butterflies are decoratively arranged. Sprinkled gold and silver are used as colours for the motifs, which are placed in varying degrees of density. The design is reminiscent of the famous decorated papers of the *Sanjūroku-nin-shū* in the Nishihongan-ji.

former performed in an energetic running tempo, the latter in the elegant flowing movements of what were called peace dances. The dancers mostly appeared in pairs, fours or sixes, and moved in unison. In principle only men danced, but there were also boys' and women's dances, many of which have fallen into oblivion.

The transition from the Music Office (gaku-ryō) to the Court Music School (gaku-sho) was effected by Emperor Murakami in the tenth century. Antiquated dances were suppressed and new duet dances developed. The great days of bugaku began in the reign of Emperor Ichijō (986–1011). Treatises were written on the art of the dance; a basic work was written and illustrated by Fujiwara no Shinzei (Michinori) in 1159.

The art of bugaku was among the obligatory accomplishments of a courtier. In court festivities princes and courtiers often danced quite spontaneously, but always without masks. In the Genji-monogatari the dance performed by the shining Prince Genji at the Autumn Leaf Festival is described in adoring terms. Genji danced the 'waves of the Blue Ocean' with Tō no Chūjō before the emperor in the Suzaku-in Palace. Forty flautists in unison provided the accompaniment. At this feast dance followed dance, rewarded by the emperor with gifts and promotions of rank. A special artistic event at court was the gosechi dance on the second dragon day of the Eleventh Month. Four young ladies-in-waiting danced it on the stage, elegantly swinging their sleeves.

But music was not reserved for official occasions. For the ladies and gentlemen of the aristocracy the cultivation of their musical accomplishments was quite as important as their skill in writing verse and fine calligraphy. Ladies could express the nobility of their 155–156 sentiments on the string instruments: the wagon or sō no koto zithers or the biwa lute; the gentlemen could also, or they could turn to the art of the transverse flute to reveal the depths of their souls. Instruments with particularly beautiful tone quality were treasured, became heirlooms and possessed personal names.

More than a hundred bugaku dances have been handed down from the Heian period; thirty-two different facial masks were used in their performance. Of these, twenty-four types can be identified today.[40] The masks of the Heian period appear to have been made for performances in temples or, at any rate, were certainly worn on these occasions. In the Tōdai-ji bugaku masks are still preserved that were worn in the kegon-e festivals of 1042, 1086, 1160 and 1162 and are inscribed with

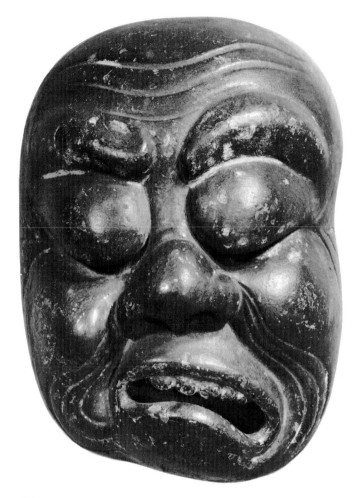

157
Hare Mask for the *bugaku* dance called *ninomai:* by Gyōmyō. Wood with lacquered and painted dressing. H. 29.8 cm. 1173. Itsukushima-jinja, Hiroshima.
In *bugaku* the *ninomai* dance followed the *ama* dance and parodied it. Two dancers appeared, one with the mask of a laughing man (*Emi-men*), the other with a woman's face swollen with leprosy (*Hare-men*). The most famous pair of these masks is preserved in the Itsukushima-jinja. The grotesque expression of the *hare* mask was intensified by the sculptor Gyōmyō into something hideously tragic.

these dates. There are masks with dates in the twelfth century in the possession of the Hōryū-ji too. Shintō shrines also had bugaku masks dedicated to them: the collection in the Itsukushima-jinja bears the date 1173 157–158 and is remarkable in having masters' signatures. From the end of the twelfth century, wood sculptors of the great studios also signed the masks they carved.

Japanese sculptors made the bugaku face masks, like the monumental Buddha images, into outstanding and expressive works of art. The bizarre spirit masks for the

158
Emi Mask for the *bugaku* dance called *ninomai:* by Gyōmyō. Wood with lacquered and painted dressing and horsehair. H. 27 cm. 1173. Itsukushima-jinja, Hiroshima.
The male part in the *ninomai* dance is that of a wrinkled, laughing old man with long eyebrows and beard. The comic and burlesque elements of the role are grasped here in masterly fashion.

Buddhist masks for processions are close to the *bugaku* masks in time and often in form; they were not used for dancing but exclusively for a cult practice that can be described as a Progress.[41] A central cult image, Shōtoku Taishi in the Hōryū-ji, the Buddha Amida for *raigō* processions, was taken to make a holy circumambulation *(gyōdō),* carried by bearers and attendants in masks. They represented the lower deities, the gods, demons, demi-gods and animal-men taken over from Hinduism, who appear in Buddhism as protective deities. The noblest masks were the Bodhisattvas, whose sublime celestial being was embodied in the form of the mask's expression. These *gyōdō* masks were also made in the Buddha-carving studios, and they show a very direct relation with the monumental sculpture of the Heian period. They follow the period style of Japanese sculpture of the eleventh and twelfth centuries. As in the *bugaku* masks, the technical means for enhancing the artistic impact were fully integrated; the *yosegi* technique of carving replaced the *ichiboku* method.

The Annual Festivals

The life of the emperor and his royal household was shaped by the ceremonies and feasts that the calendars prescribed for the whole year. The Tennō presided as chief priest at the Shintō observances, since he was the descendant of the Sun-Goddess Amaterasu-Ōmikami. He also led all the Confucian practices adopted from China and, with his household, followed the Buddhist exercises that brought prosperity to himself and the country. Only a handful of the thirty-three emperors of the Heian period made use of the opportunities for independent political activity. These unusual characters

ryō-ō and *genjō-raku* dances, for the sometimes grotesque sometimes lascivious *ninomai* and *kotoku-raku* dances, and equally the deeply serious *shintoriso* and *ayagiri* masks, all give expression to every essential feature of the character being danced.

159   ▷
Bosatsu Mask. Wood, lacquered and painted. H. 24.9 cm. Mid-twelfth century. The Cleveland Museum of Art, John L. Severence Fund, Cleveland (50.581).
The mask shows the dignified face of a Bodhisattva. Masks like these were worn in *gyōdō* processions by twenty-five monks who represented the *raigō* of Amida Nyorai as a healing ceremony. *Bosatsu* masks are preserved in the Hōryū-ji, in the Tōdai-ji and in the Jōdo-ji in Hyōgo. It is thought likely that a Buddha sculptor in the circle of Unkei in Nara made these masks.

160
Nenjū-gyōji-emaki (copy after the original of *c.* 1160): Scroll I, scene 2. Ink and colours on paper. H. 45.2 cm. Private collection.
In the forecourt of the Shishin-den palace hall, the imperial suite is standing on both sides of the gate, waiting on the arrival of the Tennō with the phoenix litter. The emperor repairs at the New Year to the palace of the ex-emperor, his father.

on the imperial throne were not connected by blood relationship with the Fujiwara regents.

The annual sequence of ceremonies *(nenjū-gyōji)* were prescribed by Saga-Tennō in 821. The three-volume work bears the title *Palace Ceremonies during the Kōnin Period (Kōnin-dairi-shiki)*. It gives for the first time the names of the old traditional ceremonies and those introduced at the beginning of the ninth century. Emperor Kammu, the founder of Heian-kyō, indeed had more pressing obligations than dealing with matters of court ceremonial. The book includes the Feast of

the Blue (White) Horse connected with 'stamp-singing' on the seventh day of the First Month; a Poetry Festival at the Stream's Edge in the palace garden and the Chrysanthemum Feast on the ninth day of the Ninth Month. These three festivals were taken from the Chinese. At the same time two essentially Japanese festivals were introduced: the Cherry-Blossom Feast and the Feast of Red Autumn Foliage, which were determined by the state of the vegetation and could not be decided by the calendar. Though these two feasts do not appear in the *nenjū-gyōji* they are each given a complete chapter by Murasaki Shikibu in the *Genji-monogatari*.

A pictorial record of the court ceremonies and feasts is said to have been made for the first time under Daigo-Tennō in about 930, by the court painter Kose no Kanaoka; it appears to have been lost. Therefore, at the end of the Heian period, Goshirakawa-Tennō, perhaps already conscious of the change of era due be-

tween 1158 and 1166, had a new series of *emaki* of the *nenjū-gyōji* painted. Fujiwara no Mitsunaga, painter of the *Ban-Dainagon-ekotoba,* is thought to be the chief painter of this formidable work of sixty hand scrolls. The ex-emperor kept the lacquer containers with the scrolls under his care, at first in his temple treasury in the Myōhō-in. After it was destroyed in the thirteenth century, the imperial house received them back. Emperor Gomizunoo took a lively interest in them, and in 1661 he had the whole work copied in the court studio by the painters of the Sumiyoshi family. The original having been lost, we have only the copies today: seven scrolls of the series in exact colour reproduction, nine scrolls in black-and-white. There are also quite a number of replicas from copies of the nineteenth and twentieth centuries.

What is to be learnt from the scenes of the *Nenjū-gyōji-emaki* about life in the Heian period? First we are shown the exclusive rituals of the imperial court, for instance the riding forth of the emperor to visit the ex-emperor at the New Year; we also see how all levels of the population participate, some as guards, some as servants, others simply as the gaping crowd in the street. We see too the festivals such as the Kamo Feast in the

161

Kitano Tenjin-engi: Scroll 2, scene 2. Ink and colours on paper. H. 52.1 cm. *c.* 1219. Kitano-jinja, Kyōto.
In the courtyard of the palace of the noble Miyako no Yoshika there is a display of archery. The famous statesman Sugawara no Michizane is knocking his arrow and aiming at the target; behind him the master of the house is seated on a mat, and round him guests, servants and the general public watch fascinated.

Fourth Month with the regent's procession, that accompanies the priestess, an imperial princess, to the Upper and Lower Kamo Shrines, to carry out the purification ritual at the river. Simultaneously in the imperial palace there are *bugaku* performances going on and banquets for archers.

Court games (a type of football in the palace garden) are shown together with the popular cock fights, for the lower nobility in the inner *Shinden* Palace and for the plebeians in the street. The New Year banquets of the court are shown, taking place after the archery contests 161 of the Palace Watch on the eighteenth day of the First Month, the *bugaku* dances before the emperor and the ceremonial poetry readings. We also see the very formal functions in the official hall of the palace, the Daigoku-den, at the great harvest festival, the Gosai-

en. The thrones of the emperor and empress are hidden while a long procession of Buddhist priests makes its entry into the palace. We see the reception of the empress and of the second wife of the emperor.

The hand scrolls also show Buddhist rites of exor- 35 cism. Secret ceremonies take place in the Shingon-in Hall west of the palace. *Kakemono* with the five great *Myōō* hang over the altar, flanked to left and right by the two mandala: The Womb World Mandala to the east, and The Diamond World Mandala to the west. The paintings of the *Jūni-ten* are placed in the eastern anteroom.

In these religious scenes and again in the picture of the six court dancers who are performing on a stage in the 137 East Garden of the Ryōki-den after the Naien banquet, the painter has employed central perspective so as to guide attention to the very important cult scenes.

In the next scroll we are shown the Gion Feast and folk dances, thus giving a full and graphic account of the year as experienced both at court and among the common people, from the most dignified occasions to carefree enjoyment. In addition the *Nenjū-gyōji-emaki* is 162 our unique source for seeing past customs and buildings. We are shown not only the official halls of the Chōdō-in and Buraku-in but also the buildings of the 175 inner palace, the Shishin-den, Seiryō-den and Jijū-den occupied by the empress. In part the interior arrangements are shown, with painted curtains and folding screens in the ladies' apartments. The costumes of the

163

Genji-monogatari-emaki: Chapter 36, 'Kashiwagi', scene 3 (detail of Pl. 180). Colours and ink on paper. H. 21.9 cm, L. 48.1 cm. First quarter of the twelfth century. Tokugawa Reimeikai Foundation, Tōkyō.
Prince Genji holds his putative son Kaoru in his arms on the fiftieth day after the boy's birth. He looks pensively at the child as he considers how history has repeated itself; through his forbidden love for Fujitsubo, the wife of his father, he became the father of Emperor Reizei.

most varied ranks of nobility, of the palace guards, priests, servants and common people are transmitted to our view exactly and with a sharp eye for detail.

The *Nenjū-gyōji-emaki* thus gives us a picture parallel to that in the literature, of the great years of the Heian period, a visible and living record of a unique kind, of a culture that flourished a thousand years ago.

The Ladies and Gentlemen of the Court

Murasaki Shikibu introduces the ideal hero of her novel, 'the shining Prince Genji', as the prototype of the noble gentleman of the Heian period. This beautiful, elegant, sensitive man, easily moved by the pathos of 163 life and unheroic, became the ideal of an age, an exemplar for the men, the dream prince of the ladies. His son and his grandson perpetuated many features of his character but could not parallel him in beauty, nobility of spirit or of appearance. Generations of Japanese scholars have sought for the original of Prince Genji. It seems possible that the hero was not only the creation of the novelist's imagination, but that she also seized on features of Fujiwara no Korechika (974–1010) who, like Genji, was sent into exile because of a real or attempted

love affair with the wife of the ex-emperor but was then rehabilitated and allowed to return to Heian-kyō. In the following quotation Ivan Morris gives us a description of a Heian gentleman:

> The Heian gentleman powdered his face (the faces of badly powdered men remind Sei of dark earth over which the snow has melted in patches) and used a generous amount of scent on his hair and clothes. The technique of mixing perfumes was highly developed. In an age when bathing was perfunctory and clothing elaborate and hard to clean, scent served a very useful purpose. It was, of course, no ready-made commodity, but the product of a complex and sophisticated art. Genji himself was much admired for the skill with which he prepared his own incense, whose distinctive aroma always announced his approach and lingered after his departure. In the case of Prince Niou, who on the whole is pictured as one of the more masculine of the male characters, the preparation of scents was something of an obsession. Both he and his friend Kaoru owe their names to this art; and nothing more symbolizes the ideals of this period, and contrasts it with the subsequent age of military heroes, than the fact that two of Murasaki's most respected male characters should be named 'Lord Fragrance' and 'Prince Scent'.[42]

It was not Murasaki Shikibu alone who described her male heroes with round faces powdered white, pathetic and effeminate; even in the *Utsubo-monogatari,* written by a man, the main hero is like Prince Genji. A century later this ideal of beauty was still alive, otherwise it would have been unlikely that the painters of the *Genji-monogatari-emaki* and all the other genre pictures of the time should represent their figures so true to this description.

Prince Genji's fabulous wealth, in spite of his being reduced to subject status by his imperial father, is what makes him the paragon of the world of the Heian court. He possessed two palaces in the city, Nijō-in and Rokujō-in, and there he lodged and cared for his numerous lady-loves, not all together in a harem but separately, each in her own wing, ranked according to her standing. Although Genji groans loudly at the wearisome state business which accompanies his high offices, he none the less is able to devote much of his time and thoughts to the ladies, especially his beloved concubine Murasaki. A man of his rank had to participate in all the court ceremonies and appear at all receptions, banquets and official temple celebrations such as the Kamo Feast with a suitable entourage. He had to spend most of his time at court, entertaining their Majesties, playing the princely sport of *kemari* football, making music and joining in *bugaku* dances and poetry contests. Hunting and riding excursions, even archery or fencing, were beneath his dignity.

What Genji had to do in his political and administrative offices is not known, but whatever it was he did it with reluctance. The basis of all learning at that time, Chinese and classical Chinese literature, which of

164
Genji-monogatari-emaki: Chapter 50, 'Azumaya I' (detail of Pl. 186). Colours and ink on paper. H. 21.8 cm. L. 39.2 cm. First quarter of the twelfth century. Tokugawa Reimeikai Foundation, Tōkyō. In the lower right-hand corner sit the maid servants of Nakanogimi, while their mistress (left) is having her hair combed and dried. Ukifune, her half-sister, is looking at *monogatari* pictures. The court ladies are wearing official court costume with patterned silk garments in delicately combined colours. The three-quarter profile of one and the lost profile of the other show the standardized method of portraying women's faces in *tsukuri-e,* which is described as 'stroke for an eye, hook for a nose'.

course included poetry, formed part of the education of a noble. At the coming-of-age celebration for his son Yūgiri, he admitted that his education showed gaps due to his having been brought up in the palace. But now his son was to attend university. Poor Yūgiri now had to accept the despised sixth rank—he was entitled to the fourth. The boy had to study under the scholars and doctors of the university, described as contemptible and ludicrous, and clearly this gave him an inferiority complex.

For in the life of an aristocrat love adventures were ultimately more important. The second chapter of the novel already describes how at night Genji discussed with his brother-in-law Chūjō, and with Uma no Kami and Tō-Shikibu no Jō the psychology of the different types of women in all classes of society. They assess the types and nuances of relationship to such an extent among themselves that one wonders whether a lady could have understood this classification of her own sex. There are, of course, very sharp judgments on the other ladies of the court to be found in the diary of Murasaki Shikibu; Sei Shōnagon in particular is presented as arrogant and egocentric, and her free behaviour censured.

Daily life was restricted by prohibitions and taboos as well as by court ceremonial: by obligations of ritual hygiene, ritual uncleanliness such as contact with death, illness, birth, women's menstruation or even bad dreams, which Shintō required to be countered by claustration, or by geomantic prohibitions of certain unlucky directions (coming from the Chinese doctrine of *yin* and *yang*) which had to be circumvented by being avoided. They interfered with normal life, though at times they could provide excellent excuses and escapes from disagreeable situations.

Medical knowledge was exceptionally narrow. Acupuncture had been adopted from China, it is true, and for many afflications cautery at certain nerve centres by moxibustion was used. The sick were diagnosed and treated according to the Tao method using *yin* and *yang* doctrine. Mostly, however, sickness was attributed to possession by evil spirits or influences, which had to be driven out and transferred to a medium through the Dhārāni spells of exorcists, usually Buddhist priests.

The sensitive man of the Heian period, inclined to the Buddhist philosophy of the vanity of earthly things, aspired to become a monk. Many of the characters in the Genji novel free themselves in this way from their human ties and aberrations. Prince Genji himself often expressed his decision to became a monk, but he never did; he was a child of this world, with many loveable traits for which his contemporaries idolized him. Posterity too pays him the tribute of a millennium of admiration as the inimitable image of one of the great and distinctive periods of Japanese history.

Whercas the vision we derive from literature of the noble Heian lord is vague and blurred, our picture of Heian women is lively and clear-cut. This we owe to the boredom of the court ladies, who used their privileged position as a 'leisured class' with great diligence to write and describe, each according to her temperament and fantasy, the life she dreamed of or the life she soberly observed. In her *Pillow Book* Sei Shōnagun comments on the life of married court ladies:

> When I make myself imagine what it is like to be one of those women who live at home, faithfully serving their husbands —women who have not a single exciting prospect in life yet who believe they are perfectly happy—I am filled with scorn. Often they are of quite good birth, yet have had no opportunity to find out what the world is like. I wish they could live for a while in our society, even if it should mean taking service as Attendants, so that they might come to know the delights it has to offer.
>
> I cannot bear men who believe that women serving in the Palace are bound to be frivolous and wicked. Yet I suppose their prejudice is understandable. After all, women at Court do not spend their time hiding modestly behind fans and screens, but walk about, looking openly at people they chance to meet. Yes, they see everyone face to face, not only ladies-in-waiting like themselves, but even Their Imperial Majesties (whose august names I hardly dare mention), High Court Nobles, senior courtiers, and other gentlemen of high rank. In the presence of such exalted personages the women in the Palace are all equally brazen, whether they be the maids of ladies-in-waiting, or the relations of court ladies who have come to visit them, or housekeepers, or latrine-cleaners, or women who are of no more value than a roof-tile or a pebble. Small wonder that the young men regard them as immodest: Yet are the gentlemen themselves any less so? They are not exactly bashful when it comes to looking at the great people of the Palace. No, everyone at Court is much the same in this respect.[43]

A woman at the court sat with the eyes of the world, and of men, upon her, enveloped in many layers of costly silk garments and rather restricted in her movements, on a platform behind her state screen, with a writing desk in front of her. We find her thus in the poem paintings. She watched the great events of court life that went on outside in the open air, from behind bamboo curtains or from her ox-drawn carriage. Only the stiff cuffs of her sleeves, with their elegantly graded shades of colour, were visible to the outer world. Faces remained hidden, and even when the lady had to appear, she always hid her face—which was thickly made up with artificial eyebrows and blackened teeth according to the ideal of the time—behind a fan.

A woman was given in marriage by her father or else vanquished on the spot by a lover, who was able to steal in behind her curtain after a ritual exchange of poems. In the *Genji-monogatari* the gentlemen's attempts at conquest were not at all always successful and sometimes led to disaster. Murasaki describes with great psychological perspicacity how ambiguous the reactions of the ladies could be to the numerous amorous advances of Prince Genji.

Lady Shikibu also writes very informatively in her journal about the life of the royal family. The confinement of Empress Akiko, daughter of Fujiwara no Michinaga, in 1001 is recounted with a great sense of drama. The picture of the room of the birth, all decorated in white, in Michinaga's palace is placed vividly before our eyes, with the crowds of priests and courtiers all reciting sutras or performing magical rites until
208 the crown prince at last sees the light. The *Gaki-no-sōshi-emaki* also gives a representation of a birth scene, but in a lesser house, threatened eerily by invisible hunger spirits of a lower level of existence.

Every heart beat with deep devotion to children. The Murasaki in the novel, whom Genji took when she was still a child, is deeply sad that she herself cannot have children. She therefore took Genji's daughter by Princess Akashi with great affection, albeit not without a certain tinge of jealousy, to take the place of one of her own.

According to the status of the marriage (wife or concubine), the woman remained in her parent's house or might move into her husband's. Little difference was made in rank between the chief wives and the concubines, apparently.[44] Of course in normal life writing and composing poems was not the essential activity of a woman. The housewife's tasks were much more prosaic: washing and sewing her husband's clothes. Dyeing too was among the feminine arts, and the Murasaki of the novel was highly gifted in this art. Clothes were needed not only for wearing but also as gifts on every occasion, such as the New Year, and as rewards, so sewing and dyeing were important activities in the house. The mother-in-law of the great Fujiwara no Michinaga is said to have sewn new clothes for the Chancellor twice each year, according to W. McCul-

lough. In the case of the magnificent court robes of the high dignitaries, this task of the lady of the house and her servants provided plenty of occupation. Nothing was so ridiculed as old-fashion clothes, especially when they were given as gifts. One has only to think of Suetsumuhana's gift of clothing to Prince Genji!

All the same, equal rights for women, if one may use this newly fashionable expression, went unchallenged in the sphere of literature, though only there, and only in literature in the Japanese language. Without consideration of gender, poems by women had been as highly valued as those by men ever since the Nara period. A man of education expected a woman to have mastered the art of writing thirty-one-syllable *waka* poems using all relevant vocabulary, allusions and evocations of nature that make a poem a work of art. And not only the poem itself but also an accomplished copy in a hand that corresponded specially to a woman's style and character, 'woman's hand', was expected. Women's calligraphy in the Heian period was so highly esteemed as a cultivated and genuinely Japanese art and as an individual form of expression that the great poet Ki no Tsurayuki wrote his journal, *Tosa-nikki,* as though it had been written by a woman.

Poetry owes its special aura to this specifically feminine variant of aesthetic sensibility, but in later, harder times the visual arts of the Heian court were often described in derogatory tones as effeminate. In fact, the depth of feeling and heightened sensibility that have indelibly stamped many elements of Japanese art stem precisely from this period, when the ladies of the imperial court were permitted to speak in words not only of feeling but of reason, wit and malice in a manner quite inimitable.

Costume

With court ceremony continuing unchanged into the Heian period, the costume required for these functions naturally underwent no change either. At court the emperor and empress no less than the nobility down to the fifth rank still wore the appropriate state robes adopted from China. The emperor's robes will not have altered in the mid-Heian period to anything like the extent that the hair styles and dresses of the ladies did. These conformed increasingly to the Japanese taste at this time.

The emperor's festive robe for the coronation, harvest thanksgiving and New Year celebrations was the height of magnificence, a simple 'large sleeve garment' called *ōsode*. It was scarlet and cut like a kimono with long sleeves, had a wide overlap from the left to the right armpit and was profusely embroidered with emblems of good luck. The *ōsode* was held together by a pleated apron *(mo)*, and a precious jewel-studded girdle with a pendant of embroidered and painted silk belted it in. Beneath the *ōsode* the emperor wore a short-sleeved kimono over a white shirt *(hitoe)*. Both these garments were visible at neck and arm openings as bands. Two pairs of trousers belonged to the *ōsode*, red and white, worn one over the other. On his feet, the emperor wore silk socks and shoes of black lacquered leather. Emperor and nobles all held a sceptre in their right hand as an emblem of dignity. The emperor wore a *kammuri* cap of black gauze on his head, under a golden crown with a square frame and a sun-disc as the symbol of majesty.

Imperial princes were in somewhat simpler apparel, being mostly of the first, second or third ranks. They wore a monochrome *ōsode*, pulled over the *mo* apron in front. The embroidered belt had a fringed band hanging from it to which the richly fashioned court sword was attached, and on their heads the princes wore small crowns over the *kammuri* cap.

165 For all other court ceremonies the emperor and the nobles down to the ninth rank wore a *sokutai* robe. This was an overgarment like a coat, with a narrow round collar and broad straight sleeves. It closed from the left and had a broad flared hem. The girdle fastening it was only visible at the back. The material varied according to rank; only the high nobles could wear black damask. Under it was a brocade jacket and a short white kimono

165
Ban-Dainagon-ekotoba: Scroll 1, last scene. Ink and colours on paper. H. 31.5 cm. *c.* 1170. Private collection, Tōkyō.
Fujiwara no Yoshifusa receives permission to speak to Emperor Seiwa on behalf of the innocent Minamoto no Makoto, wrongly accused of arson by Ban Dainagon. The Chancellor of the Left leaves the palace, dressed in a summery *sokutai* robe.

166
Murasaki-Shikibu-nikki-ekotoba: Section 5, scene 10. Colours and ink on paper. H. 20.9 cm. Mid-thirteenth century. Fujita Art Museum, Ōsaka.
On the fiftieth day after the birth of the future Ichijō-Tennō, his grandfather, High Chancellor Fujiwara no Michinaga, stands on the verandah of his palace and looks at the new pleasure boats in the moonlight. He wears a *naoshi* cloak over his full *sashinuki* trousers and has covered his head with a *kammuri* cap.

173

167
Nenjū-gyōji-emaki (detail of a copy of the original of *c.* 1160): Scroll 5, scene 4. Ink and colour on paper. H. 45.2 cm. Private collection.
Court servants in white *kariginu* garments with *eboshi* caps wait in front of the palace. One of them sits on a lacquered stool.

168
Murasaki-Shikibu-nikki-ekotoba: Section 4, scene 14. Colours and ink on paper. H. 20.9 cm. Mid-thirteenth century. Private collection.
After the feast celebrating the fiftieth day after the birth of the crown prince the courtiers, inebriated with *sake,* dally with the ladies-in-waiting of the empress on the veran-dahs of the palace.

169
Genji-monogatari-emaki: Chapter 49, 'Yadorigi III', scene 2. Colours and ink on paper. H. 21.4 cm, L. 37.8 cm. First quarter of the twelfth century. Tokugawa Reimeikai Foundation, Tōkyō.
After the third night of love, Prince Niou and his young wife Rokunogimi awake on their marriage bed. In the anteroom a crowd of maid servants is waiting; Niou sees his wife for the first time in daylight.

49 with a long train, in the case of the regents as much as 4 metres long. Nobles let their train hang over the railing of the verandah when they were seated. Next to the skin was a shirt of fine white linen to which a coloured collar and arm band were attached.

With the *sokutai* the high nobles wore flat caps of black gauze with a 'pigtail' trailing at the back and a stiff lacquered band hanging down; lords of the sixth rank downwards had fine caps with two flaps. The court cap *(eboshi)* like a tall stiff bonnet, was less formal.

The *ikan* costume too was less official, with no train and the overgarment belted with a cord and the leather strap of the sword; at the back the coat bloused over the belt. Beneath the outer garment, baggy breeches were worn, joined together at the ankles.

Inside the palace and at home the lords wore a light garment *(naoshi)* (in which Genji, we are told, was quite 166 irresistible), of a cut similar to the *sokutai* overcoat. A red and a white undergarment went with the simple trousers. Court caps and fans went with the suit.

Hunting costume *(kariginu)* was also worn by the 167 lesser nobles; the sleeves, only sewn to the back, al-

175

lowed plenty of freedom of movement. Servants were only allowed to wear white *kariginu.* Even more comfortable was a suit consisting of a short jacket-like overcoat that tucked into the trousers.

The state robes of the empress corresponded to the ceremonial costume of the emperor. There were twelve 125 layers *(jūni-hitoe)* of narrow kimonos under a divided skirt, scarlet in colour. The garment next to the skin had long sleeves in which the hands could be hidden. 168 The middle *hitoe* had five false collars and sleeve bands, the colour grading of which was strictly regulated, for personal taste was expressed not in the cut of the garment but only in the nuances of its colours. At court this costume was covered by a brocade jacket reaching to the waist, and on top of this the *uwagi* was worn. Over that was bound a back train of thin white embroidered silk.

But the crowning glory of feminine beauty and 169 toilette was long trailing hair, sometimes bound but usually left free and often supplemented with false locks. The empress, like the emperor, had a crown-like ornament of gold and a fan to hide her face, like every lady at court.

For informal court wear, the ladies only needed four garments that were left unbelted. The court serving women wore white silk garments, often with painted designs, and over them a brocade jacket. For going out, noble ladies threw a veiling cloak over their heads.

The women among the commoners, as they are 51 shown in the *Shigisan-engi-emaki* often only wore a linen garment, held in at the waist with a cord or an apron. Richer ladies wore several coloured, kimono-like gowns. In the city women wore large straw hats shaped like plant pots, covered with a veil on journeys.

Monks and priests are recognizable by the simple kimono with a pleated skirt and a black cloak of linen or 173 grass. Over this was worn the priestly scarf, a broad cloth sewn together from pieces of brocade, intended to imitate the patched garment of the Buddha. Police and knights dressed hardly differently from civilians. The palace watch were recognizable by their caps, which had a fan-like cockade of horsehair at the side. They were regularly armed with a sword and a mighty bow, and carried a quiver full of arrows at their backs. For fighting the knights had their decoratively laced ar- 145, 172 mour worn over a kimono and gaiter-like trousers. On their heads they wore small folded *eboshi,* while the generals wore finely forged iron helmets crested with imposing horn-like ornaments.

170
Portrait of Taira no Shigemori (1138–1179): traditionally ascribed to Fujiwara no Takanobu. Ink and colours on paper. H. 139 cm, W. 112 cm. Jingo-ji, Kyōto.
This portrait belongs to the group produced in the entourage of the Ex-emperor Goshirakawa; it is said to be of Shigemori. He wears the court robe with *kammuri* cap and has a *shaku* sceptre and dress sword. The sparsely drawn facial features of this *nise-e* portrait in *Yamato-e* style are very individually characterized.

All the costumes described here are represented in the *Nenjū-gyōji-emaki,* from the emperor—though not in his highest state robes—down to policemen and the women of the plebians. Fujiwara no Takanobu portrayed the lords of the upper nobility in grand *sokutai* 170, 202 costume in the portraits in the Jingo-ji. The ladies and gentlemen of the court appear in the *Genji-monogatari-emaki* in the more intimate *naoshi* costume. Official court robes are worn by the ladies in the chapter entitled

171
Heiji-monogatari-emaki: Scroll 3: Rokuhara-gyōkō. Colours and ink on paper. H. 42.4 cm. Late thirteenth century. Tōkyō National Museum, Tōkyō.
The scene shows the flight of Emperor Nijō from the imperial palace, to escape from rebellious troops. He is disguised as a woman and leaves the palace in a cart under the eyes of suspicious Minamoto warriors.

172
Hampi Coat. Woven silk. H. 36.1 cm. Mid-twelfth century. Itsukushima-jinja, Hiroshima.
This little sleeveless silk coat came to the shrine in Hiroshima as a votive offering. It is woven in a refined Chinese 'brocade' style, with a repeat pattern of circles containing cranes and *kishi* flowers. *Hampi* were worn under armour.

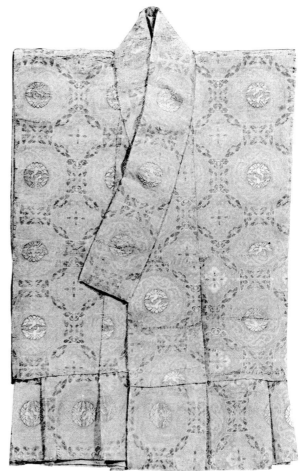

9 Yadorigi, they wear a brocade jacket and *mo* apron as they attend on the emperor and Prince Kaoru playing in the anteroom at a game of *gō*.

The artist has throughout the work taken great delight in the colour schemes of the ladies' robes, seen in rainbow gradations at the wide sleeve openings. Often, as in the *Nenjū-gyōji-emaki,* the presence of great ladies is betrayed solely by a sleeve protruding from under the bamboo curtain.

The officers and men of the palace guard and other single warriors are met, with or without their armour but always with their bow and arrows, in the *Ban-Dainagon-ekotoba*. In the Kamakura period they are

173

Fragment of silk with Buddhist motifs. *Nishiki* silk. H. 204 cm, W. 57 cm. Late Heian period. Ninna-ji, Kyōto.

The motif of the sacred pearl on a lotus and the ground pattern with thunderbolts identifies this splendid silk as a piece of a priest's scarf (*ōhi*). According to tradition it belonged to Prince Abbot Shōshin Hōshinnō, who died in 1085. Judging by the sophisticated weaving technique, it might be of a later date.

174

Ban-Dainagon-ekotoba: Scroll 3, scene 5, attributed to Fujiwara (Tokiwa) no Mitsunaga. Ink and colours on paper. H. 31.5 cm. *c.* 1170. T. Sakai Collection, Tōkyō.

After the guilty Ban Danaigon has been seized, his palace is given over to great distress; the ladies and servant girls succumb to their sorrow. In the room we see the daily utensils of a noble family.

175
Nenjū-gyōji-emaki (detail of a copy of the original of *c.* 1160): Scroll 5, scene 4. Ink and light colours on paper. H. 45.8 cm. Private collection.
Following the New Year banquet a contest in the composition of Chinese poems is being held in the Jijū-den Hall behind the Shishinden. The emperor is participating in disguise. Behind the great men stands a laid table and stools for the diners.

176
Nenjū-gyōji-emaki (copy of the original of *c.* 1160): Scroll 5, scene 5. Ink and light colours on paper. H. 45.8 cm. Private collection.
After the poetic contest we see the gentlemen seated at table.

mostly promoted to being the heroes of the stories. In 171 the *Heiji-monogatari-e* we are eye-witnesses of the events of the year 1159 to 1160, when the lovely city of Heian-kyō was occupied by the mounted hosts of the Taira and Minamoto clans, the emperor and ex-emperor taken prisoner and the palaces burnt down. Despite this and later *inferni* the state apparel of the emperor and empress, of the court nobles and ladies has persisted to this day and is still worn on ceremonial occasions.

Food and Drink

While at court supreme importance was attached to the elegance of robes and the minutiae of costume, the pleasures of the palate do not seem to have played an essential part in the life of the Heian aristocracy. More importance was attached to the arrangement of the food than to its taste, and much attention was paid to the lacquer and ceramic on which it was served.

At court there were two main meals, described in detail by I. Morris.[45] It was customary to serve every person of rank on a tall standing tray of lacquered wood. 174 Polished rice, the food of the upper classes, was piled in a pyramid in the centre of a plate, surrounded by little dishes with a variety of vegetables and fish, shell fish, radishes or seaweed. Fish was eaten boiled, baked or pickled. The food was all served in small pieces that could be comfortably managed with chopsticks. Meat was entirely avoided on Buddhist principles, though an exception was made sometimes for wild fowl.

Water and rice wine were the usual drinks. *Sake* at that time contained less alcohol than the modern spirit. Thus we can understand how the gentlemen of the court enjoyed drinking their wine at every festive occasion and were always falling into sentimental or amorous moods. Murasaki Shikibu describes in her diary such scenes in the palace of Fujiwara no Michinaga. 168

Nuts and fruit were served with the wine and sometimes a sorbet, made from ice kept in cellars and mixed with liana syrup.

The *Nenjū-gyōji-emaki* shows the lower nobles at a 175–176 common table for a great banquet. The *literati* who have taken part in the poetry contests sit on bamboo stools at flat tables. For other groups, such as the priests, meals are laid out on mats in the palace courtyard, and the diners sit on the ground. Palace servants hold burning torches to light the proceedings. The festive hustle and bustle of these occasions can be vividly imagined.

On special occasions rice cakes with all kinds of delicious additions were served. On the Day of the Boar in the Tenth Month one partook of seven different colours of cake, to prevent sickness and promote fertility. In the *Genji-monogatari* Murasaki is offered these cakes in a pretty *hinoki* wood box. Prince Genji later orders white cakes for her, which are to be placed with gifts on her pillow after the third night of love—a wedding custom.[46]

Page-girls called *uneme* are shown waiting on Their Majesties at table. They wear particularly enchanting painted garments and brocade jackets, adding a cheerful note to the ceremonial scenes of palace life.

IV Literature and Life as Reflected in Painting

Yamato-e and the Genji-monogatari-emaki

> The rains of early summer continued without a break, even gloomier than in most years. The ladies at Rokujō-in amused themselves with illustrated romances. The Akashi lady, a talented painter, sent pictures to her daughter.
>
> (*The Tale of Genji*, translated by E. G. Seidensticker, p. 437)

All writing in Japan was done, right from the earliest contact with Chinese culture, not in books but on hand scrolls *(makimono)*. These were made of sheets of paper or strips of silk glued together horizontally, and they might be many metres in length. The handy *makimono* was also used for the kind of painting intended for private contemplation, for it was equally suitable for sketching and for finished works of art of high quality.

Fragments survive in Japan of a hand-scroll edition of eight scrolls of Buddhist content, the *Illustrated Sutra of Cause and Effect*, or *Sutra of Past and Present Karma (Kakō-genzai-e-inga-kyō)*, from the first half of the eighth century. In the form transmitted from China it depicts details from the previous and historical lives of the Buddha Shaka in such a way that, in parallel above the text, the wonderful events are rendered in a series of separate little scenes.

Two and a half centuries later, the highly developed narrative literature of the Heian period gave the first incentive to the really great original creations of Japanese painting: the *Yamato-e* scrolls, *emakimono* or *emaki*. *Waka* poetry had already inspired an individual Japanese lyrical style of painting. The delight in multiple aesthetic expression brought forth a composite work of language, calligraphy and picture very early in Japan, a form of art supported by the dominant taste of the court nobility. First, as was explained above, came the pictorial responses to *waka* poems, which gave the germ, the 'heart picture' *(kokoro-e)*, the mood of the poem. The sliding doors and folding screens in noble palaces provided the decorative frame for them.

Around the year 1000, when Murasaki Shikibu was writing the novel of the 'Shining Prince Genji', it was one of the favorite past-times of courtiers to contem-

186 plate illustrations of novels *(monogatari-e)*, to paint them in a dilettante way and to compete among each other in painting contests. We are told in the novel in chapter 17, 'E-awase', that scrolls with pictures of the

Taketori-monogatari, Ise-monogatari, Utsubo-monogatari and the *Shō-Sammi-monogatari* were all submitted by artists of the time for the picture contests, so there must already have been outstanding representations of Japanese people in their surroundings.

Where are the earliest illustrations of typical Japanese people to be seen today? A few sketches, hidden from the public, showing men in Japanese costume, were discovered in 1955 on the frames of the wall paintings in the Hōō-dō of the Byōdō-in at Uji. The haughty lords with round faces are clearly distinguishable from the Chinese figures, depicted as the Japanese saw or imagined them, on a chest in Kyōōgokoku-ji and on the 177 famous *senzui-byōbu* formerly in the same temple in a 138 similar manner. The gaunt gesticulating Chinese diverge not only in their clothing from the ideal Japanese aristocrat, but also in their faces. The former are grotesque, ugly or comical in comparison to the latter, who are dignified and measured, with rounded faces.

The paintings with scenes from the life of Prince Regent Shōtoku Taishi (574–622) are now mounted on five-fold wall screens; originally they decorated the Pic- 178 ture Hall of the Hōryū-ji. They are by the painter Hata no Chitei (Munesada), who also painted the statue of Shōtoku, and are dated to the year 1069. A landscape seen as though from afar and from above is the background for fifty-eight separate scenes of episodes from the life of Shōtoku; they are on three planes but irregu-

177
Karabitsu Trunk. Wood with colour painting and red outlines. H. 49.2 cm, W. 82.3 cm. Ninth century. Kyōōgokoku-ji (Tōji), Kyōto.
The wooden trunk in the Tōji is important in the history of painting: it has on its sides, though rather naively portrayed, pictures of Chinese playing a variety of games. The delight in caricature is a feature that can be observed throughout *Kara-e* of the Heian period.

178
Shōtoku Taishi eden (detail): by Hata no Chitei (Munesada). Formerly decorating the walls of the Edono of the Hōryū-ji; now five two-part standing screens. H. (each) 181.3 cm, L. 272.7 cm. 1069. Tōkyō National Museum, Tōkyō.
The esoteric Buddhist sects saw Crown Prince Shōtoku Taishi as a reincarnation of the Buddha and recorded the episodes of his life and previous existences. In his fourteenth year took place the destruction of Buddhist sanctuaries, instigated by Mononobe and Nakatomi. A pagoda is being pulled down, and the statue of the Buddha thrown into the Naniwa Canal. This painting of 1069 marks the beginning of Japanese *Yamato-e*: the houses, people and landscape details all have Japanese features.

larly placed, and there are cartouches of inscription for the lay. Unmistakably Japanese, the overcrowded and very animated landscape shows Mount Fuji on the horizon of the third panel; Shōtoku is said to have climbed to the top on his horse in his twenty-seventh year. Though the core of the picture is Buddhist in inspiration, since Shōtoku is equated with the Buddha Shaka, unambiguous Japanese figures appear here. The women are all court ladies, wearing many-layered silk robes; their hair hangs free, a fashion only known in Japan at the time.

The earliest hand-scroll work of *Yamato-e,* as famous as it is characteristically Japanese, is the *Genji-monogatari-emaki,* the scrolls of the Genji novel. Fragments have survived in four scrolls from the first half of the twelfth century. The twenty painted scenes and twenty-nine pieces of text from 2 to 109 lines in length, are now in separate rigid frames. Fifteen of the paintings belong to the Tokugawa Reimeikai Foundation and four to the Gotoh Art Museum (formerly Masuda Collection), both in Tōkyō. A fragment with later overpainting is in the Tōkyō National Museum. The extremely lavish execution of the paintings and the precious decorated papers on which the text fragments are written suggest that the work was a commission from the imperial court. Fujiwara no Mototoki's journal, *Chōshū-ki,* records that in 1119 a series of Genji paintings were made in ten scrolls, commissioned by Ex-emperor Shirakawa; whether or not these were the very ones we now have is not known. The painter or painters, who perhaps belonged to the court Painting Bureau, are not known, though there is an old tradition that Fujiwara no Takayoshi was the artist. The calligraphy of the text shows five distinct hands. It is precisely in the context of a court commission that artists of all the arts would be recruited to work on such a communal project, in the same way as for the deluxe sutras. Perhaps the *Genji-monogatari-emaki* we know today date from ten or twelve years after Ex-emperor Toba held the government and power in his own hands following the death of his grandfather Shirakawa in 1129. He himself and his wives, Taikemmon-in (Tama-ko, 1101–1145) and Bifukumon-in (Toku-ko, 1117–1160), all encouraged the arts. Like the court ladies of a century earlier at the time of Murasaki Shikibu, they took a burning interest in illustrations for novels, for these showed them a perpetuation of their own world of feeling and thoughts and of their own sphere of life. Each separate section of the work

measures 21.4 to 22 centimetres in height by 39 or 48–49 centimetres in length. The sections can be conveniently looked at as a whole and do not, like the later continuous narrative pictures, press the eye ever onward. The composition of the pictures is completely new. As in the novel, the stress is on people and their moods, not on events. To make the figures visible in the interiors of the palace, the houses are without roofs, 'with blown-away roofs' *(fukinuki yatai)* so that a bird's-eye view of the interiors is created in a kind of isometric drawing. Since the sides of the houses and the rooms are rarely parallel to the plane of the picture but lead diagonally into the distance, the picture space is bounded vertically by columns and pillars. Often a building protrudes into the picture plane, however, to emphasize the continuity and accidental nature of the confines of the picture. In this armature of architectural space rendered geometrically and lineally, the people are revealed as though lifelessly given up to their feelings, hardly ever involved in any activity.

Following the mode and taste of the time, stiff clothes envelop the figures. The ladies in their rigidly pleated silk garments and cascades of black hair look like butterflies. The men wear the tall black court caps that show their ranks, even on their deathbed. The faces have no personal features, though in their noble reserve there are many nuances of feeling. They are drawn according to the formula 'a line for the eye, a hook for the nose' *(hikime-kagihana).* We have an exception however in Emperor Suzaku, who became a monk: he sits weeping at the sickbed of his favourite daughter Onna Sanno Miya because she has decided to become a nun.

The strong use of colour gives these pictures an almost ornamental emphasis. This is achieved by means of a painting technique called 'built-up, made-up painting' *(tsukuri-e).* It was started with a drawing in ink. Over this was put a layer of burnt shell-lime ground

179

Genji-monogatari-emaki: Chapter 36, 'Kashiwagi I.' Colours and ink on paper. H. 21.9 cm, L. 48.3 cm. First quarter of the twelfth century. Tokugawa Reimeikai Foundation, Tōkyō.
Ex-emperor Suzaku sits in the centre of a room that is divided by curtains on rails. He is wiping tears from his face, distressed because his daughter, Princess Onno Sanno Miya, who is lying sick in a bed on the left, has decided to become a nun. Prince Genji in the foreground is also deeply moved. The mood of despair and sorrow is echoed by the court ladies on the right, and even the colour composition emphasizes the profound melancholy of the scene.

179, 183

179

179–187

180
Genji-monogatari-emaki: Chapter 36, 'Kashiwagi III.' Colours and ink on paper. H. 21.9 cm, L. 48.1 cm. First quarter of the twelfth century. Tokugawa Reimeikai Foundation, Tōkyō.
This scene takes place inside the palace where Prince Genji, on the fiftieth day after the birth of his alleged son Kaoru is holding the baby in his arms and looking at him thoughtfully. Six red lacquer trays with food are ceremonially laid out in a row. The baby's mother, Princess Onna Sanno Miya, is resting concealed on the left at the back; her maid servants are seated in front. Only the splendid coloured hems of the sleeves of one of them is peeping out from behind the curtains.

Genji-monogatari-emaki: Chapter 37, 'Yokobue'. Colours and ink on paper. H. 21.9 cm, L. 38.7 cm. First quarter of the twelfth century. Tokugawa Reimeikai Foundation, Tōkyō.
As Genji's son Yūgiri comes home secretly at night, he sees a delightful scene: his wife Kumoinokari gives suck to her baby. The group of the mother and her maid servants behind the drawn curtains is lit up by lamp light. On the left, the room is enclosed by a decorative landscape on a sliding door.

182
Genji-monogatari-emaki: Chapter 38, 'Suzumushi I'. Colours and ink on paper. H. 21.8 cm, L. 47.4 cm. First quarter of the twelfth century. Gotoh Art Museum, Tōkyō.
On the night of the full moon of the fifteenth day of the Eighth Month, Prince Genji visits Princess Onna Sanno Miya, who has become a nun, in the Sanjō Palace. The princess is in an inner room, leaning in prayer against a doorpost, while a young nun, who has made her sacrifice to the Buddha, is listening to the insects in the garden.

('Chinese powder') that made a basis for the colours, which were mainly powdered minerals. Right at the end, after the application of the colours, came the fine lines in ink, drawn without accents, and the black parts—hair and caps—were overlaid with brilliant India ink mixed with lime. In places a ground was painted over in thin silver paint and a few lines of drapery were picked out in gold.

One picture—the second in the series—falls completely outside the norm in the *Genji-monogatari-emaki* series because it takes place in an open landscape and not indoors. Chapter 16 of the novel, 'Sekiya', describes the meeting between Genji, who is on a pilgrimage to Ishiyama with his attendants, and the cortege of the governor of Hitachi, who is returning to the capital. Genji had once loved Utsusemi, the wife of the governor; feeling moved, he sends her a poem. The two trains appear in the middle ground of the picture between rounded and steep mountains. In the left-hand third of the picture, riders and ox carriages are con-

183
Genji-monogatari-emaki: Chapter 40, 'Minori'. Colours and ink on paper. H. 21.8 cm, L. 48.3 cm. First quarter of the twelfth century. Gotoh Art Museum, Tōkyō.
On a stormy autumn night, Prince Genji visits his concubine Murasaki, who is dying. In an inner room on the right, Murasaki lies, hiding her face, with her arm on an arm-rest (cf. Pl. 125). In the foreground, on the right, the head of Empress Akashi is visible. Genji sits facing the sick woman on the verandah, his face hidden in his sleeve. The melancholy of the meeting is intensified by the silvery autumnal atmosphere in the garden.

184 ▷
Genji-monogatari-emaki: Chapter 39, 'Yūgiri'. Colours and ink on paper. H. 21.8 cm, L. 39.5 cm. First quarter of the twelfth century. Gotoh Art Museum, Tōkyō.
In the Sanjō-in Prince Yūgiri is at his writing desk reading a letter from Ochiba, written on richly patterned paper. Driven by jealousy, his wife Kumoinokari approaches and seizes the letter. Servants are sitting in the neighbouring room.

185 ▷
Genji-monogatari-emaki: Chapter 48, 'Sawarabi'. Colours and ink on paper. H. 21.4 cm, L. 39.2 cm. First quarter of the twelfth century. Tokugawa Reimeikai Foundation, Tōkyō.
In a mountain villa in Uji, preparations are going on for the departure of Lady Nakanogimi to Heian-kyō, where she will become the official concubine of Prince Niou. Unhappy at leaving, Nakanogimi lies in her back room. Separated from her by simple cloth screens, her attendants are preparing fabrics, while Bennogimi speaks comfortingly to her mistress.

fronted. On the right rise a *torii* and shrine buildings, and *kana* characters from the poem to Utsusemi are almost invisibly inserted as *uta-e* into the landscape; they refer to the spring in the frontier mountain pass. On the horizon above is a distant view of the shore of Lake Biwa. There is no tension nor activity in this scene either; as in all the other pictures, the landscape and the figures float in uncertainty. Unfortunately the picture is very worn and details are hard to recognize.

'Egg-coloured paper' was used as the support for the paintings of the *Genji-monogatari-emaki*. It is a specially firm, smooth and absorbent paper made from rice and paper-mulberry fibres, stiffened with fillers and lime.

The mineral colours used on it were ground malachite for the bright green, azurite for blue, lead and mercury combinations for the cinnabar and orange-red tones. The white, of white lead or burnt shell-lime, is a colour that often tends to oxidize to violet or to discolour. Yel-

Genji-monogatari-emaki: Chapter 50, 'Azumaya I'. Colours and ink on paper. H. 21.5 cm, L. 48.9 cm. First quarter of the twelfth century. Tokugawa Reimeikai Foundation, Tōkyō.
Nakanogimi has her half sister Ukifune in her house, concealed from the Nijō Palace. While Ukifune is having her hair washed, she is being entertained with *monogatari-e*, which she looks at while a servant reads the text to her.

low and tea-coloured hues were obtained from ochres or organic materials.

The decorated papers of the text parts came from the same workshops that supplied the sutra scribes.

In the imperial palace there was a special Office for Writing Materials from which, in chapter 37 of the novel, Prince Genji orders particularly beautiful writing paper. On it he writes the *Amida Sutra* for Onna Sanno Miya. The calligraphic elements of the *Genji-monogatari-emaki* are written on just such select court writing paper. The variations of ground colouring and the cloud scatter with all the usual patterns in leaves, grains and strips of gold and silver foil from the workshop's repertory are often enriched here with pictorial motifs in gold and silver paint: whirlpools, butterflies, snow crystals.

The calligraphy is the work of several hands. If, as T. Akiyama claims,[47] the work originally consisted of about ten scrolls, the enormous task of copying could only be done with a team of scribes, and they would certainly be *nōsho* of the court atelier. Even though, in

130

187
Genji-monogatari-emaki: Chapter 44, 'Takegawa II.' Colours and ink
on paper. H. 22 cm, L. 48.1 cm. First quarter of the twelfth century.
Tokugawa Reimeikai Foundation, Tōkyō.
The figures are grouped round a flowering cherry tree in the inner
garden. On the left the daughters of Tamakazura are playing *gō;* the
stake is the cherry tree. The spring-like atmosphere is stressed by the
splendid garments of the servants on the verandah. On the right Tō
no Chūjō is watching the scene through the blinds.

Legend and History in the *Emaki*

keeping with the text of the novel, the writing was in
the cursive *kana* of the women's style, it is still possible
to distinguish five different hands.

The picture narratives devoted to women's writing
were described as women's painting. The laws of representation for the composition of the picture and the
rendering of figures were fully mastered and firmly applied in the *Genji-monogatari-emaki*. Henceforth the later
hand scrolls, with their illustrations of novels and
women's journals, faithfully followed this totally
Japanese method of painting with its very decorative
abstractions.

The antithesis of this style arose in one developed as a
matter of course for eventful dramatic narrative. It is
called 'report painting' and was art for men. These reports might deal with legendary material such as the
foundation of temples or else with historical events.
The drawing here is executed with rapid brush movements; space stretches into the infinite over the whole
length of the scroll, and the painter was able to capture
the whole space-time continuum of the happening in a
vivid rhythm.

The three scrolls of the *Shigisan-engi-emaki* were 51, 188-191
painted between 1160 and 1170. They are devoted to
representations of legends pertaining to the miracles of
the god of Mount Shigisan in Yamato and were intended as a chronicle for the temple itself. The scrolls
were perhaps dedicated to the temple by the court in
Heian-kyō, for the Shigisan and its protecting deity,
Bishamon-ten, were protectors of the whole country.
The concept of the narrative, stretching over three

188
Shigisan-engi-emaki: Scroll 1, scene 2. Ink and colours on paper. H.
31.7 cm. *c.* 1160–1170. Chōgosonshi-ji, Nara.
The second scene of the scroll of the 'Flying Storehouse' shows how
the golden begging bowl of the priest Myōren carries off the rich

man's storehouse through the air over a river, followed by the man's
family, servants and priests; the man is mounting his horse. The
rapid slightly caricatural brush strokes add to the drama of the
event.

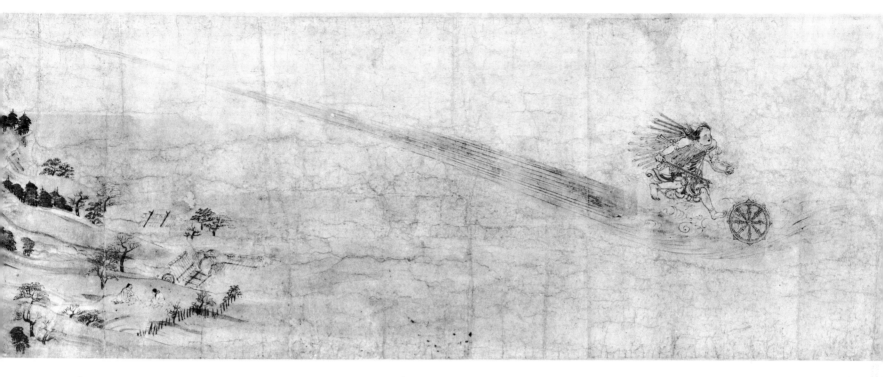

189

Shigisan-engi-emaki. Scroll 2, scene 6. Ink and colours on paper. H. 31.8 cm. *c.* 1160–1170. Chōgonsonshi-ji, Nara.

The figure of a boy, the heavenly sword deity, is running along a wisp of cloud, rolling the Wheel of the Law in front of him; he is running from Mount Shigisan to the Imperial Palace to cure Emperor Daigo, who is sick. The landscape on the left, seen as from on high, resembles in its striking and rapid stylization the frontispieces of the sutras painted in gold and silver.

190

Shigisan-engi-emaki. Scroll 3, scene 6. Ink and colours on paper. H. 31.7 cm. *c.* 1160–1170. Chōgonsonshi-ji, Nara.

The focus of the story, and of this picture, in the third scroll ('the Nun') is the Great Buddha of the Tōdai-ji in Nara. There the nun is informed that her lost brother is Abbot Myōren of Mount Shigisan. The powerful gilt bronze cult image is shown inside the open hall, which is rendered in central perspective.

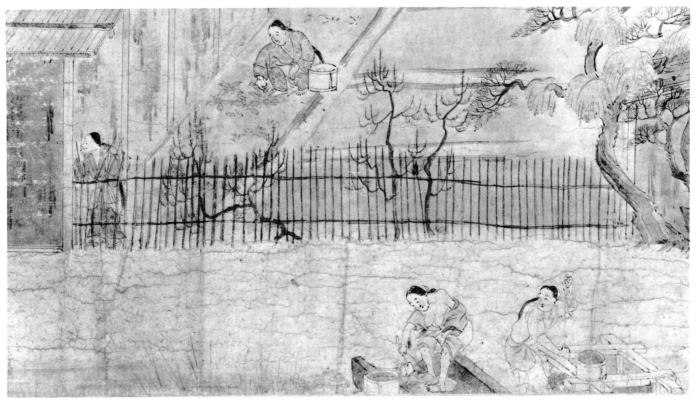

191

Shigisan-engi-emaki. Scroll 3, scene 4. Ink and colours on paper. H. 31.7 cm. *c.* 1160–1170. Chōgonsonshi-ji, Nara.

On the quest for her brother the nun comes to a village. This picture shows the daily life of the peasant women: in the foreground one is taking water from the well, another is stamping her washing with her feet. Across the street a third is picking vegetables, while a fourth is eagerly watching the nun through the fence.

192

Ban-Dainagon-ekotoba: Scroll 1, scene 5, attributed to Fujiwara (Tokiwa) no Mitsunaga. Ink and colours on paper. H. 31.5 cm. *c.* 1170. T. Sakai Collection, Tōkyō.

The onlookers press back to the Eshō-mon. People of all ranks crowd together in fascination and horror, and flee from the sparks.

scrolls, is a work of genius. Like the *Genji-monogatari-emaki* it is a National Treasure.

The miracles begin in the first scroll with the begging bowl of the priest Myōren, which is disregarded by a rich peasant, flys itself with his storehouse, full of sacks 188 of rice, lock stock and barrel, to the Shigisan, to the blank astonishment of the onlookers and the victim. At the victim's request, the priest sends back the sacks of rice but keeps the storehouse for the temple. In the second scroll an imperial messenger rides to the Shigisan to ask Myōren to use his supernatural power to help Emperor Daigo who is sick. Myōren, however, does not travel to Kyōto himself but sends Bishamon-ten's di- 189 vine messenger. The Imperial Palace with the emperor's Dwelling Hall, Seiryō-den, is naturalistically rendered and gives a sure indication of the date. In the third scroll we follow the pilgrimage of a noble nun who went to seek her brother. On the threshold of the 190–191 Hall of the Great Buddha in the Tōdai-ji in Nara, the Buddha directs her in a dream to the Shigisan; she discovers her lost brother in the priest Myōren.

196

193–194
Ban-Dainagon-ekotoba: Scroll 2, scene 2, attributed to Fujiwara (Tokiwa) no Mitsunaga. Ink and colours on paper. H. 31.5 cm. *c.* 1170. T. Sakai Collection, Tōkyō.
A fight between the child of a policeman and that of a servant of Ban Dainagon brings the misdeed of the latter to light. The mother angrily drags her son away. The crowd on the street gives uninhibited vent to its horror at the crime.

The scrolls are 8.47, 12.60 and 14 metres long. Only in the two last scrolls are there pictures and text; however, the legends were written down in the book *Kokon-setsuwa-shū* in the first half of the twelfth century and a century later in the *Ujishūi-monogatari* so that the events recounted in the paintings can be reconstructed by scholars.

In the *Shigisan-engi-emaki* both drawing and text are executed with a rapid brush, and colour is used sparsely only to stress an accent or to make important figures stand out. The artist used gold paint for objects connected with religion such as the floating lotus-shaped begging bowl, the figure of the Great Buddha, and the radiance and jewels of the divine messenger.

The direction of the figures involved in the action goes from right to left following the unwinding of the scroll. The scene is seldom lost in the distance, nor does it often come forward out of the picture, although in the 'framelessness'[48] of Japanese composition the relative positions of the details are undecided. The buildings here lie parallel to the edge of the painting, unlike those in the *Genji-monogatari-emaki*, but parallel perspective is consistently used for the lines running into the distance. The sacred space of the Great Hall of the Tōdai-ji alone has vanishing-point perspective, as the distancing lines all converge on the carving of the Great Buddha.[49]

Antecedents for the humorous and fresh elements of caricature in the figures and for the moving rhythms of the landscapes can be found in Chinese-style paintings, for example the *senzui-byōbu* formerly in the Kyōōgokoku-ji. The only typically Chinese element is the painting technique: the contours and washes done with rhythmic movements of the brush, some with slanting brush; otherwise the painter transposes the Chinese technique completely into his Japanese world. He depicts his figures with an effervescent delight in humanity: the lesser folk with their uninhibited surrendering to their feelings are seen with a certain scorn; the members of the imperial court, cool and dignified. The heroes of the scrolls are unmistakable individuals. The priest Myōren and his sister, the noble nun, are both treated like portraits; they are immediately recognizable in each episode by their facial features.

Only an artist from the imperial court could come into question for this work, probably (unlike the case of the *Genji-monogatari-emaki*) a specialist in ink painting in the imperial workshop. The landscape details are faithful pictures of the Yamato countryside, shown with a few running lines for hills and dashes and dabs for trees.

In contrast to the Genji pictures, the real and poetic beauty of the lovely landscape is fully grasped here.

The dating of the work is established by two buildings portrayed in it. The rebuilding of the Dwelling Hall of the emperor, the Seiryō-den (in the second scroll), after a fire, was only completed in 1157. On the other hand, the Main Hall of the Tōdai-ji with the statue of the Great Buddha, which is illustrated with every architectural detail by the artist, was completely burnt down in 1180. There is, therefore, a firm basis for dating the work between 1160 and 1170.

Another hand scroll with historical subjects, the *Ban-Dainagon-ekotoba*, is very close to the *Shigisan-engi-emaki* both in time and formally. Once more it is a court painter who describes, in three successive scrolls, a historical event. It takes place in the year 866. The scheming councillor Ban (Tomo no) Dainagon set fire to the main gate, Ōten-mon, of the Main Hall (Chōdō-in) in the Imperial Palace and caused suspicion to fall on his political rival, the Minister of the Left, Minamoto no Makoto. The first half of the first scroll gives the scene of the sacrilege. From the right the crowd of fleeing bystanders and police presses towards the Suzaku-mon Gate and in the direction of the billowing clouds of smoke that rise leftward from the burning gateway in the centre. A corresponding crowd on the left watches the fire, anxious and curious, from the Eshō-mon Gate. The work has been thus described by Otto Kümmel: 'In the centre towers the burning gateway, all alone, while blood-red tongues of flame lick its heavy black swathes of smoke. At an apprehensive distance from this raging inferno, on either side, a bawling half demented crowd, at first sight a formless mass. But on a closer look it resolves into quite unforgettable individuals, more memorable than most people in real life, though their faces and bodies are only suggested by a couple of ingenious brush strokes'.[50]

In the second half of the scroll the accused Minamoto no Makoto faces exile, but Fujiwara no Yoshifusa betakes himself to Emperor Seiwa and proves Makoto's innocence.

The second scroll begins with an imperial messenger hurrying to Makoto to announce the remission of his punishment. The action speeds up after this: one of the children of the major-domo of Tomo no Dainagon has a fight with the son of a policeman who had by chance seen the act of arson. In the cycle of events—above the children are scrapping, below the fathers are accusing each other—the policeman lets his secret escape.

188, 190
189

190

138

192

165

193-194

198

195
Kibi-Daijin-Nittō-ekotoba: (detail). Ink and colours on paper. H. 32 cm. Second half of the twelfth century. Museum of Fine Arts, Boston (32.131).
In this witty illustrated narrative, the Japanese envoy Kibi no Makibi (693–775) is helped by a demon to beat the Chinese in their own land at their own game. Kibi escapes death in an enchanted tower by magic and is entertained to a meal by the astounded Chinese. The attitude of superiority of Heian-period Japan vis-à-vis its great model, China, is clearly expressed here.

The third scroll is devoted to the just punishment of the offender. Tomo no Dainagon's servant is interrogated, Dainagon is arrested, and while his wives shriek 174 and lament in grief and despair indoors, the prison wa- 196 gon drives off, and a group of faithful servants watches the departing culprit from the courtyard gate.

The painter of the *Ban-Dainagon-ekotoba* employed direct brush drawing in equal measure with bright colour, but much more frugally than in the *Genji-monogatari-emaki.* The outlines and inner lines are drawn like written characters with pronounced extensions but with short strokes, and very deliberately laid on the paper. He has caught the dramatic movements of the people and of the horses too with great vitality. The figures are brought to life with applications of colour both flat and shaded, even the faces shine with excitement from the addition of red to their cheeks. To divide the scenes the painter sometimes used the same banks of cloud that are inserted in the *Genji-monogatari-emaki* to create a mood; they play a central part on the folding screens with *Yamato-e* scenes as a means of separating or joining space. Another type of division used by the painter is tall trees set between the changing scenes, and these are just as carefully observed and particularized as are his men and women.

This series of scrolls is traditionally ascribed to the court painter Fujiwara (also Minamoto or Tokiwa) no Mitsunaga, who was active at the court around 1173. At this time Mitsunaga was working for Ex-emperor

Goshirakawa on the long *emaki* series on the Yearly Observances *(Nenjū-gyōji-ekotoba)*, a work in sixty scrolls, which he either painted or designed, and legend has unconcernedly attributed any similar work to him as well. Among these are the *Ban-Dainagon-ekotoba* and

195 the humorous scrolls recounting 'Kibi Daijin's Journey to China' *(Kibi-Daijin-Nittō-ekotoba)*, during which cunning and magic allow the Japanese emissary to triumph over the Chinese.

Women's Literature in the *Emaki*

The illustrations of novels enjoyed great popularity among the ladies of the court. In chapter 50, 'Azumaya', of the *Genji-monogatari-emaki*, we are shown the

186 Lady Ukifune in the house of her stepsister; she is being entertained by a servant's reading aloud to her the text of a novel from one volume, while she herself follows the story in another volume of illustrations. Thus these volumes of wide format *(sōshi)* already existed in the Heian period as well as the *emaki*. It is possible that many of the individual novel illustrations were intended for such books and were only mounted on hand scrolls in a later period.

196
Ban-Dainagon-ekotoba: Scroll 3, scene 6, attributed to Fujiwara (Tokiwa) no Mitsunaga. Ink and colours on paper. H. 31.5 cm. *c.* 1170. T. Sakai Collection, Tōkyō.
After the company conducting the convicted Ban Dainagon into exile has gone through the palace gate, the servants look sadly after their master.

197 ▷
Nezame-monogatari-emaki. Ink and colours on paper decorated with gold and silver leaf. H. 25 cm. Twelfth century. Yamato Bunka-kan Museum, Nara.
The Nezame Tale illustrations, like those of the *Genji-monogatari-emaki,* make use of *tsukuri-e* technique. The first scene shows, on the right, an idyllic flower garden with three girls making music, while in the centre can be seen the cap of the hero, who is spying into the house where the ladies are concealed. In comparison with the *Genji-monogatari-emaki* the decorative element is given greater prominence; the figures are lost in the ornamental play of lines and patterns.

198 ▷
Murasaki-Shikibu-nikki-ekotoba: Section 5, scene 10. Colours and ink on paper. H. 20.9 cm. Mid-thirteenth century. Fujita Art Museum, Ōsaka.
On the fiftieth day after the birth of Crown Prince Ichijō, High Chancellor Fujiwara no Michinaga stands on the verandah of his palace and observes the new pleasure boats with a dragon head and a cock head. Though the *tsukuri-e* medium of the Heian period persists, there is a new force of movement and expression in this work of the Kamakura period.

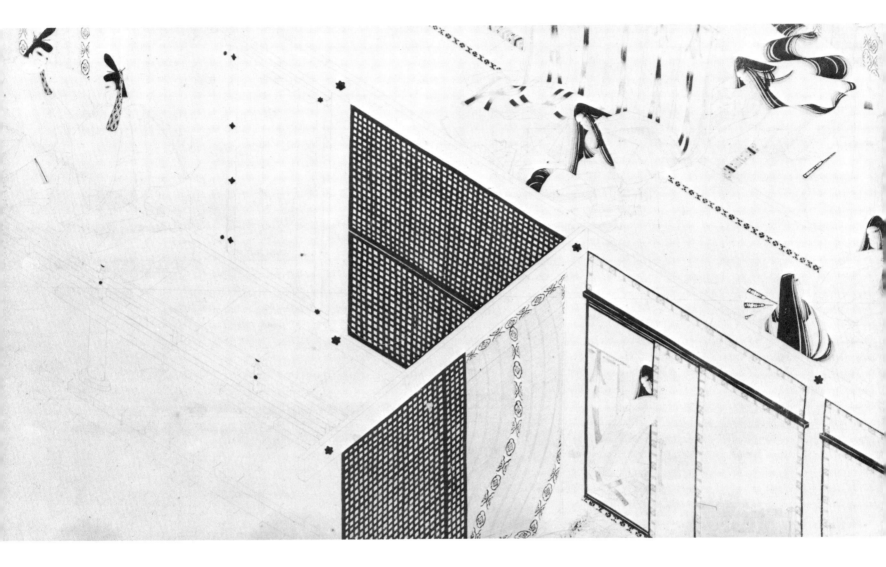

199
Makura-no-sōshi-emaki: Scene 3. Ink on paper. H. 25.5 cm. First half of the fourteenth century. N. Asano Collection, Tōkyō.
This late version of the famous *Pillow Book* by Sei Shōnagon shows an entry for the Fifth Month in a highly refined black-and-white technique. A bamboo branch is handed to the ladies in the palace, whose room is partitioned off by beams, *shitomi* lattice and *sudare* blinds. Sei Shōnagon receives it and knows its meaning: bamboo in Chinese stands for 'noble'—here it signifies 'this Lord'.

Unfortunately the quantity of new novels so diligently written in the wake of the *Genji-monogatari* by the ladies at court was in inverse proportion to their quality. But since the court gave an enthusiastic welcome to illustrations for novels the court studios produced more and more series of pictures. It is an astonishing fact that the artistic level of these paintings did not deteriorate, but on the contrary, every *monogatari-e* well into the fourteenth century maintained its individual form. We find the elaborate *tsukuri-e* form once again at the end of the twelfth century in the *Nezame-monogatari-emaki,* of which sadly 197 only four paintings and five parts of text survive. As far as the contents can be reconstituted, the work described the fantastic amorous adventures of the lovely court lady Yowa no Nezame and of her son Masako.

The writer of the romance in the mid-eleventh century is said to have been the daughter of Sugawara no Takasue, to whom is also attributed the diary *Sarashina-* 135 *nikki.* In the *emaki* ('picture scrolls'), the painting technique of the *tsukuri-e* is allied to that of the *Genji-monogatari-emaki.* The drawing of the architecture and figures also remains in this tradition. However the painting was done on writing paper patterned with

Genji-monogatari: Ukifune Album, Scene 1. Ink on paper. H. 23.9cm, L. 18.6cm. Fourteenth century. Yamato Bunka-kan Museum, Nara.

This late version of the *Genji-monogatari* survives in an album fragment. The illustrations are painted solely in ink in black-and-white technique. Court caps and flowing hair provide black accents. Prince Niou is depicted indoors writing his morning poem for Ukifune, while the presence of servants is suggested by their heads in the foreground.

mica and gold and silver foil; the scenes themselves are thus transposed into an ornamental vein. Even the drawing of the trees approximates in its playful ductus to a 'reed hand', although no character can be identified. This emphasis on the decorative brings these illustrations close to the end papers of illustrated sutras and also 122 to the fan sutras of the Shitennō-ji.

Murasaki Shikibu's diary is known today in an illustrated edition of the thirteenth century. In both form and content it too resembles the *Genji-monogatari-emaki,*

though it is evident how the new spirit of the Kamakura era favoured a suggestively dramatic conception that would have been quite impossible earlier.

A picture of the times that is Japanese through and through is the *Murasaki-Shikibu-nikki-ekotoba,* in which 45, 198 the events of the years 1008 to 1010 are described at the court of Empress Akiko in a lively chronicle of the regency of the great Fujiwara no Michinaga. There exist twenty-four scenes of varying widths from this work, divided between three scrolls and six single sheets. The description begins, like the diary, with the birth of the first crown prince of Empress Akiko and Emperor Ichijō. The celebrations in the palace of Fujiwara no 166 Michinaga in honour of this event are shown in the next pictures. They give a lively rendering of the pompous way of life, the elegance of the architecture and the furnishings in the Tsuchimikado Palace. The scenes of drunken courtiers dallying with the empress's ladies- 168 in-waiting are in a light humorous vein.

An illustrated copy of the *Pillow Book (Makura-no-* 199 *sōshi-emaki)* by Lady Sei Shōnagon survives from the fourteenth century. The painting has relinquished the colourful splendour of *tsukuri-e* in favour of pure ink painting. One has the impression that it is the preliminary drawing for a painting in colour. The lines are precise and delicate, as though drawn with a pencil, and the black-and-white effects produced with great refinement; there are only rare washes and accents of red on lips. This type of performance is also described as a 'white (or a left-blank) picture'. 200

The artistic style of the *monogatari-emaki,* like the *Yamato-e,* led into the formation of the Tosa school's style of painting. Narrative pictures in the form of a continuous scroll became less and less frequent and, on the whole, were only commissioned at court. On the other hand we often find the classic themes of the novels, like the *Genji-monogatari* or the descriptions of the wars of the Heike and Minamoto, from which the hand-scroll form had emancipated itself in the tenth and eleventh centuries, transferred to the standing screen.

Portraits and Poets

Japanese secular painting first found its individual expression in the poetic mood-landscapes of *Yamato-e.* The charming landscapes with flowering trees or fiery autumn colours gave a more cheerful character to the

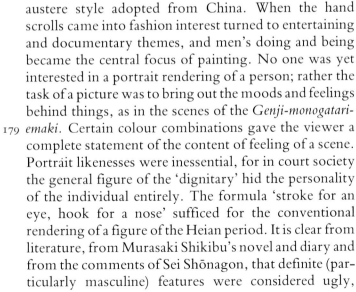

austere style adopted from China. When the hand scrolls came into fashion interest turned to entertaining and documentary themes, and men's doing and being became the central focus of painting. No one was yet interested in a portrait rendering of a person; rather the task of a picture was to bring out the moods and feelings behind things, as in the scenes of the *Genji-monogatari-emaki*. Certain colour combinations gave the viewer a complete statement of the content of feeling of a scene. Portrait likenesses were inessential, for in court society the general figure of the 'dignitary' hid the personality of the individual entirely. The formula 'stroke for an eye, hook for a nose' sufficed for the conventional rendering of a figure of the Heian period. It is clear from literature, from Murasaki Shikibu's novel and diary and from the comments of Sei Shōnagon, that definite (particularly masculine) features were considered ugly,

179

201
Prince Shōtoku Taishi with Attendants. Ink and colours on silk, H. 126.8 cm, W. 72 cm. Second half of the eleventh century. Ichijō-ji, Hyōgo.
Crown Prince Shōtoku Taishi (574–622) was added in Japan to the series of hanging scrolls with ideal portraits of the patriarchs of the Tendai sect. He is represented preaching at sixteen years of age, dressed as a priest, holding an incense burner. The large cult figure is surrounded by ten small boys, worshipping him.

202
Minamoto no Yoritomo: attributed to Fujiwara no Takanobu (1145-1205) Colours on silk. H. 138 cm, W. 112.5 cm. Jingo-ji, Kyōto.
The striking facial features make this portrait of Yoritomo particularly impressive. It belongs to the same cycle as the *Portrait of Taira no Shigemori* (Pl. 170). *Yamato-e* created real cult pictures in these so-called 'likenesses' of regents and high dignitaries posing in their robes of state. Yoritomo's cold and brutal detachment radiates the spirit of the new epoch of which he was the founder.

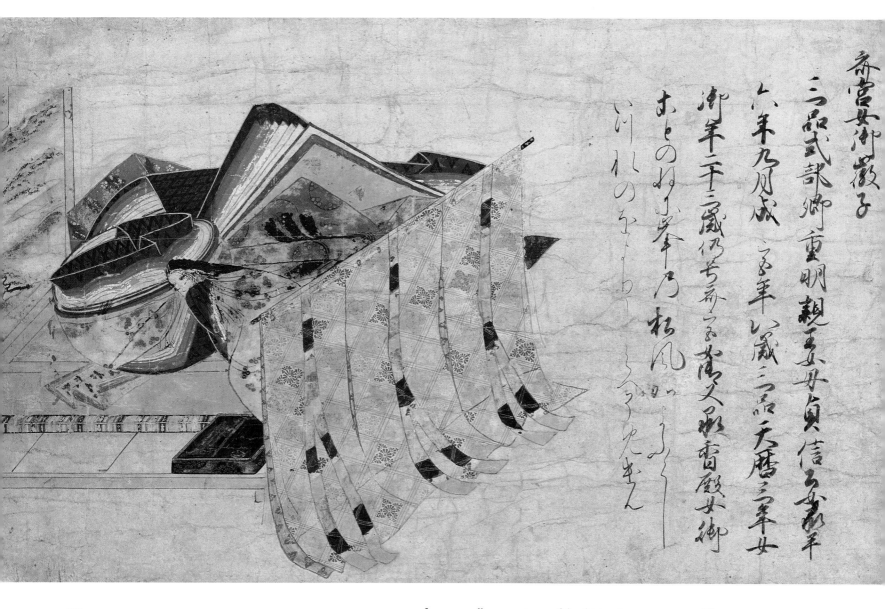

斎宮女御徽子
三品式部卿重明親王女母貞信公敦
六年九月成三承平三品天暦三年女
御年二十二歳仍弖著爲廣文服香殿女御
おものか小峯乃　松風か○さ
汗れの○ま

203
The Poetess and Empress Saigu Nyōgo Yoshiko: attributed to Fujiwara no Nobuzane (1176–1268). Colours and ink on paper. H. 27.9 cm, L. 51.1 cm. Mid-thirteenth century. Freer Gallery of Art, Washington, D.C. (50.24).
This picture of Empress Saigu Nyōgo Yoshiko (929–985) comes from a scroll, now cut up, of the thirty-six poets on mats. The great lady sits on a platform between her screen of state and *senzui-byōbu*. Her costly robes with their hems folded one over the other, the brocade jacket and *mo* apron are visible. Her long hair is spread out over them in three locks. The text gives biographical details and one of her poems.

even plebeian. The ideal of the beautiful nobleman was the smooth, round, apple-faced man with a small beard on his chin.

In the scrolls with historical and legendary tales, however, certain characters in the story, for instance the priest Myōren in the *Shigisan-engi-emaki,* may be given quite definite personal traits. These make it pos-sible to identify the hero throughout the various inci-dents of the tale as it unfolds.

In the sphere of Buddhist cult painting, on the other hand, the traditional ideal portrait of important patri-archs and founders of sects played an important role. At some ceremonies the portraits stood at the centre of the rite and were honoured as members of the Buddhist

205

pantheon. The patriarchs of the Shingon and Tendai sects also enjoyed worship and honour. Shōtoku Taishi, the Prince Regent of the sixth-seventh century, and the priest Ennin were included among the patri-201 archs of the Tendai sect. Their portraits are preserved in the Ichijō-ji together with the continental patriarchs. Even before these portraits there were the famous Nara-period portraits of Shōtoku Taishi and his brothers. This early portrait corresponds to the central cult figure of a Shaka trinity.[51]

Though Shintō deities were represented in sculpture as 'traces' of Buddhist beings and powers in the guise of Japanese princesses and priests, like the Trinity of the Yakushi-ji, painting did not followed suit with representations of Shintō deities until the Kamakura period.

An answer to the question of when the first portraits of Japanese emperors, not of priests, were painted is given in literature: the prologue to a poem in the tenth volume of the *Goshūi-waka-shū*, an anthology by the poetess Dewa no Ben, describes a portrait of Emperor Goichijō (1008–1036). There are in fact no such portraits surviving until the imposing group of men of the twelfth century, preserved in the Jingo-ji. These are the crowning glory of *Yamato-e* portrait art. It seems possible to deduce from diaries that the painters of the court studio prepared sketches of the most important men of the court for an imperial commission, on festive occasions. From these sketches, apparently, portraits of leading men of the time at the court of Ex-emperor Goshirakawa were turned into cult paintings. From what was probably a larger group the portraits of Minamoto no Yoritomo, Taira no Shigemori and Fujiwara no Mitsuyoshi have been preserved. These portraits convey the dignity and nobility of their characters. Clothed in official ceremonial costume in court style with stiff, girdled, black damask robe, a parade sword, *shaku* sceptre and stiff *kammuri* cap, only the faces stand out from the ornament of the costume in 170 clear, accurate, linear drawing. Shigemori (d. 1176), son of General Taira no Kiyomori, betrays scepticism and passivity in his features. Fujiwara no Mitsuyoshi represents the typical courtier of the ex-emperor. In the tradition of the court his face is withdrawn and imper-202 sonal. Minamoto no Yoritomo, on the other hand, the founder of the Kamakura shōgunate, has decision and unscrupulousness written in his face. This, the latest portrait of the group, tells us sufficiently that a new epoch in Japanese history had begun.

The *Yamato-e* produced another very characteristic branch of portrait art: the portraits of poets *(kasen-e)*. These are ideal portraits, painted from imagination and not from life. It was felt desirable to see the poet in person and honour him in the calligraphic collections of his works. Here too cult worship played a part, for the poets were equated with Shintō deities and elevated to *kami*. Though the earliest *kasen-e* belong to the Kama- 203 kura period—they are attributed to Fujiwara no Nobuzane (1176–1265)—they show retrospectively the figures of courtiers and court ladies of the Nara and Heian periods.

In two early scrolls, partly dismantled now, the poets are illustrated singly with a short accompanying text that includes a poem and a biography. One scroll shows them seated on mats, the other without. The men are mostly of middle court rank, shown in official or unofficial costume. Most of them are full of upright dignity, the priests often more human and full of character, the court ladies with their faces hidden in the colourful cascades of their costly garments.

Caricatures and the 'Six Stages of Existence'

Of all the *emaki* of the Heian period, the scrolls with caricatures in the Kōzan-ji have achieved the highest fame. They are without titles or text. There are four hand scrolls that begin with animals imitating human activities; then animals fighting among themselves are shown, and finally there are quite merciless caricatures of people—always including monks—gambling and testing their strength.

The scrolls are called *Chōjū-jimbutsu-giga* or *Chōjū-giga* ('Satirical Pictures of Animals and Men'). The first has hares, frogs, monkeys and foxes playing human 204–206 games that the weaker always win. At the start hares and monkeys compete in swimming, then follows an archery contest between hares and frogs ending with a victory dance for the frogs. Other contests follow and then a blasphemous scene in which a monkey dressed as a monk worships at the cult image of a frog. It would seem that a monk of high rank is mocking not only humanity in general but court society and the priesthood in particular.

In the second scroll sixteen groups of fighting animals are introduced. Birds, horses, bulls, fabulous

204
Chōjū-giga: Scroll 1, scene 3. Ink on paper. H. 31.8 cm. Twelfth century. Kōzan-ji, Kyōto.
Hares and frogs bring trays with food and a water jug to the hares' archery contest. The calligraphic fluency of the painting renders in a lively manner the animals and groups of plants, the latter placed rather like stage scenery. The early parts of the four scrolls are traditionally attributed to Abbot Toba Sōjō.

205
Chōjū-giga: Scroll 1, scene 5. Ink on paper. H. 31.8 cm. Twelfth century. Kōzan-ji, Kyōto.
In this section various animals are represented as caricatures of humans. On the right hares and foxes are concerned with a dead frog; on the left hares, foxes and a cat—dressed like humble folk—are watching two frogs who are performing a *dengaku* folk dance.

beasts and dogs are all battling without any apparent reason.

The third scroll falls into two parts: first there are nine scenes showing men gambling, with four kinds of board game and the favorite Japanese trials of strength (head, belly and ear pulling, and finally a staring contest). A cock fight and a dog fight are then observed by a ring of fascinated watchers. The second half of the scroll is again devoted to animal caricatures. A race between a hare on a stag and hares riding foxes is followed abruptly by a scene with frogs and monkeys feasting and playing, while a snake and three frogs run away from them.

The fourth scroll shows men: eleven sketches portray, in burlesque fashion, deformed beings, Buddhist ceremonies, archery on horseback and various contests.

207

206

Chōjū-giga: Scroll 1, last scene. Ink on paper. H. 31.8 cm. Twelfth century. Kōzan-ji, Kyōto.

A monkey dressed as a priest is telling his prayer beads. In front of him lies a bundle and a table with offerings of peaches. Hares and a frog hurry in from the left, as servants bring in more offerings; they accompany a hare in court costume who is carrying a tiger skin.

207

Chōjū-giga: Scroll 4, last scene. Ink on paper. H. 30.9 cm. Thirteenth century. Kōzan-ji, Kyōto.

The last scene of the fourth scroll shows masterly caricatures of humans doing strange things. An abbot with a fan is praying at an altar; the cult image represents the skeleton of a frog. Behind him monks are reading a sutra and evidently fascinating their audience of common folk. The painter of this thirteenth-century persiflage has inverted the theme from the end of the first scroll: there a monkey was celebrating before a cult image of a frog.

208

Gaki-no-sōshi-emaki: Scene 2. Ink and colours on paper. H. 27.2 cm. Late twelfth century. Formerly Kawamoto Collection. Tōkyō National Museum, Tōkyō.

In a roofless house, a seated woman is giving birth. Surrounded by women, containers and sherds, an invisible hunger spirit *(gaki)* is snatching at the afterbirth; in the anteroom a priest is reciting spells.

The *Chōjū-giga* thus presents no uniform whole. The first two scrolls have long—though with no adequate reason—been attributed to Abbot Toba Sōjō, Kakuyū (1053–1140). Kakuyū, the son of the court noble Minamoto no Takakuni, became abbot of the Onjō-ji and later bishop of the Shōkongō-ji in the imperial palace at Toba. Although the work was produced some decades after his death, caricatures have been called *toba-e* in Japanese since the Edo period. The third scroll bears the date 1253 at the end. It shows different hands in both parts, and the fourth scroll too has another different style of drawing.

All the artists were of the clergy however. The precise ample line drawing, used in such an original way in the caricatures, is known from the ductus of the iconographic Buddhist sketches. It is also found in another medium, in gold and silver paint, in the pictures of the frontispieces of sutra manuscripts.[52]

Today sketches done with bravura in ink only, as well as the meticulous drawings in the style of the *Genji-monogatari-emaki,* are given the common designation 'white painting' *(haku-byō)* to distinguish them 200

209

Yamai-no-sōshi-emaki. Ink and colours on paper. H. 21.2 cm. Late twelfth century. Formerly Matsunaga Collection. Fukuoka Municipal Museum, Matsunaga Memorial Museum Foundation, Fukuoka.

Obesity is one of the diseases included in the Sickness Scrolls depicting the 'Six Stages of Existence'. A bloated woman suffering from this misfortune can only move about with the help of two attendants. In the street two men do not disguise their amazement, while a young mother devotedly nurses her child without paying attention.

210 ▷

Jigoku-no-sōshi-emaki. Ink and colours on paper. H. 26.4 cm. Second half of the twelfth century. Formerly in the Anju-in Temple. Tōkyō National Museum, Tōkyō.

The third scene in these Scrolls of Hell shows the fifteenth of the sixteen hells, where murderers, thieves, lechers and drunkards must roast in flames. To the left and right are devils who throw or drive the sinners into the fire. The sinners are seen screaming in agony among the flames. The painter depicts the inferno with a real gusto for the macabre; his aim, after all, is to lead the observer into the path of righteousness.

やくがくのとてやむ
れまたすがつてさみてまた、
やくがくのとてやむらう小
もて天をしつう致

たゝこの地獄よ別昕ありなほ
とふこのゝゝろの衆生じう人開まそ
畜生 偸盗邪婬おもしたうそ
雨炎火石

clearly from ink painting *(sumi-e* or *suiboku-ga)*. Ink painting came anew from China to Japan in the fourteenth century and is essentially the painting of Chan (Zen) Buddhism.

Clerical *emaki* include the scrolls—of a different type—with representations of the 'Six Stages of Existence' *(Rokudō)*. Interest in the disturbing and frightening portrayal of the lower forms of existence came with the concepts of the Amida faith. Those of the spirits of Hell, Hunger and Sickness survive from what were originally perhaps more comprehensive repertoires. Imagination was most powerfully set alight by the macabre themes, and sometimes it is easy to see that traits of caricature are used, there in particular, as an antidote. The 'Six Stages of Existence' brought nothing new in the way of themes, for the palace had screens with just those pictures by the end of the ninth century. They were used as pictures at the Butsumyō-e Feast in the Twelfth Month. It may be as S. Ienaga suggests,[53] that the brutal power struggles between the Taira and Minamoto clans—so realistically portrayed in the 171 *Heiji-monogatari-emaki*—brought the court elite into direct contact with the horrors of war and promoted a taste for realism.

At that time, around 1180, the *Rokudō-no-sōshi-emaki* were published. The Scrolls of Hell *(Jigoku-no-sōshi-* 210 *emaki)* have survived in four scroll fragments; twenty-three separate pictures show episodes from the ten main and sixteen subsidiary hells. The hells of the firecock, of snakes, of insects and of the iron mortar show the torments of sinners, torments that do not bring death but can lead to rebirth in Paradise for the repentant sinner, through the grace of the Bodhisattva Jizō.

The same glee in macabre detail is shown in the *Gaki-no-sōshi-emaki* in the depictions of bloated hunger 208 spirits *(gaki)*, small and large, who must sustain their lives on excrement, refuse and blood. They are present in every level of society and in every walk of life: at the banquets of nobles, at the birth of children, in cemeteries and at the Obon Feast of All Souls.

A closely related style and similar view appear in the Sickness Scrolls *(Yamai-no-sōshi-emaki)* which parade 209 human suffering. Uncomfortable and ridiculous maladies are depicted with sober matter-of-factness. Two scrolls of the Heian period with twenty-one separate pictures and their corresponding texts survive. Hardly any work from this time has represented the inevitable sufferings of human existence so universally.

Conclusion: The End of the Period

The Earthquake

Then there was the great earthquake of 1185, of an intensity not known before. Mountains crumbled and rivers were buried, the sea tilted over and immersed the land. The earth split and water gushed up; boulders were sundered and rolled into the valleys. Boats that rowed along the shores were swept out to sea. Horses walking along the roads lost their footing. It is needless to speak of the damage throughout the capital—not a single mansion, pagoda, or shrine was left whole. As some collapsed and others tumbled over, dust and ashes rose like voluminous smoke. The rumble of the earth shaking and the houses crashing was exactly like that of thunder. Those who were in their houses, fearing that they would presently be crushed to death, ran outside, only to meet with a new cracking of the earth.

Hōjōki ('An Account of My Hut')
by Kamo no Chōmei, 1212[54]

The political and economic end of the Heian period was already heralded in the civil wars of the years 1156 and 1159 to 1160. The noble military clans, the Taira and Minamoto, supported by the adherents of the emperor, ex-emperor or monastic troops, waged a relentless struggle for power that did not stop short at treachery, deceit or brutal slaughter. After the death of Taira no Kiyomori in 1181, fortune favoured the Minamoto. The last phase of the civil war was the Gempei War, and here the battles between the two clans reached a climax of ferocity. Yoshitsune, brother of Minamoto no Yoritomo, acted as his general and in 1185 annihilated the fleet of the Taira at Dannoura. Though the empire collapsed after this battle, the imperial regime in Heian-kyō continued without interruption. The child-emperor Antoku, who died in 1185, was replaced on the throne by his brother Gotoba (1180–1239), and Ex-emperor Goshirakawa retained the reins of government in his hands as before.

The clan chief of the Minamoto, Minamoto no Yoritomo, however, set up a counter-government, the 'tent government' *(bakufu)* in the city of Kamakura in the Kantō region. In a cooly calculated move he laid the necessary economic foundations for a new social order, first recruiting the agreement of the Tennō. Feudalism was thus established in Japan. Alongside the existing governors he appointed his vassals, military governors and territorial rulers, and financed his regime with drastically increased taxes. He only lived to exercise his appointment as Military Dictator (Sei-i Tai-shōgun) for seven years, but in that time he established a new era in Japanese history.

The new models of the military nobility corresponded to the traditional Japanese clan ideals, ideals of loyalty to the clan chief and intrepid, death-defying zeal in battle, which had been overlaid in the Heian period by the elitist and over-refined way of life of the court nobility. The old ideals found new expression in the Kamakura period in the code of knighthood of the *bushi* or *samurai*. Zen Buddhism provided the philosophical guidance, brought by a new generation of monks from China to Japan. The spiritual goal was now individual enlightenment, achievable in this life through the self-knowledge obtained through meditation and discipline. The dream of Paradise had lost its validity for both the *bushi* and the Zen monk. The Jōdo and *nembutsu* sects only survived among the common folk. The Zen priest Eisai (1141–1215) travelled twice through China and, under the patronage of Minamoto no Yoriie, the second shōgun in Kamakura, he founded the Rinzai sect in 1191, which still remains active today.

Zen Buddhism brought new artistic styles and aesthetic maxims to Japan in its wake. Such arts as pure ink painting represented a total reversal of the Heian values and a new artistic language of spiritual abstraction. On the other hand, the striving for dramatic realism grew stronger in Buddhist sculpture, while a 'new Realism' assumed greater importance in literature.

However, the new spirit of the times did not have a completely clear field and was unable to oust the specifically Japanese creations of the Heian period entirely, since, in the entourage of the imperial court and in the old capital of Heian-kyō, the *wa-yō* ideal remained inviolable and vital, though its forms might undergo changes. Later generations consciously and repeatedly drew inspiration from the old repertoire. The great decorative painting of the Momoyama period or the Rimpa School of the Edo period and their great representatives Kōetsu, Sōtatsu and Kōrin are unthinkable without Heian art and *Yamato-e* painting. The concept of nature and the manner of representing human figures of *emakimono* survived right into the popular wood-cut art of *ukiyo-e* up to the nineteenth century.

Perhaps the highly refined art of the Heian period, with its stress on feeling and its elegant decadence, was able to remain alive because it arose from that sphere of Japan's being that might be called Japan's soul.

202

Appendices

Notes

1 J. E. Kidder, Jr., *Japanese Temples*, London, 1964, p. 35.
2 The end of the Heian period is considered to be either 1185, the defeat of the Taira clan at the sea battle of Dannoura, or 1192, the date Minamoto no Yoritomo was named Sei-i Tai-shōgan and his *bakufu* government in Kamakura was recognized. See also: B. Lewin, *Kleines Wörterbuch der Japanologie*, Wiesbaden, 1968, p. 337.
3 Sir G. B. Sansom, *A History of Japan*, vol. I: *A History of Japan to 1334*, London, 1958, pp. 178–196.
4 See: D. Seckel, *Emakimono: The Art of the Japanese Painted Hand-Scroll*, photos and foreword by Akihisa Hasé, New York, 1959.
5 I. Morris, *The Nobility of Failure: Tragic Heroes in the History of Japan*, 2nd ed. Harmondsworth, 1980.
6 B. Lewin, *Aya and Hata: Bevölkerungsgruppen Altjapans kontinentaler Herkunft,* Studien zur Japanologie, vol. 3, Wiesbaden, 1962.
7 J. and R. K. Reischauer, *Early Japanese History*, 2 vols., Princeton, 1937.
8 'The very fact that the first important literary achievement, apart from historical records, is a collection of native verse testifies to the singular eminence of poetry in the national tradition.' (after Sir G. B. Sansom, *A History of Japan,* vol. I, London, 1958, p. 93).
9 G. Cameron Hurst III, *Insei: Abdicated Sovereigns in the Politics of Late Heian Japan, 1086–1185*, New York, London, 1976, p. 65.
10 *Shinkokin-waka-shū: Japanische Gedichte,* trans. by H. Hammitzsch and L. Brüll, Stuttgart, 1964, p. 151.
11 See: Ennin, *Diary: The Record of a Pilgrimage to China . . .,* trans. by E. O. Reischauer, New York, 1955.
12 Y. S. Hakeda, *Kūkai: Major Works.* New York, 1972, p. 51.
13 See the colour plates by Y. Ishimoto in *Eros + Cosmos in Mandala*, Tōkyō, 1978.
14 T. Yanigasawa in *Eros + Cosmos in Mandala*, Tōkyō, 1978.
15 The old and new prototypes and the artisanal tendency in this unified yet richly varied art is presented by B. Kurata, 'Jōgan chōkoku', *Nihon no bijutsu* 1, no. 44, Tōkyō, 1963.
16 H. Minamoto, *Shinshu Nihon Bunkashi Taikei*, vol. IV: *Heian zenki*, Tōkyō, 1943, p. 216.
17 Y. Yashiro, *Art Treasures of Japan*, vol. I. Tōkyō, 1960, p. 183.
18 R. Goepper, ed., *Shu-p'u: Der Traktat zur Schriftkunst von Sun Kuo-t'ing*, Studien zur Schriftkunst Ostasiens, vol. 2. Wiesbaden, 1974.
19 O. Benl and H. Hammitzsch, ed., *Japanische Geisteswelt: Vom Mythus zur Gegenwart*, Baden-Baden, 1956, pp. 59f.
20 S. Kato, *A History of Japanese Literature,* London, 1979, pp. 91–136.
21 Sir G. B. Sansom, *A History of Japan,* vol. I, London, 1958, p. 140.
22 See: *ibid.,* pp. 174f.
23 G. Cameron Hurst III, *Insei: Abdicated Sovereigns in the Politics of Late Heian Japan, 1086–1185.* New York, London, 1976, p. 150.
24 R. T. Paine and A. C. Soper, *The Art and Architecture of Japan,* Harmondsworth, 1955, p. 230.
25 'The appearance of this merciful Buddha, who offered Redemption to everyone, corresponded to a change in the religious practices of the faithful, a weakening of the vehement actions and efforts made to obtain salvation and a growing trust in the saving grace of the Buddha.' (translated from W. Grundert, *Japanische Religionsgeschichte*, Tōkyō, Stuttgart, 1935, p. 84).
26 D. Seckel, *Einführung in die Kunst Ostasiens*, Munich, 1960.
27 *Genji-monogatari: Die Geschichte vom Prinzen Genji,* trans. by O. Benl, vol. I, Zurich, 1966, p. 36.
28 D. Seckel, *Buddhistische Kunst Ostasiens*, Stuttgart, 1957, p. 153.
29 O. Benl, *Die Entwicklung der japanischen Poetik bis zum 16. Jahrhundert*, Hamburg, 1951, p. 71.
30 *The Gossamer Years (Kagerō Nikki): A Diary by a Noblewoman of Heian Japan*, trans. by E. Seidensticker, Tōkyō, 1964, p. 14.
31 S. Kato, *A History of Japanese Literature*, London, 1979, p. 173.
32 After *The Pillow Book of Sei Shōnagon*, trans. by I. Morris, 2nd ed., Harmondsworth, 1971, pp. 10f.
33 M. Morris, 'Sei Shōnagon's Poetic Catalogues,' *Harvard Journal of Asiatic Studies*, 40, no. 1, Cambridge, Mass., June, 1980, pp. 5–54.
34 After A. Gatten, 'The Order of the Early Chapters in the Genji Monogatari,' *Harvard Journal of Asiatic Studies*, 41, no. 1, Cambridge, Mass., 1980, pp. 5–46.
35 M. Furuya, 'Heian-jidai no sho,' *Nihon no bijutsu* 5, no. 180, Tōkyō, 1981; Pl. 21.
36 T. Akiyama, *Japanische Malerei*, Geneva, 1961, p. 66.
37 See: B. W. Robinson, *Arts of the Japanese Sword*, London, 1961, p. 18.
38 B. von Ragué, *Geschichte der japanischen Lackkunst,* Berlin, 1967, pp. 23, 25.
39 G. Gabbert, *Die Masken des Bugaku: Profane japanische Tanzmasken der Heian- und Kamakura-Zeit*, Wiesbaden, 1972, p. 38.
40 See: *ibid.* and K. Nishikawa, *Bugaku Masks*, Tōkyō, New York, San Francisco, 1978.
41 See: D. Seckel, 'Buddhistische Prozessionsmasken (Gyōdō-men) in Japan,' *Nachrichten der Gesellschaft für Natur- und Völkerkunde Ostasiens,* 76 Hamburg, 1954, pp. 29–52.
42 After I. Morris, *The World of the Shining Prince: Court Life in Ancient Japan*, London, 1964, p. 145.
43 *The Pillow Book of Sei Shōnagon*, trans. by I. Morris, London, 1967, p. 39.
44 W. McCullough, 'Japanese Marriage Institutions in the Heian Period,' *Harvard Journal of Asiatic Studies*, 27, Cambridge, Mass., 1967, pp. 103–167.
45 I. Morris, *The World of the Shining Prince: Court Life in Ancient Japan*, London, 1964, pp. 147ff.
46 *Genji-monogatari: Die Geschichte vom Prinzen Genji,* trans. by O. Benl, vol. I, Zurich, 1966, p. 304.
47 T. Akiyama, *Japanische Malerei*, Geneva, 1961, p. 70; *idem.,* 'Genji-e,' *Nihon no bijutsu* 4, no. 119, Tōkyō, 1976, p. 22.
48 On the concept of 'framelessness' see: T. Tsudsumi, *Die Kunst Japans*, Leipzig, 1929, pp. 23ff.
49 The sequence of the images has been exhaustively interpreted by

G. Armbruster, 'Das Shigisan-Emaki: Ein japanisches Rollbild aus dem 12. Jahrhundert,' *Mitteilungen der Ostasiengesellschaft* XL, Hamburg, Wiesbaden, 1959.

50 Translated from O. Kümmel, 'Die Kunst Chinas, Japans und Koreas,' *Handbuch der Kunstwissenschaft,* Potsdam, 1929.

51 Y. Shirahata, 'Shōzō-ga,' *Nihon no bijutsu* 12, no. 8, Tōkyō, 1966, p. 19.

52 K. Toda, *Japanese Scroll Painting*, 2nd ed., New York, 1969, p. 50.

53 S. Ienaga, Painting in Yamato Style, vol. X: *The Heibonsha Survey of Arts*, New York, Tokyo, 1973, p. 107.

54 After D. Keene, ed., *Anthology of Japanese Literature from the Earliest Era to the Mid-Nineteenth Century,* New York, 1955.

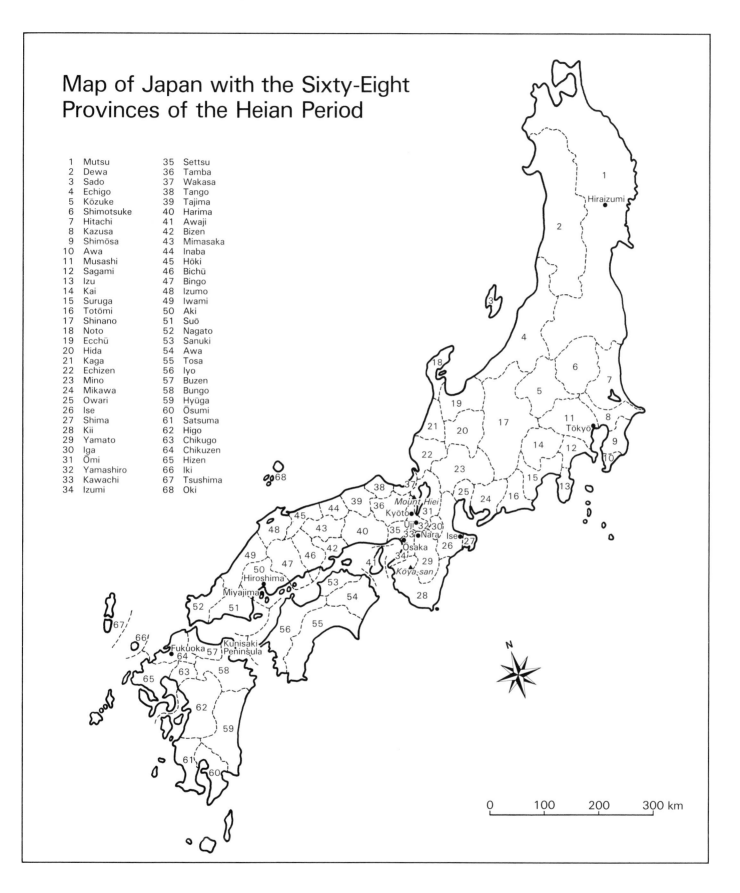

Map of Japan with the Sixty-Eight Provinces of the Heian Period

1	Mutsu	35	Settsu
2	Dewa	36	Tamba
3	Sado	37	Wakasa
4	Echigo	38	Tango
5	Kōzuke	39	Tajima
6	Shimotsuke	40	Harima
7	Hitachi	41	Awaji
8	Kazusa	42	Bizen
9	Shimōsa	43	Mimasaka
10	Awa	44	Inaba
11	Musashi	45	Hōki
12	Sagami	46	Bichū
13	Izu	47	Bingo
14	Kai	48	Izumo
15	Suruga	49	Iwami
16	Totōmi	50	Aki
17	Shinano	51	Suō
18	Noto	52	Nagato
19	Ecchū	53	Sanuki
20	Hida	54	Awa
21	Kaga	55	Tosa
22	Echizen	56	Iyo
23	Mino	57	Buzen
24	Mikawa	58	Bungo
25	Owari	59	Hyūga
26	Ise	60	Ōsumi
27	Shima	61	Satsuma
28	Kii	62	Higo
29	Yamato	63	Chikugo
30	Iga	64	Chikuzen
31	Ōmi	65	Hizen
32	Yamashiro	66	Iki
33	Kawachi	67	Tsushima
34	Izumi	68	Oki

Layout of the Greater Imperial Palace (Daidairi)

Gates:

A   Anka-mon
B   Ikam-mon
C   Datchi-mon
D   Jōtō-mon
E   Yōmei-mon
F   Taikem-mon
G   Ikuhō-mon
H   Bifuku-mon
I   Suzaku-mon
J   Kōka-mon
K   Dantem-mon
L   Sōheki-mon
M   Impu-mon
N   Jōsai-mon
O   Furō-mon
P   Yōroku-mon
Q   Emmei-mon
R   Kaimei-mon
S   Buraku-mon
T   Fukurai-mon
U   Banshū-mon
V   Ryūtoku-mon
W   Kōgi-mon
X   Eifuku-mon
Y   Shōkei-mon
Z   Kaki-mon
A'   Eiyō-mon
B'   Tsūyō-mon
C'   Sensei-mon
D'   Kanka-mon
E'   Ganyō-mon
F'   Chōraku-mon
G'   Ōten-mon
H'   Eika-mon
I'   Shōgi-mon
J'   Keihō-mon
K'   Shōzem-mon
L'   Kenshim-mon
M'   Kōrai-mon
N'   Kaishō-mon
O'   Shōtoku-mon
a   Shikkam-mon
b   Sakuhei-mon
c   a small north gate
d   Kenshum-mon
e   Shunka-mon
f   Kenrei-mon
g   Sumei-mon
h   Kyūjū-mon
i   Chūka-mon
j   Gishū-mon
k   Kiam-mon
l   Genki-mon
m   Anki-mon
n   Kayō-mon
o   Senyō-mon
p   Ensei-mon
q   Chōraku-mon
r   Shōmei-mon
s   Eiam-mon
t   Butoku-mon
u   Ommei-mon
v   Yūgi-mon

Buildings:

1   Urushi-muro
2   Hyōgo-ryō
3   storehouse
4   storehouse
5   storehouse
6   storehouse
7   Tonomo-ryō oder Shuden-ryō
8   'Tea Garden'
9   Ōkimi-no-tsukasa
10   Uneme-no-tsukasa
11   Ōkura-shō
12   storehouse
13   storehouse
14   Naga-dono
15   Ritsu-bunzō
16   guard post
17   Ōtonoi-dokoro
18   Naikyō-bō
19   Ukon-efu
20   Zusho-ryō
21   Ōuta-dokoro
22   Komon-ryō
23   Kura-ryō
24   Nanin
25   Nui-dono-ryō
26   Nashimoto-no-in
27   Sakon-efu
28   Uhyō-efu
29   Butoku-den
30   Utage-no-matsubara
31   Shingon-in
32   Ito-dokoro
33   Naizen-shi
34   Uneme-no-machi
35   Moku-no-naikō
36   Chūka-in
37   Ranrim-bō
38   Keihō-bō
39   Kahō-bō
40   Gohi-dono
41   Dairi
42   Shiki-no-onzō-shi
43   Geki-no-chō
44   Minami-dokoro
45   Ippon-no-gosho-dokoro
46   Kama-dokoro
47   Sake-dono
48   Naiju-no-machi
49   Saiga-in
50   Sahyō-efu
51   Tōga-in
52   Takumi-ryō
53   Zōshu-shi
54   Sama-ryō
55   Tenyaku-ryō
56   Mii
57   Nakazukasa-no-kuriya
58   Buraku-den, within the Buraku-in
59   Daigoku-den (above) Ryūbi-dō (below)
60   Chōdō-in or Hasshō-in
61   Shōran-rō
62   Seihō-rō
63   Jijūkyoku
64   Nakatsukasa-shō
65   Udoneri
66   Kemmotsu
67   Shurei
68   Tenyaku
69   Onyō-ryō
70   Kageyushi
71   Fumi-dono
72   Dajō-kanchō
73   Chōsho
74   Saiin
75   Shōin
76   Shusuishi
77   Enkan-jinja
78   Kunai-shō
79   Daizenshiki
80   Gugo-in
81   Ōi-ryō
82   Uma-ryō
83   Jibu-shō
84   Shoryō-ryō
85   Gemba-ryō
86   Hanji
87   Kyōbu-shō
88   Danjōdai
89   Hyōbu-shō
90   Mimbu-shō
91   Shuzei-ryō
92   Shukei-ryō
93   Zōsha
94   Zōsha
95   Shikibu-shō
96   Shuzei-no-kuriya
97   Mimbu-no-kuriya
98   Shukei-no-kuriya
99   Shikibu-no-kuriya
100   Rinin
101   Saiin
102   Tōin
103   Ōtoneri-ryō
104   Jijūsho-no-kuriya
105   Gagaku-ryō

(after J. and R. K. Reischauer, *Early Japanese History,* Princeton, 1937)

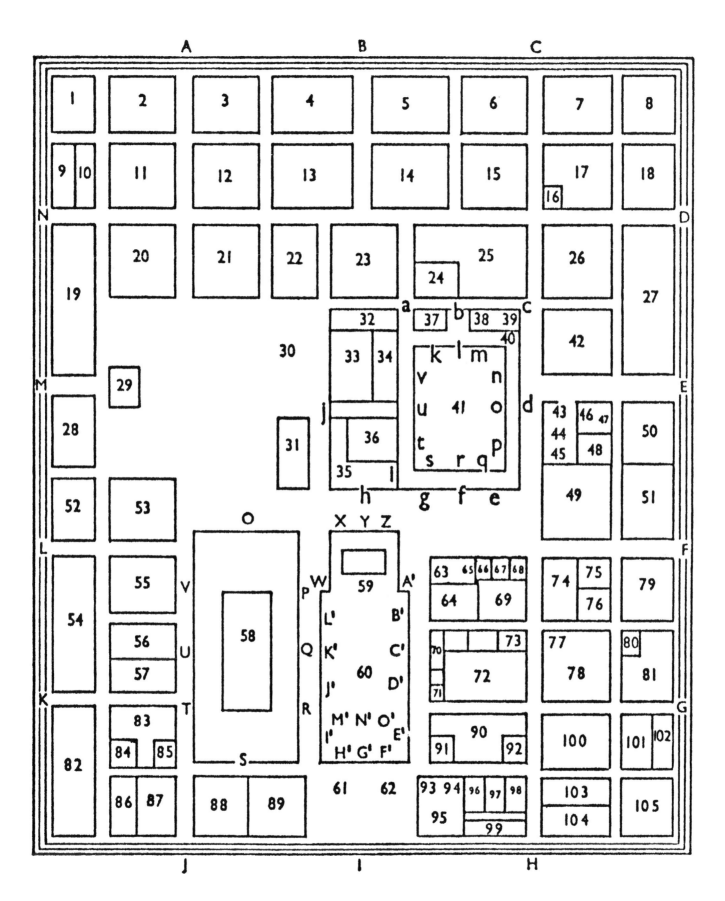

Layout of the Imperial Palace (Dairi)

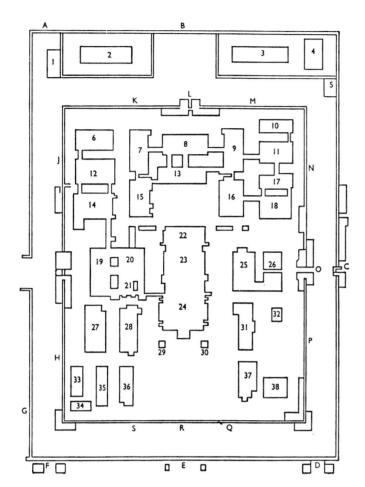

(after J. and R. K. Reischauer, *Early Japanese History*, Princeton, 1937)

Gates:

A   Shikkam-mon
B   Sakuhei-mon
C   Kenshum-mon
D   Shunka-mon
E   Kenrei-mon
F   Sumei-mon
G   Chūka-mon
H   Butoku-mon
I   Ommei-mon
J   Yūgi-mon
K   Kiam-mon
L   Genki-mon
M   Anki-mon
N   Kayō-mon
O   Senyō-mon
P   Ensei-mon
Q   Chōraku-mon
R   Shōmei-mon
S   Eiam-mon

Buildings:

1   Gosho-dokoro
2   Ranrim-bō
3   Keihō-bō
4   Kahō-bō
5   Gohi-dono
6   Shihō-sha
7   Tōka-den
8   Jōgan-den
9   Senyō-den
10   Shigeihoku-sha
11   Shigei-sha
12   Gyōke-sha
13   Jōnei-sha
14   Higyō-sha
15   Koki-den
16   Reikei-den
17   Shōyōhoku-sha
18   Shōyō-sha
19   Kōrō-den
20   Seiryō-den
21   Denjō-no-ma
22   Jōkyō-den
23   Jijū-den
24   Shishin-den
25   Ryōki-den
26   Ummei-den
27   Kurōdo-dokoro-machiya
28   Kyōsho-den
29   Ukon-no-tachibana (orange tree)
30   Sakon-no-sakura (cherry tree)
31   Giyō-den
32   Mikoshi-yadoriya
33   Tsukumo-dokoro
34   Tsukumo-dokoro-nansha
35   Shimmotsu-dokoro
36   Anfuku-den
37   Shunkō-den
38   Shuki-den

The Emperors of the Heian Period

(after G. B. Sansom)

Emperor	Birth	Accession	Abdication	Death
Kammu	737	781	—	806
Heizei (Heijō)	774	806	809	824
Saga	786	809	823	842
Junna	786	823	833	840
Nimmyō	810	833	—	850
Montoku	827	850	—	858
Seiwa	850	858	876	880
Yōzei	868	877	884	949
Kōkō	830	884	—	887
Uda	867	887	897	931
Daigo	885	897	—	930
Suzaku	923	930	946	952
Murakami	926	946	—	967
Reizei	950	967	969	1011
Enyū	959	969	984	991
Kazan	968	984	986	1008
Ichijō	980	986	—	1011
Sanjō	976	1011	1016	1017
Goichijō	1008	1016	—	1036
Gosuzaku	1009	1036	—	1045
Goreizei	1025	1045	—	1068
Gosanjō	1034	1068	1072	1073
Shirakawa	1053	1072	1086	1129
Horikawa	1079	1086	—	1107
Toba	1103	1107	1123	1156
Sutoku	1119	1123	1141	1164
Konoe	1139	1141	—	1155
Goshirakawa	1127	1155	1158	1192
Nijō	1143	1158	—	1165
Rokujō	1164	1165	1168	1176
Takakura	1161	1168	1180	1181
Antoku	1178	1180	(deposed)	1185
Gotoba	1180	1184	1198	1239

The Fujiwara Regents (866–1184)

	Sesshō	Kampaku		Sesshō	Kampaku
Yoshifusa (804–872)	866–872	–	Norimichi (996–1075)	–	1068–1075
Mototsune (836–891)	873–880	880–891	Morozane (1042–1101)	1086–1090	1075–1086; 1090–1094
Tadahira (880–949)	930–941	941–949			
Saneyori (900–970)	969–970	967–969	Moromichi (1062–1099)	–	1094–1099
Koretada (924–972)	970–972	–	Tadazane (1078–1162)	1107–1113	1105–1107; 1113–1121
Kanemichi (925–977)	–	972–977			
Yoritada (924–989)	–	977–986	Tadamichi (1097–1164)	1123–1129; 1141–1150	1121–1123; 1129–1141
Kaneie (929–990)	986–990	990			
Michitaka (957–995)	990–993	993–995	Motozane (1143–1166)	1165–1166	1158–1165
Michikane (961–995)	–	995	Motofusa (1144–1230)	1166–1172	1172–1179
Michinaga (966–1027)	1016–1017	[996–1017] Nairan	Motomichi (1160–1233)	1180–1183; 1184–1186	1179–1180
Yorimichi (922–1074)	1017–1019	1019–1068	Moroie (1172–1238)	1183–1184	–

The Minamoto (Genji) Clan

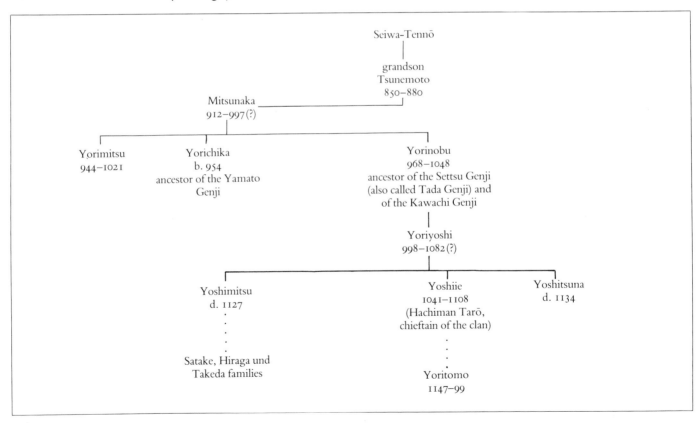

(after G. B. Sansom, *A History of Japan,* vol. I, London, 1959)

The Most Important Events in the Art and Architecture of the Heian Period

924	Thousand-armed Kannon for the Hosshō-ji
926	Priest Jōei (Jinin): figures of Buddha for the Daigo-ji
927	Book of ceremonies, *Engi-shiki,* written
935	*Tosa-nikki,* travel diary by Ki no Tsurayuki
937	*Busshi* Kōshō: two Ni-ō for the Kiyomizu-dera
945	Prose tales, *Ise-monogatari,* written
951	Jūichimen Kannon for the Rokuharamitsu-ji
951–952	Pagoda of the Daigo-ji decorated with the Mandala of the 'Two Worlds' and the Shingon patriarchs and consecrated
951–980	*Yamato-monogatari* written
985	Genshin (Eshin Sōzu): *Ojō Yō-shū*
987	Chōnen brings from China a statue of Shaka (Seiryō-ji) and paintings of 16 Rakan
990	Kōdō of the Hōryū-ji built
991	Yakushi trinity for the Kōdō of the Hōryū-ji
c. 996	*Makura no sōshi* ('Pillow Book') by Sei Shōnagon
1002	*Portrait of Jion Daishi* for the Yakushi-ji Central image of the Amida trinity for the Hokke-ji
c. 1002–1010	*Genji-monogatari* by Murasaki Shikibu
1003	Jūni-ten masks for the Kyōōgokoku-ji
1006	Fujiwara no Michinaga builds the Godai Hall in the Hosshō-ji, for which the statue of Fudō-myōō, now in the Dōshu-in, was carved
1007	Fujiwara no Michinaga consecrates the sutra grave on Mount Kimpusen
1010	Murasaki Shikibu writes her diary, *Murasaki-Shikibu-nikki*
1012	Thousand-armed Kannon for the Kōryū-ji
1013	Statue of Yakushi for the Kōfuku-ji Poetry anthology, *Wakan-rōei-shū*
1020	Fujiwara no Michinaga founds the Hōjō-ji
1022	Kondō and Godai-dō of the Hōjō-ji consecrated
1042	*Bugaku* masks for the shrine, Temukeyama-jinja
1047	Statue of Yakushi for the Saimyō-ji
1051	Statue of Yakushi for the Hōkai-ji
c. 1050	*Senzui-byōbu* for the Kyōōgokoku-ji
1053	Byōdō-in consecrated *Busshi* Jōchō: statue of Amida for the Hōō-dō of the Byōdō-in; doors of the Hōō-dō of the Byōdō-in painted with the *raigō* of Amida and with landscapes
1064	*Busshi* Chōsei: statues of the Jūni-ten for the Kōryū-ji
1066	Yakushi trinity for the Ryōzen-ji, Nara
1069	*Busshi* Enkai: statue of Shōtoku Taishi for the Hōryū-ji Hata no Chitei (Munesada): wall painting *Shōtoku Taishi eden* for the Edono of the Hōryū-ji

226

1078	Statues of Bishamon-ten and Kichijō-ten for the Hōryū-ji
1086	Painting: *Buddha's Entry into Nirvana* for the Kongōbu-ji
1096	Hondō of the Ishiyama-dera built
1098	Amida Hall of the Hōkai-ji built
c. 1100	Painting: *Resurrection of the Buddha from the Golden Coffin*
1102	*Gyōdō* masks for the *raigō* festival in the Hōryū-ji
1105	Amida Hall of the Sonshō-ji consecrated
1107	Hondō of the Jōruri-ji: nine statues of Amida
1108	Kōdō of the Chūson-ji in Hiraizumi built
1116	Fujiwara no Mototoshi does calligraphy for the anthology *Wakan-rōei-shū*
1119	*Genji-monogatari-emaki* mentioned in literature
1120	Calligraphy: *Sanjūroku-nin-shū* for the Nishihongan-ji
1120–1140?	*Genji-monogatari-emaki* painted
1121	Eye-opening ceremony for the statue of Shōtoku Taishi in the Shōryō-in of the Hōryū-ji Yakushi Hall of the Daigo-ji built
1124–1126	'Golden Hall' of the Chūson-ji built
1126	Sutra Hall of the Chūson-ji built
1127	Painting of the *Jūni-ten* for the Kyōōgokoku-ji Painting of the *Five Great Kings of Wisdom* for the Kyōōgokoku-ji
1130	*Busshi* Inkaku: statue of Amida for the Hōkongō-in, consecrated at this date
1135–1140	*Busshi* Kenen: statue of Amida for the Anraku-ji, Toba
1137	Anraku-ji in Toba consecrated
1139	Seijō-ji consecrated
c. 1140	Scrolls with satirical pictures, *Chōjū-giga,* produced
1141	Wall paintings from the *Lotus Sutra* for the Kunō-ji
1144	*Bugaku* masks for the Hōryū-ji
1148	Amida trinity for the Sanzen-in, Ōhara
1149	Enshō-ji founded
1151	Amida trinity with crystal eyes for the Chōgaku-ji
1154	Statue of Senju Kannon for the Būjō-ji
c. 1157	*Nenjū-gyōgi-emaki* by Tokiwa no Mitsunaga
1160	Fujiwara no Tadayuki does calligraphy for the anthology *Wakan-rōei-shū* Shiramizu-Amida-dō (or Ganjō-ji) built and decorated with Amida trinity and Ni-ten
1164	Scroll *Heike-Nōkyō* for the Itsukushima-jinja; Rengeō-in (or Myōhō-in) consecrated, containing 1,001 statues of the Thousand-armed Kannon by Kōchō, Kōkei and Unkei
1173	*Bugaku* masks for the Itsukushima-jinga
1175–1177	Scrolls of the *Ban-Dainagon-ekotoba* produced
1176	*Busshi* Unkei: statue of the Buddha Dainichi for the Enjō-ji

1178	Pagoda brought to the Jōruri-ji
before 1180	Scrolls of the *Shigisan-engi-emaki* painted
1180	Taira no Shigehira has the Tōdai-ji and Kōfuku-ji burnt down
1181	Chūgen has the Tōdai-ji rebuilt
1185	*Bugaku* masks for the Kasuga-jinja
1186	Portraits by the Inson school for the Kōdō of the Kōfuku-ji
1188	Portraits by the Kōkei school for the Nanen-dō of the Kōfuku-ji
1190–1192	Calligraphy of the 'Eyeless Sutra' for Ex-emperor Goshirakawa
1194	Portraits by the Myōen school for the Kondō of the Kōfuku-ji *Busshi* Unkei: statues of two Ni-ō for the Nanchū-mon Gate of the Kōfuku-ji

List of Works of the Buddha Sculptors Kōshō and Jōchō

> Dimensions:
> 1 *shaku* = 30.3 cm
> *jōroku* = 16 *shaku* = *c.* 500 cm for standing figure and
>   *c.* 250–290 cm for seated figure
> *tōshin* = life size

Kōshō
(active *c.* 990–1021 in Kyōto, administrator of the Kiyomizu-dera Temple, father of Jōchō)

990–995	Shaka for the Ryōzen-in, built by Genshin (Eshin Sōzu)
991	Shaka *(jōroku)* for the Kawara-in Palace of Sadaijin Minamoto no Tōru. The work was transferred in 1000 to the Gidarin-ji.
988?	Shaka Trinity for the Enkyō-ji
c. 989	Jūichimen Kannon for the Henjō-ji
990?	Yakushi trinity for the Kōdō of the Hōryū-ji
c. 992?	Amida for the Gokuraku-ji
993?	Yakushi for the Zensui-ji
c. 995	Miroku trinity for the Zenshō-ji
998	Receives the clerical title of *Tosa Kōshi*
999?	Miroku trinity for the Miroku-ji
999	Dainichi, Fugen and Jūichimen Kannon for the Chōen-ji
	Nyoirin Kannon in silver
999–1000	Improvements to the image of Myōken in the Myōken-dō of the Reigan-ji
	Shō-Kannon, Bon-ten and Taishaku-ten for the Jijū-den Hall
1001	Cult image for the Kedai-in Temple built by Genshin (Eshin Sōzu)
1002	Amida with Fugen and Monju of sandalwood, for readings of the *Lotus Sutra* in the Higashi Sanjō-in Palace of the Fujiwara
1003?	Yakushi for the Byōdō-in
1004	Material for four Shi-tennō statues received from Fujiwara no Yukinari
1005	Life-size figures of Yakushi, gilt Jūichimen Kannon and Fudō, gessoed and painted, begun for Empress Gofūzu
	Fugen for the Sammai-dō Hall of the Jōmyō-ji of Fujiwara no Michinaga
1006	Gilt Amida for the Seson-ji
1006?	Fudō-myōō for the Dōshu-in Temple
1007	Five Buddhas for the pagoda of the Kongōbu-ji on Kōya-san

1008	Yakushi of sandalwood for Empress Goshūzen
1010	Yakushi and Kannon of silver for the Ninnō-e Festival
1012?	Senjū Kannon for the Kōryū-ji
1013?	Yakushi for the Kōfuku-ji
1013	Amida for the Shōrin-in Temple in Ōhara
	Gold leaf for three statues received from Fujiwara no Michinaga
1018–1022	Miroku (2 *jōroku*) for the Seki-dera built by Genshin (Eshin Sōzu)
1020	Nine Amida images *(jōroku)* for the Muryōju-in of the Hōjō-ji

Jōchō
(active: ?–1057 in Kyōto, son of Kōshō)

1020	Nine gilt Amida figures *(jōroku)*; Kannon and Seishi (both 10 *shaku)*; (with Kōshō) four Shi-tennō with gesso and paint, for the Muryōju-in of the Hōjō-ji
1022	Gilt Dainichi (32 *shaku*); four gilt figures of Shaka, Yakushi, Monju and Miroku (each 20 *shaku*); Bon-ten, Taishaku-ten and four Shi-tennō (each 9 *shaku*), gessoed and painted, for the Kondō of the Hōjō-ji
	Fudō and four Myōō (each 20 *shaku*) four Shi-tennō (each 16 *shaku*); all gessoed and painted, for the Godai-dō of the Hōjō-ji
	Both halls were consecrated on 14 July 1022, and on 16 July 1022 Jōchō received the clerical rank of *Hokkyō*
1023	Seven gilt Yakushi figures *(jōroku)*; six gilt Kannon figures *(jōroku)*; a gilt Nikkō and a Gakkō Bosatsu; twelve Jūni Shinshō (each 8 *shaku),* gessoed and painted, for the Yakushi-dō of the Hōjō-ji
1026	For the confinement of the empress: twenty-seven life-size figures: Shaka, Fugen, Monju, seven Yakushi, six Kannon, five Dai-myōō, Bon-ten, Taishaku-ten and four Shi-tennō
1036	Three Buddha figures for the funeral of Emperor Goichijō
1040	Silver figure of Yakushi (1 *shaku*) for the memorial service for Emperor Gosuzaku
1041	Renovation of the figurehead on the dragon-head galley for the Cherry Blossom Festival
1047	Yakushi trinity for the reconstructed Kōfuku-ji; Jōchō receives the clerical rank of *Hōgen*
1053	Gilt Amida *(jōroku)* and twenty-five small relief figures of Bodhisattvas for the Hōō-dō of the Byōdō-in in Uji

Works Ascribed to Jōchō:

Copy of the Shaka figure of the Daian-ji for the Hakkaku-dō of the Tō-in Temple in the Yakushi-ji

Shaka figure *(jōroku)* for the Saiin of the nobleman Kunitsune no Ason

Jizō figure *(tōshin)* for the Rokuharamitsu-ji

Dainichi in sandalwood, Yakushi and Shaka for the Sambō-in of the Daigo-ji

Amida for the Katoku-in in Sakamoto

(List of works of Jōchō after K. Mizuno, 'Dai-busshi Jōchō'. *Nihon no Bijutsu* I, no. 164 [Tōkyō, 1980])

Genealogical Tree of the Sculptors of the School of Jōchō

——————— Blood relatives

– – – – – – – Pupils

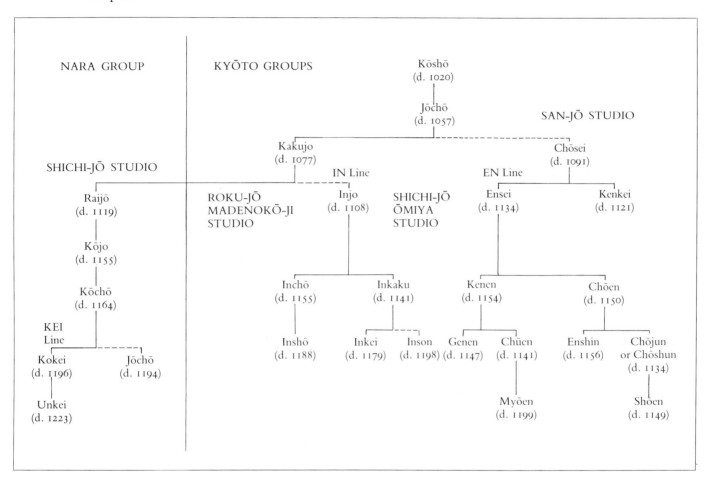

NARA GROUP

KYŌTO GROUPS

Kōshō
(d. 1020)

Jōchō
(d. 1057)

SAN-JŌ STUDIO

Kakujo
(d. 1077)

Chōsei
(d. 1091)

SHICHI-JŌ STUDIO

IN Line

EN Line

Raijō
(d. 1119)

Injo
(d. 1108)

Ensei
(d. 1134)

Kenkei
(d. 1121)

ROKU-JŌ
MADENOKŌ-JI
STUDIO

SHICHI-JŌ
ŌMIYA
STUDIO

Kōjo
(d. 1155)

Kōchō
(d. 1164)

Inchō
(d. 1155)

Inkaku
(d. 1141)

Kenen
(d. 1154)

Chōen
(d. 1150)

KEI
Line

Inshō
(d. 1188)

Inkei
(d. 1179)

Inson
(d. 1198)

Genen
(d. 1147)

Chūen
(d. 1141)

Enshin
(d. 1156)

Chōjun
or Chōshun
(d. 1134)

Kokei
(d. 1196)

Jōchō
(d. 1194)

Unkei
(d. 1223)

Myōen
(d. 1199)

Shōen
(d. 1149)

Glossary

Abbreviations:
Chin. = Chinese
Skr. = Sanskrit

ACALANĀTHA (Skr.) See Fudō-myōō.

AIZEN-MYŌŌ (Skr. Rāgarāja) 'The god who vanquishes lust and greed,' manifestation of Dainichi and Kongōsātta and incarnation of the highest benevolence. The colour of his body is red; he has three eyes and six arms; his head is crowned with a lion's head and he sits on a red lotus.

AMATERASU-ŌMIKAMI 'The great noble goddess who shines in Heaven,' in Shintō the mythological ancestress of the imperial house. Her grandson Ninigi is regarded as the great-grandfather of Jimmu-Tennō, the first Japanese emperor. Her shrine was set up in Ise under Suinin-Tennō.

AMIDA NYORAI (Skr. Amitābha, Amitāyus tathāgata; in Japanese also Muryokō and Muryoju) 'Buddha of Eternal Radiance and Life'. Dhyāni Buddha of the West, Lord of the Western Paradise, also of the 'Pure Land' *(Jōdo)*. The colour of his body is gold; his hair is swept to the right. His mudras: *jōin* (Skr. *dhyāna*) = Meditation; *tempōrin-in* (Skr. *dharmacakra*) = Turning the Wheel of the Law; *raigō-in* (Skr. *vitarka*) = Promise of Deliverance.

AMIDA-DŌ ('Amida Hall', also Yūshin-dō) Hall of Worship for the Buddha Amida. In Japan usually a square hall of 3, 5 or 7 bays with a pyramidal roof; the interior an imitation of Amida's Paradise (Jōdo) with an image of Amida, also an Amida trinity in sculpture and scenes of the Western Paradise in painting, forming a synthesis of the arts.

ashi-de ('reed hand') Decorative and illustrative scattering of script characters in a *Yamato-e* picture. In Heian art used as an ornamental element in the decoration of writing paper and lacquer.

bettō Administrator or director of an office.

BHAISHAJYAGURU TATHĀGATA (Skr.) See Yakushi Nyorai.

BIRUSHANA NYORAI, also Rushana (Skr. Vairocana) 'Buddha of all-embracing Radiance.' The original Buddha of all following manifestations of the Buddha; in Japan equated with the Shintō sun goddess, Amaterasu-Ōmikami. Birushana is seated on a thousand-petalled lotus surrounded by a nimbus containing hundreds of small Buddhas.

BISHAMON-TEN, also Tamono-ten (Skr. Vaishravana) Guardian deity of the North under the Shitennō; later god of Good Luck. Represented as an armoured knight, standing, with spear and pagoda, on a rock with two demons.

BODHISATTVA (Skr.) See Bosatsu.

BOSATSU (Skr. Bodhisattva) 'Whose being is Enlightenment.' A being who has achieved the ten perfections of Buddhist doctrine but has renounced Buddhahood in order to help those trapped in suffering towards Enlightenment (Nirvana).

BON-TEN (Skr. Brahmā) The third great creator, in Hinduism, with Vishnu and Shiva. In esoteric Buddhism represented as a man with four heads and four arms, riding on three geese.

BUDDHA (Skr.) See Nyorai.

BUTSU (Skr. Buddha) In Japan, normally only the name of Shaka Nyorai.

bugaku ('dance music') Dance following continental models, executed on a stage with an orchestra, by clergy and lay nobles at dedication feasts. Sometimes danced with masks (twenty-four types are now known), the earliest of which are from the beginning of the eleventh century.

bushi, also *samurai* ('knight')　A member of the nobility of the sword, which during the Heian period, in contrast to the court nobility, was building itself up as a power in the provinces.

busshi ('Buddha master')　In Japan, a sculptor *(ki-busshi)* or painter *(e-busshi)* of Buddhist cult images.

bussho ('Buddha [carving] studio')　The studios of the *busshi* who, from the tenth century, became independent of the temples and worked on commission.

byōbu ('folding screen' with two or six panels)　Generally a pair of screens with continuous or complementary subjects pictured on them. In the Heian period there were *byōbu* with Chinese themes *(Kara-e)* and others with Japanese themes *(Yamato-e).* The former were five feet high, the latter four feet.

CHAN (Chin.)　See Zen.

DAIDAIRI ('Greater Imperial Palace')　The enclosed area of administrative and private buildings of the Imperial Palace, based on the model of the Chinese metropolis of Chang'an (cf. pp. 220–221).

DAIJŌ-E ('Feast of the Rice Tasting')　Main Shintō ceremony after the accession of an emperor.

DAINICHI NYORAI (Skr. Mahāvairocana)　'Buddha of the Great Light.' The ultimate and central Buddha of esoteric Buddhism, the nucleus of Buddhist wisdom and the central figure of the Mandala of the 'Two Worlds'.

DAIRI ('palace')　Residence of the emperor (cf. p. 222).

DAJŌ TENNŌ, also *Jōkō* ('Great Emperor')　Title given the emperor after his abdication.

danzō ('figure of scented wood')　Sculptures of sandalwood, usually neither dressed nor painted, at first imported from China.

dazaifu　Seat of the military command of Kyūshū (Tsukushi) from the sixth century; played an important role as link with the continent.

dengaku ('field music')　Popular dances that came into fashion in the Heian period and celebrated the planting of rice in a religious ceremony.

DEVA　See Ten.

e-busshi　See *busshi.*

e-dokoro ('Painting Office')　An office in the imperial court to which painters and arrangements for painted decoration in the palaces were subject; founded in 886.

ekotoba ('picture narrative')　See also *emakimono.*

emakimono, also *emaki* ('picture scroll')　Term for hand scrolls with picture narratives in *Yamato-e.*

eshi ('painter')　Term for professional painters who executed secular pictures for the court or for noblemen.

FUDŌ-MYŌŌ (Skr. Acalanātha)　'The Immovable King of Wisdom (or Light).' A frightening figure who protects Buddhism with sword, lasso and flames; a manifestation of Dainichi in esoteric Buddhism.

FUGEN BOSATSU (Skr. Samantabhadra)　'Bodhisattva of Limitless Wish-Fulfillment' and highest wisdom. He is seated on a white elephant that has six tusks, and in esoteric Buddhism he holds thunderbolts in his hands. In the Heian period he was regarded as a healer of women's troubles, following a chapter of the *Lotus Sutra.*

fukinuki-yatai ('blown-off-roof style')　In *Yamato-e* a method of representation for revealing scenes happening indoors.

gagaku ('elegant music')　Concert music, also performed to accompany *bugaku* dances in unison with wind, percussion and string instruments.

GENJI ('Minamoto clan')　Name of the families split off from the imperial house that were demoted back into subject rank. The various lines were named after the emperors from whom they descended.

giga ('joke picture') Term for caricature-like, sketchy pictures done in rapid ink painting.

gigaku ('art music') Dances with head masks introduced from the continent during the seventh century. About 240 masks survive from the late seventh to the mid-eighth century.

GODAI KOKŪZŌ (Skr. Akasagarbha) The 'Five Great Kukūzō,' 'Manifestations of Space-embracing Wisdom,' represent the virtues of the five Buddhas of Wisdom (Godai Nyorai). They provide protection from catastrophes and promote good fortune.

GODAI-MYŌŌ (Skr. Dharmapāla) The 'Five Great Kings of Wisdom' (lit. 'Brilliant Kings' or 'Kings of Light'). Emanations of Dainichi Nyorai in frightening aspect. Round the central figure of Fudō-myōō are placed Gozanze-myōō in the East, Gundari-myōō in the south, Daiitoku-myōō in the West and Kongōyasha-myōō in the North.

Gyōdō Temple processions in connection with the cult of Amida representing the *raigō,* the Descent of Amida Nyorai, with his following of twenty-five Bodhisattvas.

gyōdō-men Masks for *gyōdō* processions, representing Bosatsu or Jūni-ten.

HACHIMAN Shintō god of war and protector of the nation. In Buddhism adopted as Dai-Bosatsu and represented as a monk (Sōgyō Hachiman).

HAIDEN ('Prayer Hall') Hall or anteroom at a Shintō shrine for worshippers. An architectural innovation of the mid-Heian period.

haji ('earth potter') Simple low-fired earthenware, made on the wheel by members of the *haji* guild and used as plain household crockery.

hakubyō-e ('painting [left] white') A technique of *Yamato-e* in which only outlines were drawn in black ink, and a few accents provided such as the black areas of women's hair or men's caps and touches of red for the lips.

hensō See mandala.

hikime-kagihana ('stroke for an eye, hook for a nose') Term for the calligraphic method of portraying the human face in *Yamato-e*.

hisashi Roof extension in palace buildings and temples.

hiten ('flying deity') A floating Bosatsu-like figure who brings votive offerings in the *raigō* of Amida.

Hōgen ('Eye of the Law') Second rank of the Buddhist church, to which artists might be appointed in the Heian period, if they specialized in Buddhist sculpture and painting; see also *Hōin* and *Hokkyō*.

Hōin ('Sign of the Law') Highest rank of the Buddhist church; see also *Hōgen* and *Hokkyō*.

Hokkyō ('Bridge of the Law') Third and lowest rank of the Buddhist church; see also *Hōgen* and *Hōin*.

hompa-shiki ('rolling-wave style') The style of carving drapery folds in Jōgan sculpture. The ridges are alternately higher and flatter, like breaking waves.

HONDEN Main hall of a Shintō shrine.

HONDŌ Main hall of a Buddhist temple complex.

honzon Principal cult image in a temple hall.

HŌŌ ('Phoenix') Title of an ex-emperor who has become a monk.

hōsōge ('flowers of precious appearance') Fantastic blossoms in the style of Tang art that fall from Heaven during holy events; also an ornament in Buddhist art.

ichiboku-zukuri ('single-block technique') Term for wooden sculptures carved from one block, often hollowed out at the back. The earliest Japanese carving technique, which reached its acme in Jōgan sculpture.

insei ('cloister or palace government') The regency of an abdicated emperor with his own administrative apparatus; after 1068, the term for the third phase of the Heian period.

issai-kyō ('a set of sutras')   A collection of all the known sutra texts consisting of 5,000 to 6,900 scrolls.

jinja ('gods' shrine')   A Shintō shrine.

JIZŌ BOSATSU (Skr. Kshitigarbha) 'Womb of the Earth.' Bosatsu who delivers and leads living things, active between the Nirvana of Shaka Nyorai and the coming of the Buddha of the future, Miroku. In the guise of a monk with jewel and rattle he saves people from Hell and is the protector of children.

Jōdo ('Pure Land')   Name of the Western Paradise of Amida Nyorai.

jōroku ('16 feet')   Size of the Buddha, usually *c.* 5 metres for standing figures and 2.50–2.90 metres for sitting figures.

JŪICHIMEN KANNON (Skr. Ekadashamukhāvalokitesh-vara)   An aspect of Kannon, venerated as a Saviour from demons. Ten small heads, symbolizing the stages of Enlightenment, sit atop his head, which looks behind him.

JŪNI SHINSHŌ ('twelve generals of Yakushi Nyorai')   These twelve terrifying guardians sometimes have the heads of the twelve beasts of the Zodiac. The generals symbolize the twelve vows of Yakushi Nyorai to deliver mankind.

JŪNI-TEN ('twelve deva')   Protective deities of the country and of Buddhist doctrine, who played an essential role in esoteric Buddhism in place of the Shi-tennō.

kami ('deity')   A divine Shintō being.

kana   Characters of the Japanese syllabic script.

kanji ('Chinese characters')   The ideograms adopted from China that can be read in either Japanese or Sino-Japanese.

KANNON BOSATSU, also Kanzeon (Skr. Avalokitesh-vara)   'The Lord who looks down on the world's cry of suffering.' An emanation of Amida Buddha, whose image he wears in his crown. With Seishi, the attendant of Amida. In the *raigō* he holds a lotus throne for the deceased. In the Heian period portrayed as eleven-headed Kannon, thousand-armed Kannon and Nyoirin Kannon.

kanshi ('Chinese poem')   The form, adopted from China, of five-word or seven-word poems *(shi)*, which rhyme at the end of the lines.

Kara-e ('Chinese painting')   Paintings in Chinese style with Chinese themes, in contrast to *Yamato-e*, paintings with Japanese style and content.

kara-kami ('China paper')   Decorated paper produced in China, or from Chinese models in Japanese workshops, coloured and printed with various patterns in mica, or decorated with stencils.

kara-yō ('Chinese style')   Term for the trend in art and culture in Japan that turned to China and copied it directly, in contrast to 'Japanese style,' *(wa-yō)*.

kasen-e ('poet picture')   Term for ideal portraits of famous poets in *Yamato-e* style.

keman ('flower banner')   Fan-shaped decorative hanging of bronze or leather, for altars, temple carts and consecrated objects.

ki-busshi   See *busshi*.

KICHIJŌ-TEN, also Kisshō-ten (Skr. Srī-mahā-deva)   Goddess of good harvests, luck and virtues; Indian consort of Bishamon-ten (Vaishravana). Usually represented as a lady of the Tang period with a lucky jewel in her hand.

kichō ('curtain stand')   T-shaped frame with free-hanging length of cloth, behind which the ladies of the court could sit protected from inquisitive eyes.

kirikane ('cut gold')   Term for the decoration of Buddhist paintings and sculpture with patterns in cut gold leaf.

kokoro-e ('heart picture')   Term for the significance of a work of art as represented in one picture, or for the frontispiece of a sutra that represents its content.

KONDŌ ('Golden Hall')   The main hall of a Buddhist temple, also called Hondō.

konshi ('blue paper')   Dark blue writing paper dyed with indigo, used for writing sutras.

maki-e ('sprinkled picture')   Lacquer technique, in which pictures are made by sprinkling gold and silver powder into the moist lacquer.

manyō-gana or *mana-gana* ('writing form of the *Manyō-shū*')   The use of Chinese characters phonetically as syllabic characters, in order to write down poems and texts in the Japanese language.

mandara, also *hensō* (Skr. mandala)   Schematic representation of the Buddhist pantheon in the form of diagrams.

MONJU BOSATSU (Skr. Mañjushrī) 'The happy Youth.' Bodhisattva of wisdom, whose attributes are a sword and a book.

mappō ('end of time' or 'latter days of the Law')   The last of the three Buddhist epochs, which was to begin in 1053 in Japan.

mikkyō ('secret teaching')   Term for the tantric Shingon and Tendai sects of esoteric Buddhism, introduced at the beginning of the Heian period.

MIROKU BOSATSU (Skr. Maitreya) 'The Loving One.' Buddha of the Future Era, represented as Bodhisattva in the Paradise of the East, Tosotsu-ten (Tushita). Sometimes represented as a Buddha, sometimes as a Bodhisattva.

miyabi ('noble elegance')   The particular elegance of the high nobles of the imperial court that stamped the life-style of the aristocracy of Heian-kyō.

mokushin-kanshitsu ('dry lacquer over wooden core')   Technique of sculpture in which a thick layer of hemp, soaked in lacquer, was applied over a wooden core and the final modelling done in dry lacquer; in use from the second half of the Nara period into the early Heian period.

monogatari ('tale')   Prose literature in the form of a novel.

monogatari-e ('novel pictures')   Illustrations to famous stories of the Heian period, painted in the style of *Yamato-e,* mostly as *tsukuri-e.*

mudrā (Skr.) ('seal')   Symbolic hand positions and gestures of the Buddhas and Bodhisattvas.

nehanzu ('picture of Nirvana')   Representation of the entry of Shaka Nyorai into Nirvana.

nikki ('diary')   Diaries with autobiographical features; in Japan since the Heian period, supposed to be written by men in Chinese and by women in Japanese in *kana* syllabic script.

nembutsu ('Buddha invocation')   The invocation *namu Amida butsu* proclaimed first by preachers, later by sects as the Way to Rebirth in the Western Paradise of Amida Nyorai.

Ni-ō, also Ni-ten (Skr. Vajradhara) ('Two Kings')   Two frightening guardians placed at the Chū-mon Gate of Buddhist temples to protect the Law.

nise-e ('likeness picture')   Official portrait of a high dignitary, painted in state robes with realistic facial features.

nōsho ('outstanding writer')   From the late tenth century, the term for the great calligraphers who worked in court service.

NYOIRIN KANNON (Cintāmanicakrāvalokiteshvara) ('She Who Quenches Desire')   A form of the 'Six Kannon' with two, four or generally six arms.

onna-de ('women's hand')   The form of *kana* syllabic script written by women.

onoko-de ('men's hand') The script with Chinese characters, preferred by men.

RAIDŌ ('Prayer Hall') Annex or extension of the Hondō of a Buddhist temple.

raigō ('welcoming descent' of Amida Nyorai who comes to conduct the dying believer to his Paradise). The Buddha Amida is represented on clouds, floating down with Kannon, Seishi and other Bosatsu. The *raigō* is the central theme of Amida Buddhism as portrayed in art.

Rikushō-ji ('Six Shō Temples') Six temples east of Kyōto, in Shirakawa, laid out by ex-emperors during the *insei* period.

ROKKASEN ('six poetic geniuses') The six famous poets of the ninth century: Ariwara no Narihira, Bishop Henjō, Kisen Hōshi, Ōtomo no Kuronushi, Bunya no Yasuhide and Lady Ono no Komachi.

roku-dō, also *riku-dō* ('Six Worlds') The six stages of existence in Buddhist thinking: the lowest is the World of Hells, then follow the worlds of the Hunger Spirits, of Animals, of Demons, of Humans and of the Mortal Gods.

RUSHANA See Birushana Nyorai.

saishiki-emaki ('coloured *emaki*') The *emakimono* built up as *tsukuri-e* in a technique of multi-layered drawing and colouring. The classic examples are the *Genji-monogatari-emaki,* the *Nezame-monogatari-emaki* and the *Murasaki-Shikibu-nikki-emaki.*

samurai See *bushi.*

sanzon ('trinity') Group of three cult images as a con-figuration of the World of Buddha.

SEISHI BOSATSU (Skr. Mahāsthāmaprāpta) 'Exceptional Strength.' The Bodhisattva who represents the Wisdom of Amida. Together with Kannon Bosatsu, attendant of the Buddha Amida. Characterized by hands in the gesture of worship and a vase in his crown.

SENJU KANNON (Skr. Sahasrabhujāvalokiteshvara) Universal saviour figure of Kannon with a thousand arms and eleven heads. The favourite form of Kannon Bosatsu during the *insei* period.

SHAKA NYORAI (Skr. Shakyamuni tathāgata) Name of the historical Buddha, the Indian prince Siddhārtha Gautama.

shaku Ceremonial sceptre often found on statues of Shintō gods in court dress.

shikishi ('colour paper') Almost square poem sheets, mostly of coloured paper, painted or printed, used as a ground for calligraphy or for elegant missives.

shinden-zukuri ('sleeping hall method of construction') Palace architecture of the Heian period.

shita-e ('underground picture') Painting over which text is written, for decorative or religious purposes.

SHI-TENNŌ, also *lokapāla* (Skr. Catur-mahārāja) 'Four Heavenly Kings.' Guardians for the four sides of the World Mountain, adopted from Indian iconography; in Buddhism warriors guarding a stūpa, a mandala and an altar.

shōji, also *sōji* Sliding doors in a Japanese palace hall; during the Heian period they were used as a support for painting.

sō-kana ('grass *kana*') *Kana* scripts written like the Chinese rapid grass character.

sue WARE High-fired earthenware, made in Japan from the fifth to the thirteenth century after Korean models and mostly used for ceremonial purposes.

TAISHAKU-TEN (Skr. Sakradevanam Indra) 'Mighty Lord of the Deva.' A Brahminic God who combatted the deva. In Buddhism 'Lord of the Thirty-one Heavens,' a pendant figure to Bon-ten (Skr. Brahmā).

tanka, also *waka* or *uta* ('short poem') The standard Japanese thirty-one-syllable poem. It consists of lines of 5, 7 and 7 syllables or 7 and 7 syllables.

TEN (Skr. Deva)   A non-Buddhist Indian deity.

TOBATSU-BISHAMON-TEN ('Bishamon from Turfan')
A manifestation of Bishamon-ten in armour as the
protector of a city or country. Usually he stands on
two demons and the Earth goddess.

togidashi ('polish out')   A lacquer technique: gold and
silver powder is sprinkled into the still damp lacquer
over motifs previously drawn; the surface is then
covered over with lacquer and polished until the
sprinkled motif reappears.

tsukuri-e ('built-up picture')   *Yamato-e* painting technique: over a preliminary drawing and foundation,
strong colours are employed to cover the surfaces; the
picture is completed with lines of ink on top.

uta   See *tanka*.

uta-awase ('poetry contest')   Entertainment at court
consisting of officially organized poetry 'contests'.

uta-monogatari ('poem-novel')   Short stories constructed as a frame for poems, usually dialogue poems.
Examples are the *Ise-monogatari, Yamato-monogatari,*
etc.

vajra (Skr.)   Indra's thunderbolt.

waka ('Japanese poem')   See *tanka*.

washi ('Japanese paper')   In contrast to Chinese paper
(kara-kami), paper made in Japanese mills *(kōya)* from
the fibres of the paper mulberry.

wa-yō ('Japanese style')   In contrast to 'Chinese style'
(kara-yō), characteristically Japanese forms in the art of
the Heian period.

YAKUSHI NYORAI (Skr. Bhaishajyaguru)   'Buddha of
Healing.' He made twelve vows to heal all living creatures of physical and spiritual diseases; usually shown
with a bag of medicine in his right hand.

YAMATO   The central province of Japan, including the
capital city of Nara; territory of the Yamato clan; in an-
tiquity and in poetry describes the whole of Japan.

Yamato-e ('Japanese painting')   The individual style of
Japanese painting, in contrast to the Chinese style
(Kara-e) adopted from China.

yosegi-zukuri ('sculpture of wooden blocks combined
together')   A new technique of wooden sculpture introduced at the beginning of the eleventh century, that
allowed the carving of extremely thin, shell-like, large
figures. The wooden blocks or boards were combined
according to the principles of modular construction and
worked by division of labour.

ZEN (Skr. Dhyāna, Chin. Chan) ('meditation')   The
practice of meditation common to all Buddhist sects,
that came from India via China to Japan.

zuzō ('drawn figures')   Outline drawings of the figures in the Buddhist pantheon. They were brought
from China or copied there, and served as models for
the iconography in art.

Bibliography

Akiyama, T. *Japanische Malerei*. Geneva, 1961.
—— *Heian jidai sezokuga no kenkyū* ('Peinture profane du haut moyen âge japonais'). Tōkyō, 1964.
—— 'Genji-e.' *Nihon no bijutsu* 4, no. 119. Tōkyō, 1976.
—— 'A New Attribution for a Painting Fragment to the Twelfth Century "Tale of Genji Scrolls"'. *Kokka* 1011. Tōkyō, 1978.
—— *et al.* 'Emakimono.' *Genshoku nihon no bijutsu* 8. Tōkyō, 1968.
Alex, W. *Architektur der Japaner*. Ravensburg, 1965.
Armbruster, G. 'Das Shigisan-Engi-Emaki. Ein japanisches Rollbild aus dem 12. Jahrhundert.' *Mitteilungen der Ostasiengesellschaft* XL. Hamburg–Wiesbaden, 1959.
—— and Brinker, H. *Pinsel und Tusche*. Munich, 1975.
Art Treasures from the Imperial Collections. Tōkyō, 1971.
Aston, W. G. *Nihongi*. Vols. 1, 2. London, 1956.

Baltzer, F. *Die Architektur der Kultbauten Japans*. Berlin, 1907.
Bary, W. T. *Sources of the Japanese Tradition*. New York, 1958.
Benl, O. 'Fujiwara Kinto, Dichter und Kritiker der Heian-Zeit.' *Monumenta Nipponica* 4, no. 2. Tōkyō, 1941.
—— *Die Entwicklung der japanischen Poetik bis zum 16. Jahrhundert*. Hamburg, 1951.
—— and Hammitzsch, H. ed. *Japanische Geisteswelt: Vom Mythus zur Gegenwart*. Baden-Baden, 1956.
Bersihand, R. *Geschichte Japans von den Anfängen bis zur Gegenwart*. Trans. by V. S. Schaarschmidt. Stuttgart, 1963.
Blaser, W. *Tempel und Teehaus in Japan*. Olten-Lausanne, 1955.
Brower, R. H. and Miner, E. *Japanese Court Poetry*. Stanford, 1961.
—— *Fujiwara Teika's Superior Poems of Our Time*. Stanford, 1967.

Dettmer, H. A. *Grundzüge der Geschichte Japans*. Darmstadt, 1965.

Eckardt, H. 'Das Kokonchomonchu des Tachibana Narisue als musikgeschichtliche Quelle.' *Göttinger asiatische Forschungen*. Vol. 6. Wiesbaden, 1956.
Elisseeff, D. and V. *La Civilisation japonaise*. Paris, 1974.
—— *Japan, Kunst und Kultur*. Freiburg, Basle, Vienna, 1981.
Ennin. *Diary: The Record of a Pilgrimage to China... (Nittō guhō junrei gyōki)*. Trans. by E. O. Reischauer. New York, 1955.

Florenz, K. *Geschichte der japanischen Literatur*. 2nd ed. Leipzig, 1909.
Fontain, J. 'Kibi's Adventures in China.' *Boston Museum Bulletin*, no. 344. Boston, 1968.

—— *The Pilgrimage of Sudhana*. The Hague, 1967.
—— and Hempel, R. *China, Korea, Japan*. Propyläen Kunstgeschichte, Vol. 17. Berlin, 1968.
Fujimura, S. *Nihon bungaku daijiten*. Vols. 1–7. Tōkyō, 1936–7.
Fukuyama, T. 'Byōdōin to Chūsonji.' *Nihon no bijutsu* 9. Tōkyō, 1964.
Furuya, M. *Heian Temples: Byōdō-in and Chūson-ji*. Trans. by R. K. Jones. The Heibonsha Survey of Japanese Art, Vol. 9. New York, Tōkyō, 1976.
—— 'Heian-jidai no sho.' *Nihon no bijutsu* 5, no. 180. Tōkyō, 1981.

Gabbert, G. *Die Masken des Bugaku: Profane japanische Tanzmasken der Heian- u. Kamakura-Zeit*. Wiesbaden, 1972.
—— *Buddhistische Plastik aus China und Japan: Bestandskatalog des Museums für Ostasiatische Kunst der Stadt Köln*. Wiesbaden, 1972.
Gatten, A. 'The Order of the Early Chapters in the Genji Monogatari.' *Harvard Journal of Asiatic Studies* 41, no. 1. Cambridge, Mass., 1980, pp. 5–46.
Goepper, R. *Kunst und Kunsthandwerk Ostasiens*, Munich, 1968; 2nd ed., 1978.
The Gossamer Years (Kagerō Nikki): A Diary by a Noblewoman of Heian Japan. Trans. by E. Seidensticker. Tōkyō, 1964.
'Gotoh bijutsukan meihin zuroku ('Catalogue of the Masterpieces in the Gotoh Art Museum').' Ex. cat. Tōkyō: Gotoh Art Museum, 1953.
Gundert, W. *Die japanische Literatur*. Potsdam, 1929.
—— *Japanische Religionsgeschichte*, Tōkyō, Stuttgart, 1935; 2nd ed., 1943.

Hakeda, Y. S. *Kūkai: Major Works*. New York, 1972.
Hammitzsch, H. (ed.). *Erzählungen des alten Japan (Konjaku Monogatari)*. [partly in German] Stuttgart, 1965.
Herberts, K. *Das Buch der ostasiatischen Lackkunst*. Düsseldorf, 1959.
Hurst III, G. Cameron. *Insei: Abdicated Sovereigns in the Politics of Late Heian Japan, 1086–1185*. New York, London, 1976.

'Idemitsu bijutsukan meihinran zuroku (Illustrated Catalogue of the Exhibition of the Masterpieces of the Idemitsu Museum, Painting and Calligraphy).' Ex. Cat. Tōkyō: Idemitsu Art Gallery, 1968; 2nd ed. 1981 [with English text].
Ienaga, S. *Jōdai yamato-e zenshi*. Tōkyō, 1966.
—— 'Yamato-e.' *Nihon no bijutsu* 10. Tōkyō, 1969.
Ishida, H. 'Mikkyō-ga.' *Nihon no bijutsu* 1, no. 33. Tōkyō, 1969.
Ishimoto, Y. *Eros + Cosmos in Mandala*. Tōkyō, 1978.
Ito, N. 'Mikkyō kenchiku.' *Nihon no bijutsu* 4, no. 143. Tōkyō, 1978.

Japan: Frühe buddhistische Malereien. UNESCO-Sammlung der Weltkunst. New York, 1959.
'Japanese Calligraphy.' Ex. Cat. Tōkyō: Tōkyō National Museum, 1978.
Japanese Poetic Diaries. Selected and trans. by E. Miner. Berkeley, Los Angeles, 1969.

Kageyama, H. *The Arts of Shinto.* Arts of Japan, Vol. 4. New York, 1973.
Kameda, T. 'Men to Shōzō.' *Genshoku nihon no bijutsu* 23. Tōkyō, 1971.
Kato, B. *et al. The Threefold Lotus Sutra.* 2nd ed., New York, 1975.
Keene, D. ed. *Anthology of Japanese Literature from the Earliest Era to the Mid-Nineteenth Century.* New York, 1955.
Kidder, Jr., J. E. *Japan before Buddhism.* 2nd ed., London, 1959.
—— *Masterpieces of Japanese Sculpture.* Tōkyō and Rutland, VT, 1961.
—— *Japanese Temples.* London, 1964.
—— *The Birth of Japanese Art.* London, 1965.
Kinoshita, M. 'Sanjūrokunin-kashu.' *Nihon no bijutsu* 5, no. 168. Tōkyō, 1980.
Kleinschmidt, P. *Die Masken der Gigaku, der ältesten Theaterform Japans.* Wiesbaden, 1967.
Kojiki or Records of Ancient Matters. Trans. by B. H. Chamberlain. 2nd ed., Kōbe, 1932.
Kokūho: National Treasures of Japan. Vols. 1–6. Tōkyō, 1963–67.
Konjaku: Tales of Times New Past. Trans. by M. Ury. Berkeley, 1979.
Koop, A. J. 'Guide to the Japanese Textiles.' *Costumes of the Victoria and Albert Museum,* Part 2. London, 1920.
Kümmel, O. *Das Kunstgewerbe in Japan.* Berlin, 1922.
—— 'Die Kunst Chinas, Japans und Koreas.' *Handbuch der Kunstwissenschaft.* Potsdam, 1929.
Kudo, Y. *et al.* 'Amidadō to Fujiwara Chōkoku.' *Genshoku nihon no bijutsu* 6. Tōkyō, 1969.
Kuno, T. *A Guide to Japanese Sculpture.* Tōkyō, 1963.
Kurata, B. 'Jōgan chōkoku.' *Nihon no bijutsu* 1, no. 44. Tōkyō, 1970.
—— *et al.* 'Mikkō jiin to Jōgan chōkoku.' *Genshoku nihon no bijutsu* 6. Tōkyō, 1967.
Kyōto, the Old Capital of Japan. Kyōto, 1956.
Kyōto National Museum: Heian jidai no bijutsu ('Fine Arts of the Heian Period'). Kyōto, 1958.

Lee, S. E. *A History of Far Eastern Art.* London, 1964.
Lewin, B. *Aya und Hata: Bevölkerungsgruppen Altjapans kontinentaler Herkunft.* Studien zur Japanologie, Vol. 3. Wiesbaden, 1962.
—— *Kleines Wörterbuch der Japanologie.* Wiesbaden, 1968.

The Manyōshū. Trans. by H. H. Honda. Tōkyō, 1967.
Masuda, T. and Futagawa, Y. *Japan,* Munich, 1969.
McCullough, H. C. *Tales of Ise.* Stanford, 1968.
McCullough, W. 'Japanese Marriage Institutions in the Heian Period.' *Harvard Journal of Asiatic Studies* 27. Cambridge, Mass., 1967, pp. 103–167.

Meech-Pekarik, J. 'Disguised Scripts and Hidden Poems in an Illustrated Heian-Sutra.' *Archives of Asian Art* 31. New York, 1977–78.
Minamoto, H. *An Illustrated History of Japanese Art.* Trans. by H. G. Henderson. Kyōto, 1935.
Miner, E. *An Introduction to Japanese Court Poetry.* Stanford, 1968.
—— *Japanese Poetic Diaries.* Berkeley, 1969.
Mizuno, K. 'Daibusshi Jōchō.' *Nihon no bijutsu* 1, no. 164. Tōkyō, 1980.
Moran, S. F. 'The Statue of Fugen Bosatsu, Okura-Museum, Tōkyō.' *Arts asiatiques* 7, no. 4. Paris, 1960.
—— 'The Statue of Amida (of Hōō-dō).' *Oriental Art* N.S.6, no. 2. London, 1960.
—— 'The Kirikane Decoration of the Statue of Fugen Bosatsu, Okura-Museum, Tōkyō.' *Oriental Art* N.S.6, no. 4. London, 1960.
Morris, I. *The World of the Shining Prince: Court Life in Ancient Japan.* London, 1964.
—— *The Tale of Genji Scroll.* Tōkyō, 1971.
—— *The Nobility of Failure: Tragic Heroes in the History of Japan.* Harmondsworth, 1975; 2nd ed. 1980.
Morris, M. 'Sei Shōnagon's Poetic Catalogues.' *Harvard Journal of Asiatic Studies.* 40, no. 1. Cambridge, Mass., June 1980, pp. 5–54.
Murase, M. *Japanese Art: Selection from the Mary and Jackson Burke Collection.* New York, 1975.
Murdoch, J. *A History of Japan.* Vols. 1, 2. London, 1925.

Nachod, W. *Geschichte von Japan.* 3 vols. Gotha, 1906; 2nd ed. Leipzig, 1929.
Nakano, G. 'Fujiwara chōkoku.' *Nihon no bijutsu* 7, no. 50. Tōkyō, 1970.
Nakata, Y. 'Sho.' *Nihon no bijutsu,* no. 27. Tōkyō, 1967.
—— *The Art of Japanese Calligraphy.* The Heibonsha Survey of Japanese Art, Vol. 27. New York and Tōkyō, 1973.
Nihon Emakimono Zenshū ('Japanese Scroll Painting'). 22 vols. [Vols. 1, 2 enlarged]. Tōkyō, 1958–65.
Nishikawa, K. *Bugaku Masks.* Tōkyō, New York, San Francisco, 1978.
Noma, S. *The Arts of Japan, Ancient and Medieval.* Vols. 1, 2. Tōkyō, 1966–67.
—— *et al. Japanese Sculpture.* Vols. 1–6. Tōkyō, 1952–53.
—— and Tani, N. *Nihon bijutsu jiten.* Tōkyō, 1964.

Okasaki, J. 'Jōdo kyōga.'. *Nihon no bijutsu* 12, no. 43. Tōkyō, 1969.
—— *Pure Land Buddhist Painting.* Tōkyō, 1977.
Okazaki, T. 'Kyōto Gosho to Sentō Gosho.' *Nihon no bijutsu* 8, no. 99. Tōkyō, 1974.
Okudaira, H. *Emaki: Japanese Picture Scrolls.* Tōkyō, 1962.
—— 'Emakimono.' *Nihon no bijutsu* 2. Tōkyō, 1966.
—— *Narrative Picture Scrolls.* Art of Japan, Vol. 5. New York, Tōkyō, 1973.
Oyama, N. 'Shakyō.' *Nihon no bijutsu* 5, no. 156. Tōkyō, 1979.

Pageant of Japanese Art. Vols. 1–6. Tōkyō, 1957–58.

Paine, R. T. and Soper, A. *The Art and Architecture of Japan.* Harmondsworth, Baltimore, 1955.

Papinot, E. *Dictionnaire d'histoire et de géographie du Japan.* Tōkyō, 1907.

The Pillow Book of Sei Shōnagon. Trans. by I. Morris, Harmondsworth, 1967; 2nd ed., 1971.

Ragué, B. von *Geschichte der japanischen Lackkunst.* Berlin, 1967.

Ramming, M. *Japan-Handbuch.* Berlin, 1941.

Reischauer, A. K. 'Genshin's Ojo Yoshu.' *Transactions of the Asiatic Society of Japan.* 2nd series. VII. Tōkyō, 1930.

Reischauer, E. O. *Japan, Past and Present.* New York, 1951; 3rd ed., 1964.

Reischauer, J. and R. K. *Early Japanese History.* 2 vols. Princeton, London 1937.

Roberts, L. P. *Dictionary of Japanese Artists.* Tokyo, 1976.

Rosenfield, J. M. *Japanese Arts of the Heian Period 794–1185.* New York, 1967.

—— and Shujiro Shimada. *Traditions of Japanese Art: Selections from the Kimiko and John Powers Collection.* Cambridge, Mass., 1970.

—— et al. *The Courtly Tradition in Japanese Art and Literature.* Cambridge, Mass., 1973.

Sansom, Sir G. B. *Japan: A Short Cultural History.* London, 1931; rev. ed. New York, 1943.

—— *A History of Japan.* 3 vols. Stanford, 1958–1963. [Especially Vol. I: *A History of Japan to 1334.*]

Sawa, T. 'Mikkyō no bijutsu.' *Nihon no bijutsu* 8. Tōkyō, 1969.

—— *Arts in Japanese Esoteric Buddhism.* Trans. by R. L. Gage. New York, Tōkyō, 1972.

Seckel, D. 'Das älteste Langrollenbild in Japan, Kako-Genzai-Ingakyō.' *Bulletin of Eastern Art* 37. Tōkyō, 1943.

—— *Grundzüge der buddhistischen Malerei.* Tōkyō, 1945.

—— 'Buddhistische Prozessionsmasken (Gyōdō-men) in Japan.' *Nachrichten der Gesellschaft für Natur- und Völkerkunde Ostasiens* 76. Hamburg, 1954, pp. 29–52.

—— *Buddhistische Kunst Ostasiens.* Stuttgart, 1957.

—— *Emakimono: The Art of the Japanese Painted Hand-Scroll.* Photos and Foreword by Akihisa Hasé. New York, 1959.

—— *Einführung in die Kunst Ostasiens.* Munich, 1960.

—— *Kunst des Buddhismus.* Baden-Baden, 1962.

Shikibu, Murasaki. *The Tale of Genji.* 2 vols. Trans. by A. Waley. Boston, 1935; 2nd ed. 1 vol. New York, 1960.

—— *The Tale of Genji.* 2 vols. Trans. by E. G. Seidensticker. Tōkyō, 1976; 4th ed., 1980.

Shimbo, T. 'Hakubyō.' *Nihon no bijutsu* 5, no. 48. Tōkyō, 1970.

Shimizu, Y. 'Seasons and Places in Yamato Landscape and Poetry.' *Ars Orientalis* 12. Ann Arbor, 1981.

Shinkokin-waka-shū: Japanische Gedichte. Trans. by H. Hammitzsch and L. Brüll. Stuttgart, 1964.

Shirahata, Y. 'Shōzō-ga.' *Nihon no bijutsu* 12, no. 8. Tōkyō, 1966.

—— 'Monogatari-emaki.' *Nihon no bijutsu* 6, no. 49. Tōkyō, 1970.

—— 'Kasen-e.' *Nihon no bijutsu* 5, no. 96. Tōkyō, 1974.

Shodō zenshū. Vols. 11–14; Japan, Vols. 2–5; Heian, Vols. 1–4. Tōkyō, 1954–56.

'Sho: Pinselschrift und Malerei in Japan vom 7.–19. Jahrhundert.' Ex. Cat. Cologne: Museum für Ostasiatische Kunst, 1975.

Snellgrove, D. L. ed. *The Image of the Buddha.* New York: UNESCO, 1978.

Soper, A. C. 'The Rise of Yamato-e.' *Art Bulletin* 24, no. 4. New York, 1942.

—— 'The Illustrated Method of the Tokugawa Genji Pictures.' *Art Bulletin* 37, no. 1. New York, 1955.

—— 'A Pictorial Biography of Prince Shōtoku.' *Metropolitan Museum of Art Bulletin.* New York, January, 1967.

Sukey, H. *Washi: The World of Japanese Paper.* Tōkyō, 1978.

Swann, P. C. *Japan, von der Jōmon- zur Tokugawa-Zeit.* Baden-Baden, 1965.

Tahara, M. *Tales of Yamato.* Honolulu, 1980.

Takeda, M. *et al.* 'Butsuga'. *Genshoku nihon no bijutsu* 7. Tōkyō, 1969.

Tanaka, I. *Nihon Emakimono zenshū.* Vols. 1–24. Tōkyō, 1958–69.

Tanaka, S. 'Inshokuki.' *Nihon no bijutsu* 1, no. 9. Tōkyō, 1967.

Tazawa, Y. *History of Japanese Sculpture.* Vols. 1–6. Tōkyō, 1953.

Toda, K. *Japanese Scroll Painting.* Chicago, 1935; 2nd ed., New York, 1969.

Tsukakoshi, S. *Konjaku.* Zurich, 1965.

Uyeno, N. *Woodblock Reproductions of the Genji Picture Scrolls.* Tōkyō, 1964.

Vos, F. *A Study of the Ise-Monogatari . . .* Vols. 1, 2. The Hague, 1957.

Waley, A. *Japanese Poetry.* 1919. Reprinted, London, 1956.

Wolz, C. *Bugaku: Japanese Court Dance.* Seattle, 1971.

Yashiro, Y. 'Scroll Paintings of the Far East.' *Transactions and Proceedings of the Japan Society* 33. London, 1935.

—— *Art Treasures of Japan.* Vols. 1, 2. Tōkyō, 1960.

—— and Swann, P. C. *Japanische Kunst.* Munich, Zurich, 1958.

Yamagiwa, J. K. *The Ōkagami: A Japanese Historical Tale.* London, 1967.

Yoshida, T. *Japanische Architektur.* Tübingen, 1952.

Yoshizawa, C. *et al. Japanische Kunst.* Vols. 1, 2. Vienna, Munich, 1975.

Zusetsu Nihon Bunkashi, Vols. 4, 5; Vols. 1, 2: *Heian jidai.* Tōkyō, 1958.

Photo Credits

The author and the publishers wish to thank Miss Aki Uyeno, National Research Institute of Cultural Properties, Tōkyō, Dr. Bunsaku Kurata, National Museum, Nara, and all those who have supplied the photographs for the book. The photo research for this book done by Ingrid de Kalbermatten. The numbers refer to the plates.

Index

The numbers in italics refer to plate numbers.

244